Rethinking Modernity
and National Identity
in Turkey

Rethinking Modernity and National Identity in Turkey

Edited by
Sibel Bozdoğan
and
Reşat Kasaba

University of Washington Press
Seattle and London

Publication of this book has been made possible
by a grant from the Institute of Turkish Studies,
Washington, D.C.

Library of Congress Cataloging-in-Publication Data
Rethinking modernity and national identity in Turkey / edited by Sibel
    Bozdoğan and Reşat Kasaba.
        p.   cm. — (Publications on the Near East)
    Includes index.
    ISBN 0–295–97597–0 (alk. paper)
    1. Turkey—Civilization—20th Century.   2. Social change—Turkey.
3. Nationalism—Turkey.   4. East and West.   I. Bozdoğan, Sibel.
II. Kasaba, Reşat, 1954–   . III. Series: Publications on Near East,
University of Washington.
DR432.R48   1997   96–51857
305.8'09561—dc21   CIP

Cover collage: Young girls look at posters of Turkish popular music and film
stars, 1990s (photo by Haluk Özözlü); portrait of Atatürk (private collection);
urban renewal in Istanbul, 1950s (photo by Ara Güler).

To Peter and Kathie,
who have been thinking
of Turkish modernity
for some time

Contents

Contents

Illustrations

Acknowledgments

E arlier versions of the essays collected in this book were presented at a conference held at the Massachusetts Institute of Technology in 1994. In addition to the authors represented in this volume, Aydan Balamir, Murat Belge, Sibel Erol, Zeynep Kezer, and Ilhan Tekeli also presented papers, and we wish to acknowledge their contribution to this project. We also wish to express our gratitude to Philip Khoury, Feroz Ahmad, Beyhan Karahan, Nasser Rabbat, and Royston Landau, whose comments greatly improved the quality and the interdisciplinary appeal of this event. The conference was made possible by a generous grant from the Aga Khan Program at MIT and Harvard, with additional support from the Department of Architecture at MIT and the Turkish Tourism Office in New York. We would like to thank Stanford Anderson, chair of the Department of Architecture at MIT, and Barbro Ek, former director of the Aga Khan Program, for their support of this event. We also thank Renee Caso, Denise Heinze and the rest of the staff at the Aga Khan Program office, Ayşen Savaş, Hande Bozdoğan, Felicia Hecker, and Nicole Watts, who helped us at various stages of this project. Finally, we are grateful to the Institute of Turkish Studies for their grant that supported the publication of this book.

Unfortunately, these acknowledgments must end on a sad note. As we were getting the essays in this volume ready for publication, we received the news of Ernest Gellner's death. Professor Gellner had carefully revised his own presentation and prepared it for publication well within the deadline we had set for our contributors. We feel privileged to have had the opportunity to host him at our conference, to have benefited from his insightful comments and criticisms, and to have been the editors of a volume that includes one of his last writings.

Rethinking Modernity
and National Identity
in Turkey

1

Introduction

SİBEL BOZDOĞAN AND REŞAT KASABA

In Turkey and around the world today, we are witnessing the eclipse of the progressive and emancipatory discourse of modernity. Some of us view the spectacle with melancholy—yet it has also produced a remarkably lively and pluralist climate in which new voices are being heard and deeply entrenched assumptions are being radically and, we believe, irreversibly challenged. At the center of the most heated theoretical debates in many disciplines is the question of whether it is possible to undertake a rigorous critique of the Enlightenment project of modernity without surrendering its liberating and humanist premises.

From the humanities and social sciences to art, architecture, and cultural studies, scholars in many disciplines are looking for new ways of critically engaging with the modern project and exploring options beyond it without falling back on an antimodern "return to tradition" or getting lost in the postmodern "global theme park." The stakes in these latter gambits are too high. As Appleby, Hunt, and Jacob explain it, turning our backs to modernity completely would amount to abandoning any notion of the "freely acting, freely knowing individual whose experiments can penetrate the secrets of nature and whose work with other individuals can make a new and better world."[1] Although the current debate on modernity is a worldwide and highly popular one, we believe it has a particular urgency in non-Western contexts where modernization has had a relatively short and contentious history. This collection of essays aims to assess the Turkish experience of modernity from a broad, interdisciplinary perspective.

In the first two decades after World War II, social scientists often heralded Turkey as one of the most successful models of a universally defined modernization process. The country's history of modernization and Westernization, extending back to the institutional reforms of the late Ottoman era and epitomized by the establishment of a secular nation-state under Kemalism in 1923, appeared to confirm all the expectations of theoretical writings in this genre. Ottoman and Turkish modernization was seen to be succeeding as an elite-driven, consensus-based, in-

3

stitution-building process that took its inspiration exclusively from the West. It is no wonder that two books whose authors studied the Turkish transformation closely from this perspective—Daniel Lerner's *The Passing of Traditional Society* and Bernard Lewis's *The Emergence of Modern Turkey*—became the classic texts of the modernization literature.[2]

In these and similar writings, Turkey's apparently successful adoption of Western norms, styles, and institutions, most conspicuously in education, law, social life, clothing, music, architecture, and the arts, was portrayed as testimony to the viability of the project of modernity even in an overwhelmingly Muslim country. As such, the Turkish case has not only been frequently cited in academic discussions on modernization but has also informed and inspired many independence movements in Muslim "Third World" countries such as Pakistan and Indonesia.

The first cracks in the celebratory tone that characterized these early writings appeared in the late 1960s and the 1970s. With the growing influence of what Şerif Mardin calls the "Marxisant" perspective,[3] new histories shifted their focus away from the elite, emphasized conflict over consensus, and studied economic structures rather than political institutions. According to these critiques, Turkish modernization, when examined from alternative vantage points, contained little that was worth celebrating. So influential was their demur that by the end of the seventies "modernization" had become a dirty word, and authors such as Lerner and Lewis were cited only as examples of the "wrong" way of studying the late Ottoman Empire and republican Turkey.

Early critiques of Turkish modernization concentrated their criticisms on the Ottoman leaders who preceded Mustafa Kemal or on those who followed him, and not on what Kemal himself attempted to do. In these writings, the "War of Independence" especially was considered a valiant effort and was even seen as a harbinger of the Third World revolutions to come. Recently, in the hands of groups ranging from advocates of liberal economy to Islamist intellectuals, the criticism of Turkish modernity has become more comprehensive. Now, people publicly debate and criticize the Kemalist doctrine as a patriarchal and antidemocratic imposition from above that has negated the historical and cultural experience of the people in Turkey. In a hitherto unprecedented tone, the Kemalist path of modernization, far from being an exemplary success story, is declared a historical failure that undermined the normative order in Ottoman-Turkish society. It is ironic that such doubts about the Turkish experience are being voiced precisely at a time when Turkey is again being promoted by Western diplomatic and press circles as an appealing model of social reform for the Central Asian republics of the former Soviet Union.

Underpinning these criticisms of Kemalist modernization is a strongly held doubt about the universalistic claims and aspirations of modernization theories. Today, many scholars and intellectuals favor and emphasize cultural identity, difference, and diversity over homogenization and unity. At the same time, concurrent with the demise of nationalist developmentalism in the world at large, the globalizing trends and high technologies of the market are also finding their way into Turkey. As these global trends ensnarl the country with all their energy and unruliness, official modernization, with its singularity, austerity, and paternalism, appears woefully inadequate both as a source of inspiration and as a mechanism of control in economics, politics, and cultural production.

Few of us would deny the democratic premises embodied in these developments, but we should realize that the theoretical, historical, and political debate in Turkey has left some important loose ends and generated several pitfalls. For example, it is sometimes ignored that regardless of how shallow Turkey's "civilizational shift" from Islam to the West has actually been, institutional, ritual, symbolic, and aesthetic manifestations of modernity have become constituent elements of the Turkish collective consciousness since the 1920s. Images and photographs of *La Turquie Kemaliste* in the 1930s, the propaganda films of the 1950s, and countless other representations of the official history of modernization still offer the most powerful visual tropes of this ethos of the making of a thoroughly modern nation out of the ruins of an old empire. Unveiled women working next to clean-shaven men in educational and professional settings, healthy children and young people in school uniforms, the modern architecture of public buildings in republican Ankara and other major cities, the spectacular performances of the national theater, symphony orchestra, opera, and ballet, and proud scenes of agriculture, railroads, factories, and dams are among the most familiar images. Not only have these been charged with a civilizing agency for the greater part of Turkey's republican history, but they have also come to set the official standards of exterior form and behavior against which people, ideas, and events have been measured and judged.

Another loose end is the inadequate way in which some aspects of recent Turkish history are studied and evaluated. As writers try to align themselves according to whether they believe Turkey has had too much or too little modernization, few have stepped up to study the real history of modernization in Turkey in all of its aspects. The serious doubts of some post-modernists notwithstanding, it is hard to ignore the relevance and reality of history. No matter how one might want to qualify it, in Turkey today more people live longer, fewer children succumb to childhood diseases, more people can read and write, and more people have access to modern means of transportation and communication than was the case in the 1920s. In other words, one would be justified in claiming that most people in Turkey now live lives that are qualitatively better than was typical in Anatolia during the early decades of the twentieth century. It seems to us that how this came about constitutes a valid and interesting research topic. Yet more than thirty-five years after its publication, Bernard Lewis's *The Emergence of Modern Turkey* remains the best introductory text for the study of the late Ottoman and early republican eras. On the other hand, despite his omnipresence in all aspects of modern Turkish history, Kemal Atatürk still does not have a scholarly biography.

A third and perhaps more important pitfall can be described as the state of extreme relativism that is associated with some forms of postmodernism and that may follow from a radical break with Kemalist modernism. Such an outcome would erode the possibility of finding any common ground or evaluative standard among different discourses and lifestyles. As editors of this volume, it is our conviction that if the recognition and celebration of pluralism and difference are not to lead to a complete "indifferentiation and indifference," as Chantal Mouffe cogently puts it, "one must be able to discriminate between differences that exist but should not exist, and differences that do not exist but should exist."4

On the basis of this conviction, we underline the importance of avoiding reductionist definitions of both modernity/modernism and postmodernity/postmodernism while embarking upon a rigorous and critical rethinking of Turkish modernization. Just as we need to distinguish between modernity as a potentially liberating historical condition and its instrumentalization for a political project of domination, we also need to distinguish between the democratic implications of the recent postmodern critique, on the one hand, and its self-closure into a new form of orthodoxy, on the other. In order to take advantage of the openings created by the former while avoiding the pitfalls of the latter, we must work toward building a new consensus that makes communication across social, political, and theoretical divides possible while upholding the universal principles of justice and truth. The parameters of this consensus must originate not in a grand theory or the political project of an elite but in the very dialogue that would take place across societal divisions. It is only through such interchange that we can support the growth of an "unfettered, uncensored domain of public discourse," which Appleby, Hunt, and Jacob describe as a "New Republic of Learning."[5]

The essays in this volume, first presented in an interdisciplinary conference titled "Rethinking the Project of Modernity in Turkey," held at the Massachusetts Institute of Technology in March 1994, bring together a wide range of writers from different disciplines and professions, all of whom are preoccupied with the critical debates over the current dilemmas and prospects of the project of modernity in Turkey and elsewhere. While keeping their essays focused on Turkey from their respective fields of expertise, they incorporate some of the most recent conceptual tools and frameworks, thereby providing an opening for theoretical and historical engagement with each other across disciplinary boundaries, as well as with specialists on other parts of the world. They represent a variety of positions, mostly complementary but at times conspicuously at odds with each other.

Rather than selecting the contributors strategically to affirm our own views, our objective was to open up space for some of the most prominent names to speak for themselves around our selected theme. We did not, however, want to reduce the debate to essentialized and mutually exclusive oppositions, especially between Kemalists and Islamists. Therefore, we avoided activists who were closely identified with these positions in favor of contributors who maintain a critical distance from essentialist and totalizing worldviews of any kind. A distance from both the self-righteous authoritarianism of Kemalist nationalism and the anti-individual and antimodern authoritarianism of certain aspects of Islamist politics characterizes most of the essays in this collection.

The range of positions notwithstanding, the common thread cutting across the essays is a two-fold observation that can also be seen as the tentative conclusion of this study. First, many of the writers find that the Turkish project of modernity, in the way it was conceived under the sponsorship and priorities of the nation-state, has been flawed and problematical from its inception, compromised precisely by some of the things that were done in the name of modernity. Second, they agree that both politically and intellectually, the current critical climate is an opportunity, albeit a precarious one (without any convincing indication so far that the opportunity has been seized), for rectifying the initial flaw toward a more democratic, pluralist, and creative unleashing of the country's potential.

The first seven essays after this introduction offer historical overviews of Turkish modernization, critically reevaluate the paradigms employed in its study, and discuss current challenges to it. In chapter 2, Reşat Kasaba distinguishes between modernization as a world-historical process and the modernization that is described in social science texts. He sees the former as a liberating process that made it possible for people to pursue their individual interests while forming meaningful collectivities. By contrast, the models of social change that were elaborated in the aftermath of the Second World War confined the analysis of this rich and complex development into separately conceived nation-states that were labeled with sterile pattern variables. Kasaba sees the current conjuncture in the world and in Turkey as fortuitous for having brought a relative relaxation of political, intellectual, and ideological constraints. He argues that it should be possible for us, as historians and as historical subjects, to take advantage of these circumstances and reclaim the universal and liberating potential of modernization.

Çağlar Keyder argues in chapter 3 that the 1980s and 1990s have been a time of momentous change for Turkish society, when all the institutions, values, and ideals of modernity have come under siege. Yet he cautions us that it would be misleading to blame modernization as such for the current sense of malaise in Turkey. Rather than agreeing with those who advocate culturally authentic models of social change, Keyder insists that modernity should be accepted as a total project, embracing and internalizing all the cultural dimensions that made Europe modern. Hence, he insists on the enduring validity of the project of modernity while emphasizing the crucial need for shifting the focus of the project away from the state to society itself. For this to take place, the society needs to be constructed around well-formulated and protected notions of freedom and citizenship.

The essays by Haldun Gülalp and Şerif Mardin address, in different ways, the primary challenge to Turkish modernization posed recently by an increasingly visible Islamic element in society. Gülalp examines the growth of Islamist politics in Turkey within a global political-economic perspective. He argues that Islamism in Turkey and other similarly situated countries is a product of the frustration of the promises of Westernist modernization and state-led economic development that preoccupied the governments of these countries for the better part of the twentieth century. According to Gülalp, Islamist politics grew in such an environment not as a backward looking premodernism but as a critique of modernity, without, however, articulating a clear alternative in economic terms.

Focusing more on the historiography than on the history of Turkish modernization, Şerif Mardin's essay takes issue with precisely the kind of macroeconomic and structural analysis proposed by Gülalp. Mardin looks at the existing literature on Turkish modernization, of both Kemalist and Marxist persuasions, and finds too heavy an emphasis on macro models and too little interest in micro aspects of social change, which he describes as "life-worlds." Only by reintegrating life-worlds as a central component of the study and practice of modernity in Turkey, Mardin suggests, will we be able to move beyond the shortcomings of the existing historical experience and analysis. This, he argues, will alleviate the authoritarian tendencies inherent in exclusively structuralist perspectives and help overcome the distance and alienation that the overwhelmingly Muslim population of Turkey has felt in the face of the social and political reforms of the past two hundred years.

Along similar lines, Nilüfer Göle, in chapter 6, takes exception with common ways of studying the rise of Islam as resulting from poverty, authoritarianism, and massive urbanization. For her, Islamist movements involve not only a rejection of and a reaction to modernity but also a positive articulation of a holistic vision for the community. She sees in these movements a reassertion of Islamic identity that had been excluded from both the practice and the history of Turkish modernization. Göle reminds us that Muslims are reclaiming their history in body and spirit, in relationship to and within the context of modern institutions that surround them. Thus Göle is inclined to see in Islamic movements "a hybridization between local and global realities." This way of thinking about Islam, however, should not deter us from critically assessing the future that is inherent in Islamic visions. As Göle herself notes in the concluding section of her essay, "the 'rise of the oppressed' can be emancipatory only if it is not itself repressive."

The last two essays in this section introduce the dimension of gender into the discussion. Yeşim Arat's chapter begins by reviewing the way the status and appearance of women in public have been among the most effective visual and symbolic expressions of the Turkish project of modernity in its various stages. After emphasizing the centrality of women's position in all discussions of modernity in Turkey, Arat compares the earlier construct of the Kemalist woman with the recent feminist critique of this idealized construct. The feminist critique, she states, represents nothing less than a major change from women's being the objects of paternalistic republican reforms that "granted them their rights" to women's claiming subjecthood in their own lives. Yet Arat refuses to cast these two in oppositional terms and sees the feminist activism of the 1980s as testimony to the strength of the republican project of modernity. Despite their revolt, she argues, these feminists, in their search for autonomy and their belief in universal rights beyond local traditions and provincial moralities, contribute to the liberal, secular, and democratizing polity that Kemalist Westernization ultimately stood for.

While agreeing with many of the recent criticisms directed at studies of Turkish modernization, Deniz Kandiyoti draws our attention to a still largely neglected area: the emergence of new identities and new forms of subjectivity through which we can begin to question the very meaning of what is "modern." She argues that certain lifestyles, identities, relationships, mannerisms, and habits came to be defined as "modern" not by virtue of their intrinsic qualities but as a result of the specific policies of the modernizing elite and, subsequently, the particular categories developed by the modernization school of social sciences. In particular, she focuses upon the central role of family, sexuality, and gender in discourses about Turkish modernity and highlights the historically and socially constructed nature of "modern" categories. More significantly, she emphasizes that the specific ways in which these categories affected the lives and status of women depended to a large extent on local conditions and class differentiations, which varied dramatically from city to village or from one region to another. This emphasis on the need to study "the local specificities of modernity," as Kandiyoti puts it, marks an important agenda of research neglected by traditional studies of modernization confined to official and institutional realms.

The book continues with four studies that more specifically address cultural aspects of the modernity debate in Turkey. These essays focus on current popular reactions to official modernism and examine the historical context of such reactions. Architecture, music, and popular culture are taken up in these essays with the underlying conviction that these fields are not autonomous and self-referential but are related to one another in meaningful ways as aspects of a larger cultural phenomenon. The predominance of architecture in this section, either directly or by implication, is neither arbitrary nor inconsequential. Apart from its being a recognized discipline and profession, we have viewed architecture (and its implication of a "rational structure") as a powerful metaphor for the project of modernity itself, in Turkey as elsewhere. The architectural terminology of the current postmodern debate is revealing: it is the modern "project" that is under attack; designs and blueprints are discredited as inherently oppressive and authoritarian; instead of construction, deconstruction occupies the cutting edge of critical thought; and architecture itself, as a metaphor for knowledge, is replaced by the archaeology of fragments.

In chapter 9, Sibel Bozdoğan presents a historical overview of the predicament of architectural modernism in Turkey through three distinct periods: its introduction in the Kemalist 1930s, its proliferation in the 1950s, and its rejection in the 1980s. She elaborates the discussion of modernity/postmodernity as it manifests itself in the discipline and profession of architecture, and she offers a visual stage-set for the following two contributions. In architecture, Bozdoğan argues, the problem lies less with the initial precepts of modernism, in the way it emerged as a critical, universal, and liberating discourse in architectural culture at large, than with the way it was reduced to an ideologically charged exterior form and scientific doctrine in the service of the nationalist modernizing elites in Turkey. At the same time, she suggests that the more recent postmodern celebration of liberation from the facelessness and sterility of modern architecture needs to be approached with caution, in order to avoid a standardless stylistic pluralism as an end in itself.

In his essay, Michael Meeker analyzes the seemingly opposite ideological and architectural statements of two state monuments, the Atatürk Memorial Tomb and the Kocatepe Mosque in Ankara—symbols of secular reason and religious faith, respectively—in terms of an underlying shared language of "popular intersubjectivity." From folktales to the "stories" that monuments tell, from the constitution of personhood to that of nationhood, this shared language constitutes a sort of collective imagination. On this basis Meeker rejects common binary oppositions that are typically employed to characterize the project of modernity in Turkey, such as nationalism versus religion, modernity versus tradition, and state versus society.

The last two essays in this section, written from the fields of architecture and music, respectively, look at the most phenomenal challenge to official culture in Turkey in recent years—the challenge coming from or informed by the experience of marginalized people in squatter settlements around major cities. In chapter 11, Gülsüm Baydar Nalbantoğlu looks at the architectural sites of encounters between urban and rural Turkey, specifically those between city dwellers and peasants and nomads. She calls for the opening up of a cultural and architectural space of difference irre-

ducible to either of the poles of this binary opposition. Nalbantoğlu focuses on architectural (re)constructions of rural dwellings, from early republican model villages to the ingenious dwellings and tactics of survival
put forward by rural migrants on the urban fringes today. In these she
finds critical tools and disruptive moments that have been excluded from
or silenced by the established architectural discourse and practice in Turkey,
including the worn-out advocacies of regionalism and contextualism.

Meral Özbek's essay addresses the relationship between modernization
and popular culture in Turkey through the example of *arabesk* music,
which, emerging out of the discontents of squatter populations in the
1960s, has become the most prolific form of popular entertainment in
the 1980s for millions of people of all classes and backgrounds. Taking
issue with "modernizers of both the right and the left," Özbek challenges
the characterization of *arabesk* as the vulgar, fatalistic, tasteless, and cheap
culture of manipulated masses. Instead, she defines it as the site of both
submission and resistance to dominant groups by real people who are at
once the source and the consumers of this culture. Focusing on the work
of Orhan Gencebay, the undisputed "King of Arabesk," she takes us through
the historical processes in the making of the prominent examples of this
genre of music. Özbek argues that *arabesk* lost its initial resistant and
utopian dimension in the 1980s as it became absorbed by the hegemonic
ideology of the Özal years in Turkey.

In the last section of the book, three authors whose primary special-
izations lie outside Turkey look at the Turkish case from their respective
vantage points and make some comparative and theoretical observations.
Ernest Gellner, in chapter 13, returns to a general theme that inspired
many early writers on the history of modern Turkey: the successful transformation of the Ottoman Empire into a secular and modern republic.
Instead of simply asserting this success, as was frequently done in earlier
writings, Gellner explains it by arguing that both popular Islam and the
scholar-elites in late Ottoman and early republican Turkey were better
positioned to adjust to the requirements of modern life. For the same reason, argues Gellner, there is a basis for remaining optimistic about the
future of Turkey, especially in comparison with its less fortunate neighbors to the north and south.

Roger Owen and Joel Migdal approach the topic from a more specifically Middle Eastern context. In chapter 14, Owen argues that modernity
became a political project in the Middle East under the uncertain conditions of the postcolonial and postimperial years of the early twentieth

century. Most states and societies in the region undertook to advance certain values, characteristics, and standards in their respective societies. The mechanisms through which these models were imposed, as well as their impacts, varied across the region. Nonetheless, Owen argues, they have transformed local circumstances to such an extent that today modernity should be seen as an irreversible reality in the Middle East. At the same time, he reminds us that this is an incomplete reality, or rather an unfinished project, and as such it leaves much room for human intervention and interpretation.

Where and how this intervention is likely to take place finds a partial answer in Joel Migdal's concluding essay. He argues that the ultimate character and direction of the project of modernity in countries like Turkey will be determined not by the will of state elites but in that zone where state forces come into contact with social structures which they try to mold after an idealized vision. Because of the larger-than-life stature of leaders such as Atatürk, Ben-Gurion, and Nasser, who dominated political life in their respective countries, it has not been easy to focus on these zones of interaction and untangle these complex relationships. But as Migdal reiterates, the general thrust, the hope, of the arguments expressed in this volume is that the current conjuncture will allow us to lift this veil and arrive at a more open and inclusive assessment of the past and future of the project of modernity in Turkey and the Middle East.

In putting together the essays in this volume, we started with a set of open-ended questions rather than with a clearly delineated, a priori agenda. Instead of trying to resolve the debates over such a complex and contentious history of modernization as Turkey's, our aspiration was to complicate a picture frequently oversimplified not only by the smooth trajectories and universally defined models of modernization theories but also by some of the more recent antimodern and postmodern trends. As we write, events unfolding in Turkey continue to complicate the picture daily. If modernity is a project fraught with uncertainty, as we believe it is, we can perhaps say this much: it is alive and well in Turkey.

Notes

1. Joyce Appleby, Lynn Hunt, and Margaret Jacob, *Telling the Truth about History*, New York: Norton, 1994, 201.

2. Daniel Lerner, *The Passing of Traditional Society,* New York: Free Press, 1958; Bernard Lewis, *The Emergence of Modern Turkey,* New York: Oxford University Press, 1961.

3. See Mardin's chapter 5, this volume.

4. Chantal Mouffe, "Democratic Politics Today," in Chantal Mouffe, ed., *Dimensions of Radical Democracy,* London: Verso, 1992, 13.

5. Appleby, Hunt, and Jacob, *Telling the Truth about History,* 282.

2/ Kemalist Certainties
and Modern Ambiguities

REŞAT KASABA

In 1983, the military junta in Turkey was making preparations to hand the government over to a civilian administration. Military leaders had already agreed to hold elections in that year, but they did not want the democratic process to unfold to its full potential without supervision on their part. They were particularly sensitive to the possibility that the parties and politicians of the pre-coup era might be returned to power to undo what the military had tried to accomplish during the preceding three years.

In order to prevent this outcome, they imposed restrictions and outright bans on the activities of a large number of people and organizations, and they labeled the prominent politicians of previous decades and their parties the embittered remnants of an old order. Military officials repeatedly warned the nation that electing these old leaders would bring the country back to the edge of the precipice from which it had been delivered by the 1980 coup. Instead of returning to these "tried and failed" parties and ideas, or, in state president Evren's colorful language, rather than "shopping at flea markets," people in Turkey were encouraged to "walk along the new path enlightened by the floodlights of the new leaders of the new parties."[1]

By describing the 1983 elections as a stark choice between the old and the new, the military leaders were reiterating a theme that had been central to political discourse in Turkey during most of the twentieth century. According to this theme, Turkey's social, economic, and political problems were caused by the continuing influence of pre-republican political, economic, and social institutions and attitudes. In order to be a serious competitor in the modern world, the argument went, Turks had to free themselves from this burden and make a clean start by cutting their ties to their recent (i.e., Ottoman) history. The core policy makers and ideologues who gathered around Atatürk after the purges of 1925 re-

15

peatedly stated such views as their convictions. According to them, anything that was newly attained, acquired, adopted, or built was naturally desirable and superior to everything that was inherited from the past and hence "old."[2]

During the early decades of the twentieth century, the tired and defeated people of Anatolia were in no position to debate or resist Atatürk's radical message. Some were even enthusiastic in supporting the national leader in his determination to remake the Turkish state. By the 1980s, the situation had changed completely. The Turkish people, few of whom now remembered the early years of the republic, had grown extremely suspicious of, and downright cynical about, the latest incarnations of the promises of "enlightened and prosperous tomorrows." Instead of making further sacrifices for a future that kept eluding them, they were starting to inquire about the histories, institutions, beliefs, identities, and cultures from which they had been forcefully separated. This reorientation of the social compass spread to all segments of the society, not only affecting people's political outlook but also influencing the way they dressed, which music they created and listened to, how they built their houses and office buildings, and how they thought about the history of modern Turkey.

This shift of focus had immediate and profound consequences for Turkish politics. For one thing, as part of the general assessment of Turkey's status in the modern world, the Kemalist program of modernization—including its economic policies, secularist tenets, and ethnonationalist foundations—came under close scrutiny and received increasingly vocal criticism. The Islamist Refah Party emerged as the standard-bearer of the anti-Kemalist opposition and within ten years transformed its shaky organization into the largest political party in Turkey.

The reshuffled political scene in Turkey got a further jolt when the Kurds, who constitute the largest non-Turkish ethnic group in the country, reclaimed and reasserted their distinct cultural and ethnic identity and used it as a basis for organizing an armed struggle against the Turkish army. In the process, not only did they test the very viability of the state but they also exposed some of the foundational weaknesses of Turkish nationalism as it had been conceived by the republican elite.

Putting together the nostalgic turn in tastes, the declining hold of secularism on everyday life and politics, and the growing precariousness of national unity, it is hard to avoid the impression that Turkish modernization reached some kind of turning point in the early eighties. The reformers, in particular Mustafa Kemal, had envisioned for Turkey an organized, well-articulated, linear process of modernization through which the whole nation was going to move simultaneously and with uniform experience. At the end of this process, there would emerge a militantly secular, ethnically homogeneous republic well on its way to catching up with the civilized nations of the West. Instead, the Turkish experience appeared to be culminating in economic backwardness and social flux, with Muslim and secularist, Turk and Kurd, reason and faith, rural and urban—in short, the old and the new—existing side by side and contending with, but more typically strengthening, each other.

Writers who approach the Turkish scene from the far corners of the new political arena have relatively simple explanations for this situation. According to Kemalists, the nation was derailed from its idealist path by reactionary forces bent on reasserting the primacy of religion in Turkish society. They claim that after 1950, under democratically elected governments, a variety of retrograde elements that included religious reactionaries, opportunist politicians, and ethnically suspect groups found ample opportunity to trick people and subvert the progressive goals of the Kemalist movement.[3]

For Muslim intellectuals, on the other hand, the problem arose not because Turkey had broken with Kemalism but because the country stayed with it as long as it did. Islamists find the goals of Kemalist modernization intrinsically antithetical to the essential qualities of Muslim culture, of which they see the people of Turkey as an integral part. They argue that under Atatürk, Muslims in Turkey were cut off from their religious tradition by force. According to them, once the restrictive cloak of Kemalist ideology is removed, Turks will rejoin the Islamic world and be perfectly capable of creating a society that is not only modern (which they take in the technological sense of the word) but also more equitable and "just" than the one created by the Kemalist elite after the Western image.[4]

When it comes to Kurdish separatism, the respective positions of the Kemalists and their critics are equally if not even more polarized. Kemalists deny the existence of a "Kurdish problem" and speak mostly in euphemisms such as "terrorism" and "underdevelopment." They insist that the draconian methods of suppression first used in the nineteenth and early twentieth centuries against the Kurds and other non-Turkish ethnic groups are still the most reliable way of dealing with Kurdish insurgency. They insist on attributing the fierceness of the uprising not to any genuine and legitimate cause but to the provocation and needling of a coterie of external forces.

At the same time, some groups within the Kurdish insurgency find themselves in an equally untenable position because they rely on primordial identities as their main basis for political organization and movement. This approach either ignores the complexities created by centuries of cohabitation among Kurdish and non-Kurdish groups across Turkey or, more seriously, believes that these ties can be undone by force. The latter attitude is shared by many ethnically based social movements in other parts of the world as well.[5]

The Kemalist, Islamist, and Kurdish nationalist ideologies share a strong intolerance for one another. Just as Kemalists are deeply antagonistic toward both Islamists and Kurdish nationalists, those two are keen on preventing each other from infringing on their respective terrains as they separately confront their common enemy, the Turkish state. What pushes these three points of view apart is that, in the eyes of their adherents, each position holds the key to absolute and complete truth. It is the sine qua non of such fundamentalisms that their partisans reject all ambiguity, whether in their own minds or in the minds of their rivals. In Ernest Gellner's words, they repudiate the "tolerant modernist claim that the faith in question means something much milder, far less exclusive, altogether less demanding and much more accommodating; above all something quite compatible with all other faiths."[6]

The nature and content of these debates and conflicts show that as a monolithic force that tried to mold Turkish society and mentality, Kemalism is losing its grip.[7] But once released from one doctrine, the people of Turkey should not inevitably be pushed toward new absolutes, either of the Islamist variety or of the ethnonationalist sort. Some of the ideas put forth by Islamists and Kurdish nationalists are no better than the Kemalist absolutisms in terms of their plausibility or capacity to provide a frame of reference for a fast-modernizing society like Turkey.

Rather than advancing another version of the "absolute truth," in this essay I take the skepticism of recent years as an opportunity to question the suprahistorical pretensions of *all* absolutist ideologies. I seek to recapture some of the early indeterminate richness of Ottoman and Turkish modernization by taking it out of the iron-clad pathways into which it was forced in subsequent years. In doing so, I am trying to resituate Ottoman-Turkish modernization into its proper historical context and reestablish some of the dynamism it had by virtue of its very uncertainty. It might be worthwhile to remember that what inspired and empowered many of the thinkers, writers, and activists of the modern era was not the certainties that were later invented but the ambivalence and excitement of modernization as it unfolded as a world-historical process.

Ottoman-Turkish Modernization: Experience and Interpretation

In the usage adopted here, "modernization" refers to Marshall Berman's "generalized images which summarize the various transformations of social life" attendant upon the rise of a market society and the nation-state.[8] Although this usage is in line with the classical applications of the term, it differs significantly from more recent canonical formulations that identify modernity in terms of a finite and distinct set of pattern variables.

In my use of the term in this essay, modernization entails, above all, the freeing of individuals and communities from some of their traditional obligations, enabling them to take part in the expanding market society. As Karl Polanyi argued in *The Great Transformation,* rather than resulting from the natural proclivities of human beings, the growth of the market society in Europe required a series of deliberate interventions.[9] Polanyi explained this process in terms of a double movement that involved, on the one hand, the development of a series of institutions and practices without which this new form of societal organization could never have taken root. On the other hand, there was the countermovement of protection, whereby these institutions and others that developed in a parallel fashion safeguarded the interests and dignity of individuals and communities who participated, willingly or otherwise, in the new market society. Depending on the time and the place, this protective movement entailed the redefinition of families and households, the recasting of local, national, and supranational identities and alliances, and the creation of national and international networks and formal institutions. Looking back from the vantage point of the last quarter of the twentieth century, we see that of all these institutions, relationships, and organizations, the nation-state has become the most typical domain and, in some ways, the apex of this protective movement in the modern era.

In addition to the continuing expansion of markets and the spread of protective ideologies and movements, there is a third cluster of ideas and their related practices and institutions that regulate relations between people and their rulers in the modern world. These ideas revolve around the influential discourse about human and civil rights and popular sovereignty that capped the western European transformations and created an attractive frame of reference for many social movements and systems of thought around the world. Although the manner in which market relations develop in a given society and the precise form taken by protective relations and discourses on freedom and participation may vary from one context to the other, the essences of these three processes are general enough for us to consider them to be applicable in all modernizing contexts.

As it went through the changes and transformations of the eighteenth and nineteenth centuries, the Ottoman Empire (and subsequently Turkey) was influenced by all three of the constituent forces of modernity. Ottoman economy and markets came to be linked to and dominated by European markets, primarily through networks that branched inland from port cities. The countermovement of protection took shape as institutional reform and local rebellion, such as the rebellions of the nationalist groups in the Balkans. And the discourse of freedom and rights was germane to the entire spectrum of political opposition in the Ottoman Empire, beginning with its very early stages in the nineteenth century. Simultaneous development of these forces dotted the history of Ottoman-Turkish modernization with many uncertainties, occasional reversals, and periodic shifts in its speed and priorities. The important point is to regard these fluxes not as anomalies but as integral parts of the process of modernization itself.

When the time came to write down and interpret the Ottoman and Turkish experience, however, the available tools and paradigms of the social sciences failed to capture this history in its full complexity. By the time Western social scientists focused on Turkey, they had abandoned the ambiguities that had shaped some of their early attitudes toward modernization and industrialization in favor of a more streamlined and unilinear interpretation.[10] Especially when it came to generalizing or theorizing, these authors drew their conclusions not from the ethnographic or historical record, of which they had a masterful grasp, but by applying to that material a preconceived picture of what modernity was supposed to be like. Bernard Lewis's classic, *The Emergence of Modern Turkey,* provides a good example of this kind of writing, in which historical detail is presented but then forced into what C. Wright Mills described as a "trans-historical strait-jacket" in order to support a limited number of generalizations about Turkey, Turks, Islam, and modernization.[11]

An ardent supporter of Ottoman-Turkish reform, Lewis began by emphasizing the "deeper affinities" between the democratic ideals of Western society and the Turkish culture.[12] He saw Turks as having made two fortuitous choices in their history that helped bridge the geographical and cultural gap separating them from the West. The first choice came during the Middle Ages, when the Turks turned away from Asia and looked westward. In Lewis's history, Turkish modernization started at this point but went through a major interruption when the institutions and practices of the Ottoman Empire fell under the influence of Arab and Islamic culture.[13] In Lewis's recounting, the Turks returned to their rightful path in the eighteenth century, when they made their second decisive choice by turning once again to the West for a model and inspiration as they struggled to reorganize their imperial institutions. Lewis regarded the Ottoman reform, the passing of the empire, and the establishment of the secular republic as having liberated the Turks from a burden that had kept them from taking their deserved place on the side of the West.[14]

If one sets aside these broad generalizations, one finds that *The Emergence of Modern Turkey* contains ample information about the complexities that underlay this long march of "progress." Some of the information does not "fit" the sweeping panorama just summarized and may even fatally undermine it. For one example, in an off-handed way Lewis observes that, in general, "the [Islamic] brotherhoods seem to have rallied to the support of the nationalists in Anatolia."[15] This statement suggests that folk Islam, especially, proved to be far more adaptive to changing circumstances in Turkey than one would expect from the way writers have commonly portrayed it, as primarily an obscurantist force.[16] For another example, Lewis's historical data show that rather than being clear-minded visionaries, all the main reformers of the late Ottoman era seem to have entertained some ambivalence toward the idea of Westernization. Sultan Selim III, whose reign Lewis sees as pivotal in Ottoman modernization, was surrounded by influential advisers who believed that the changes introduced by the French revealed "the evil intentions in their minds." The advisers argued that by erecting new principles and setting new laws the French were establishing what "Satan whispered to them."[17]

The chronicler and reforming minister of justice Cevdet Paşa was another prominent person whose outlook and ideology did not easily fit any preconceived mold. Lewis wrote that the Turkish Civil Code, which Cevdet compiled between 1870 and 1876, was "modern in form and presentation" but also "firmly based on the Şeriat." He described the result of Cevdet's work as both a "digest of Şeriat Law of the Hanefi school" and "one of the greatest achievements of Turkish jurisprudence."[18] Another individual who defied easy classification was the journalist Ali Suavi, whom Lewis described as a "turbaned revolutionary."[19] Suavi was trained as a

theologian but refined his ideas about the Islamic brand of Turkish nationalism while in exile in Europe. His background, orientation, fiery
rhetoric, and uncompromising attitude toward the sultan's autocracy made
Ali Suavi one of the most original and enigmatic thinkers of the liberal
opposition in the nineteenth century. Then there was Hizb-i Cedid, or
the New Party, which was formed in 1911 with the dual goal of "preserving general religious and national ethics and morals" and making use
of "the advances and products of Western civilization for the development of the Ottoman Empire."[20] Even Atatürk was careful to keep his options open. He cooperated with various religious leaders as he was organizing for the war against Greece, and he accepted the title "Ghazi"
(Muslim warrior fighting for Islam) that was given to him by the National
Assembly in 1921. Atatürk used this title throughout the rest of his life.

Even on the level of the ideas and motivations of the elite, then, such
nuances make it difficult to reconcile the path of Turkish modernization
with the clearly delineated, dichotomous categories of the literature that
analyzes and explains it. If we move beyond the elite level and examine
the societal underpinnings of Ottoman-Turkish modernization, the overall picture becomes even less clear. Although it has little to say about the
popular classes, Lewis's book is still helpful in revealing some of the uncertainties that underlay the reform process on this level. For example,
he cites the Englishman Slade, an adviser to the Ottoman throne in the
first half of the nineteenth century, who was far less than convinced that
the Ottoman reforms were having a positive impact on the population:

> Hitherto, the Osmanley enjoyed by custom some of the dearest priv-
> ileges of freeman, for which Christian nations have so long strug-
> gled. He paid nothing to the government beyond a moderate land
> tax. . . . He traveled, where he pleased without passports; no custom-
> house officer intruded his eyes or dirty fingers among his baggage;
> no police watched his motions, or listened for his words. . . . For
> this freedom, this capability of realizing the wildest wishes, what
> equivalent does the Sultan offer? It may be said none. . . . Instead
> of engrafting his plans on the old system . . . he . . . prematurely
> disclosed his schemes of self-aggrandizement and appropriation
> which disgusted his subjects.[21]

And in 1962, almost two hundred years after the beginnings of Ottoman
reform, Bernard Lewis wrote: "Religious revival in Turkey in recent years

has attracted the attention of many writers." He cited a series of books and articles spanning the years between 1947 and 1958.[22]

To find other instances of the profound ambiguities that affected Turkish society as it became modern, we can turn to another classic text, Daniel Lerner's *The Passing of Traditional Society*.[23] Like Lewis, Lerner stopped short of bridging the gap between his broad, confident statements about Turkish modernization and the contradictions that engulfed Turkish society as it went through this "unstoppable" transformation. Like Lewis's book, Lerner's is full of insightful descriptions about what was transpiring on the ground. These passages nicely reveal the complexity of Turkish modernization. Here is how Lerner describes the city: it is a modernizing landscape that

> contains many varied figures. Some migrants never penetrate the urban curtain and live out their lives in a miserable daily dying. Others find the industrial discipline a full and satisfying life. Still others are infused with new dreams and glory—imagining themselves at the head of an Islamic brotherhood, or of a proletarian union . . . defying all the mighty. Many, perhaps most, simply try to learn a little more, get a little more, have a little more.[24]

Rather than characterizing the effects of modernization in such a way that anomalies like these would be seen not as curiosities but as integral parts of the process, Lerner (like Lewis) tried to maintain the orderliness of his scheme by creating new categories. For example, he argued that Turkish dynamism originated in those strategically located groups who were neither "traditional" nor "modern," and that all this uncertainty notwithstanding, as a modernizing lot "Turks are the happiest people in the Middle East."[25]

Turkish Modernization and the Modernizing Elite

It is not only strict models and narrow categories of theories of social change that constrain the analyses of twentieth-century writers. In their efforts to portray modernization as a disciplined and unambiguous process, they find plenty of support in the words and deeds of the political leaders who implemented many of the reform measures in the nineteenth and early twentieth centuries.

Just like their interpreters and historians, the political elites saw themselves as the most important force for change in the Ottoman Empire and

Turkey. To them, Ottoman-Turkish society was a project, and the people who lived in Turkey could at most be the objects of their experiments. They freely used categories such as "old" and "new" or "traditional" and "Western" in order to reduce the dimensions of their task to manageable proportions and represent themselves as the sole bearers of progress. They regarded reform strictly as a top-down process. Accordingly, they directed a substantial part of their effort toward changing the Ottoman institutions and reshaping the physical environment in order to make it more similar to that of their European counterparts. The underlying assumption was that once the environment was altered, the behavior of individuals could be easily molded and made to fit the requirements of the newly created circumstances.

The antecedents of this approach to reform can be found in the seventeenth century, particularly in Russia's Peter the Great, who, according to Liah Greenfeld, had "forced the awareness of the west on Russia."[26] But it was in the French Revolution that the Ottoman and republican reformers found their most direct source of inspiration. There were many similarities between the Ottoman-Turkish reformers and, especially, the Jacobins who dominated the French state between 1793 and 1794, in terms of the puritanical zeal with which each approached the task of remaking their respective state and society.

For the Jacobins, the revolution had to be an all-encompassing undertaking, affecting every aspect of life in France. They decreed that French history began in 1792, the year they came to power. They redesigned the calendar into strictly decimal units, and they renamed the days, months, and holidays, substituting for the old Roman and imperial names new ones that were either neutral or based on revolutionary events and personalities. They redrew the administrative map of France, renamed the streets, and even encouraged people to change their names if these had any links to the old regime, the royal family, or the clergy. A distinctive style of clothing that included "trousers, an open shirt, a short jacket, boots, and a liberty cap" came to be associated with the "model revolutionary," and the Jacobins promoted it over the old uniforms of culottes, waistcoats, and powdered wigs.[27]

In the minds of many Ottoman, Young Turk, and Kemalist leaders, too, formal elements of change, such as the outward appearance of people, the cleanliness of streets, and the type and nature of institutions, became synonymous with modernization and consumed an inordinate amount of their time and energy. In 1829, for example, the turban was replaced with the fez as the appropriate and mandatory headgear for civilians, and "robes and slippers gave way to frock coats and capes, trousers and black leather boots," especially in military uniforms.[28] One hundred years later, in the early years of the republic, the fez became the symbol of conservatism and was outlawed by the well-known "hat law" in 1925. In Mustafa Kemal's words, the fez "sat on the heads of our nation as an emblem of ignorance, negligence, and fanaticism and hatred of progress and civilization."[29] Here is how he described someone in his audience who, it appears, had made an unsuccessful effort to cope with the new dress code:

> I see a man in the crowd in front of me; he has a fez on his head, a green turban on the fez, a smock on his back, and on top of that a jacket like the one I am wearing. I can't see the other half. Now, what kind of outfit is that? Would a civilized man put on this preposterous garb and go out to hold himself up for universal ridicule?[30]

In another example, in 1928 the Turkish government appointed a committee to examine the problem of reform and modernization in Islamic religion. In its report, the committee stated that "religious life, like moral and economic life, must be reformed on scientific lines." Among its recommendations were that mosques should be clean and orderly, with pews and cloakrooms, and that people should enter mosques with clean shoes.[31] As late as 1960, following the military coup of May 27, the military governor of Istanbul passed an ordinance forbidding people from speaking with loud voices in public places lest this create a bad impression among Western tourists.[32] It was not only what people wore but also where and how they lived, what kind of music they listened to, and even what they ate that had to conform to modern norms.[33]

In 1858, Mehmet Kâmil Efendi, a professor in a medical school, published one of the earliest cookbooks in the Ottoman Empire, laying down, as it were, the gastronomic foundations of Ottoman reform. In the preface to *The Refuge of Cooks,* he wrote that because of the changes in lifestyles, the old dishes were no longer satisfactory and "we need to adopt a new cuisine from the West that would go better with our new conditions."[34]

These and similar measures can be regarded as amusing, but the vision that prompted them—and the zealousness with which the bureaucratic elite carried them out—was anything but funny. This single-minded approach had some antecedents in the Ottoman approach to statecraft, but its two most important constituents lay not in the East but in the West. The first of these was a total admiration for science, not as something one engages in critically but as an omnipotent tool that can be borrowed and used for a variety of purposes, including inducing social change. To the reformers, the Ottoman-Turkish scene was a blank slate onto which they were determined to inscribe a firm signature of science and reason. According to them, this and only this could create the right conditions for the kind of social change they deemed necessary for the country. Here is "Ode to the Nineteenth Century," written by a liberal figure in the Ottoman opposition and reflecting some of these sentiments:

> The spread of science has enlightened the minds of men,
> The printed press has completed what was lacking.
> Alas, the Western lands have become the daysprings of knowledge,
> Nothing remains of the fame of Rum and Arab, of Egypt and Herat.
> The time is time of progress, the world is a world of science,
> Is the survival of societies compatible with ignorance?[35]

In the writings of leading intellectuals of the period, such as Ziya Gökalp, the idea of progress through science came to occupy such a central place that sometimes even the passage of time did not seem fast enough: "On progress we shall set our heart," Gökalp said; "We shall skip five hundred years and not stand still."[36] According to Mustafa Kemal, in measuring progress "our standards should be based not on the lethargic mentality of the past centuries but on the concepts of speed and movement that define our century."[37] In 1925, Mustafa Kemal wrote of civilization almost as if it were a supernatural force that should be worshipped:

> It is futile to try to resist the thunderous advance of civilization, for it has no pity on those who are ignorant or rebellious. The sublime force of civilization pierces mountains, crosses the skies, enlightens and explores everything from the smallest particle of dust to stars. . . . When faced with this, those nations who try to follow the superstitions of the Middle Ages are condemned to be destroyed or at least to become enslaved and debased.[38]

The second constituent element of the modern approach to Ottoman and Turkish reform derived from a peculiar inversion of Enlightenment thought that took place not in Turkey but in Europe. Originally, the European philosophers who are identified with the Enlightenment did not think of "human progress" as the preserve of any one culture, people, or geographical place but as something attainable by all of humanity, so long as people learned not to put obstacles in front of it.[39] By the end the nineteenth century, discussions of progress in Europe had lost most of their universalistic pretensions. In the hands of frustrated political leaders and the intelligentsia, this unifying ideal was transformed into its opposite and used as a marker to describe the inherent qualities of different groups of people. Now certain cultures were judged to be unsuitable to take part in progress unless they abandoned their identity. The progressive tenets of the Enlightenment had become an excuse for dividing people into rigid groups and categories.

To put it another way, the universalistic ideals of the eighteenth century were turned on their heads and used as weapons by the leaders of ethnic and official nationalisms to promote their particularistic goals. These leaders and their intellectual patrons had no liking for inclusive liberal ideologies and no tolerance for ambiguity or indeterminacy.[40] In their repertoire, progress ceased to be a universal and somewhat abstract ideal and became a vehicle for describing and justifying the desired and deserved upward movement of their ethnically defined "solid community" in history.[41]

At the close of the nineteenth century, as they were confronted by mounting political difficulties, military defeats, and economic problems, powerful groups among the Ottoman bureaucratic elite found a useful platform in these rigid reformulations of Enlightenment thought and moved in a similar direction by rigidifying their own ideology.[42] The reformers decided that their survival (which in their minds was synonymous with survival of the state and the nation) was contingent upon defining a homogeneous and unified community as the basis of their rule and legitimacy.[43] They discarded the ambiguities and the relative inclusiveness that had characterized the earlier reform measures and movements in favor of a more sharply drawn prescription for the creation of a national community of Turks. The creation and protection of such a community were deemed indispensable in order for the new nation and the state to catch up with the West. "We lived through pain," said Mustafa Kemal,

> because we did not understand the conditions of the world. Our thinking and our mentality will have to become civilized. And we

will be proud of this civilization. Take a look at the entire Turkish
and Islamic world. Because they failed to adapt to the conditions
and rise, they found themselves in such a catastrophe and suffering.
We cannot afford to hesitate any more. We have to move forward. . . .
Civilization is such a fire that it burns and destroys those who ignore it.[44]

There were two groups who found their status in the late Ottoman and
early republican society to be in fundamental conflict with the new nationalist ethos. One of these was the leaders of some of the popular religious orders (*tarikat*s) and those intellectuals who advocated an Islamist
version of reform and reorganization. The nationalist elites defined the
thoughts and deeds of this group as inherently and categorically opposed
to their civilizing mission. In their discourse, Islam became an all-purpose
bogey representing everything that reform, progress, and civilization were
not. Consequently, Islamists were harassed, persecuted, and generally
shunned as being fundamentally obscurantist and reactionary throughout the 1930s and 1940s.

The other group who suffered directly and immediately from the ideological shift of the Young Turk and early republican periods was the non-
Muslim communities of the Ottoman Empire. The Greek, Armenian, and
Jewish subjects of the empire, especially, had always exercised their preferences and priorities on a basis that was much larger than the narrowly
defined boundaries of the new national communities. For example, the
Greeks had found themselves at odds with the earlier nationalism of their
brethren in the Balkans. But the measures that followed the articulation
of the new Turkish nationalism were infinitely more serious and conse-
quential. In particular, several radical steps were followed in the forceful
nationalization of the "Turkish" middle class during the first half of the
twentieth century. These were, first, the deportation and massacre of large
numbers of Armenians in 1914–1915, followed by the exchange of populations with Greece between 1923 and 1930. Then came the imposition
of a special wealth tax of up to 75 percent on the properties of non-Muslim
entrepreneurs in 1942. The whole process culminated in the government-
instigated riots of September 6–7, 1955, when the businesses of Greeks
and other non-Muslims in Istanbul were ransacked by mobs.

Yet in the official rhetoric there has never been any room for a full ac-
counting of these deeds. The triumphalist rendering of the accepted versions of this history leaves out not only the Greeks and Armenians but

also the majority of those who were supposed to be the main beneficiaries of Turkish modernization. Its claims of populism notwithstanding, the reforming elite has always been deeply suspicious of anything smacking of individual initiative, including the notions of civil rights and personal freedoms. Liberal ideas that had been widely represented and even organized in the early phases of reform were eventually marginalized and committed to a perpetual slate of opposition. All ideas and institutions that originated outside the ruling elite and its regulations were perceived with suspicion and deemed dangerous if they could not be shaped and goaded according to the requirements of the political program at hand.[45] In short, in their quest to reorganize Ottoman-Turkish society, the reforming elite ended up isolating itself from society at large and became a close-minded and inward-looking ruling class.[46]

This outlook found its full expression in the First Historical Congress convened in July 1932 under Atatürk's direction in Ankara. The purpose of this gathering was to draw a framework for rewriting history textbooks for elementary and secondary schools. In their papers and comments, professors and teachers from across the country described how the new Turkish nation was to perceive itself and present its history to future generations. The participants generally agreed that Turks had created a rich civilization in Central Asia in prehistorical times, and this was the fount of all subsequent civilizations in human history. According to the participants, Turks had made the most significant contribution to the development and spread of Islamic civilization, but their services were not adequately appreciated. In fact, conservative interpretation of Islam had kept the Ottomans from participating in the European Renaissance and caused the Turks to fall behind Europe after the sixteenth century. In ten days the conference heard no mention of the ethnic diversity of the Ottoman Empire and no discussion of what had happened to its Christian subjects. The only non-Muslim presenter was a Jew, Avram Galanti, who was a professor of "Ancient Eastern Tribes" in the Department of Literature at Istanbul University. He gave a brief commentary on proper transliteration to be used in the writing of the textbooks.[47]

The narrow and sterile path of modernization that emerges from the deeds and discourses of the political elite agrees well with the way the major historians of Turkish modernization have represented the process retrospectively. Lewis, for example, commented on but overlooked the consequences of the blatant illiberalism that characterized most of the leaders "from Mahmud II (1784–1839) to İsmet İnönü (1884–1973)."[48]

In the 1950s and 1960s, most such authors regarded the breaking of traditional ties as so urgent a task that it seemed not to matter what methods were used to achieve that end. So long as those methods were directed
against institutions and practices portrayed as intrinsically antithetical
to progress and modernization (meaning, in most cases, Islamic), they
could be justified. Lewis echoed a common way of thinking about Turkish politics in these years when he wrote that "the Young Turks may have
failed to give Turkey constitutional government. They did, however, give
Istanbul drains."[49]

Modernizing Society: Then and Now

That in both theory and practice there was such an emphasis on institutional reform and its outward manifestations often leads us to forget that
these reforms touched a relatively small part of Ottoman and Turkish society in the nineteenth and early twentieth centuries. Outside the privileged domain of the political elite stood large numbers of people whose
visions and voices were rarely acknowledged during the initial years of
the republic. Even though the top-down formulations of reform and the
state-centered analyses of the reform process make it difficult to focus on
social forces as distinct from the state, through some innovative use of
sources we can break through these limitations and start to "bring the
society back" into our framework. Directly or indirectly, social forces had
an impact on the shape and effectiveness of many of the reform policies,
even if that impact is not always recognized.[50]

One source we can use to get an idea about what was going on beyond
the capital city is stories told in the Turkish vernacular that describe the
early years of the twentieth century from the perspective of peasants. In
addition to abject poverty resulting from decades of war and shortages,
such stories reveal a profound crisis of identity. When pressured, the heroes of these stories and epic poems end up declaring their loyalty to an
entity that had no fixed temporal point of reference whatsoever. In their
speech, the sultan-caliph, Young Turk leaders, Mustafa Kemal, the Prophet
Muhammed, and his nephew Ali often melt into one amorphous being
who claims their allegiance.[51]

The antagonistic nature of the subtle links between state forces and the
nonstate arena was thrust into the forefront of the Turkish political scene
only in 1950, when Mustafa Kemal's party was soundly defeated and voted
out of office in elections held that year. In the years leading up to and following the 1950 elections, the rural population created, at the grass roots

level, one of the most developed and widespread systems of political organization and participation in the world. To many this was a surprising development, for it went against the general descriptions found in many social science texts. After all, the peasantry was thought to be far removed from the advances of recent years; it had been described by some as "virtually unaffected by limited modernization."[52] In this respect, Daniel Lerner's observation is insightful, if somewhat condescending: in 1954, impressed by the degree of politicization in Turkey, he wrote that "the villagers have learned the basic lesson of democratic politics." On this occasion, they had just explained to him that it would be better to have a small margin between the major parties because then they would "heed our voices."[53]

Today, with the declining hold of Kemalist restrictions and other state-centered ideologies, we are better able to see most men and women living in Turkey not merely as objects of a project but also as subjects of their history. They are able to affect their own lives through the choices they make in villages, small towns, and the neighborhoods of big cities. They have "the power to change the world that is changing them, to make their way through the maelstrom and make it their own."[54] They live in a modern world that Lerner described as "expansive . . . populated more actively with imaginings and fantasies—hungering for whatever is different and unfamiliar."[55] Lerner describes a similar state of restlessness and adventurism that characterizes the modern person when he says, "In the perceptual apparatus of Modern men, all scales are in principle infinite until proved otherwise. [A modern man] locates himself not at some fixed point in the rank-order of things known, but at some moving point of desire in a scale of things imagined."[56]

For some, the conflicting voices and visions that have dominated the Turkish scene since the early 1980s signal not just a turn in but a complete collapse of the Turkish experiment with modernity. According to this perspective, the fruits of progress in Turkey have been not a rational and universally progressive middle-class society but an economically polarized, politically contentious, and ethnically divided people. Instead of well-informed and politically conscious actors, increasing literacy and media awareness have created a youthful and growing population addicted to the technological marvels of modernity but not quite equipped with adequate means to master them.

In reaction to the despair and cynicism that underlie many such descriptions, it is hard not to be sympathetic toward those who see a multiplication of possibilities in the detotalized, decentered world of the eighties and nineties. But one should be careful not to let the pendulum swing too far in the opposite direction and celebrate each and every break in the Kemalist framework as another step in liberation. The extreme relativism that underlies such a point of view sees each position and action as having its own truth and meaning and ignores the fundamental requirement that people communicate across the divides by which they find themselves separated.

Modernity makes it possible for people to imagine for themselves a common context beyond their most immediate, personal experience. In order to avoid the disorienting world of extreme relativism that Gellner has so forcefully criticized,[57] we need to remember the universal tenets of modernization as a world historical process. The widening and deepening of the market society, the protective impulses of human beings, and the assertion of human and civil rights are all aspects of modernization, and as such they are not the preserves of any one group, point of view, tradition, or culture. As students of and participants in this drama, we can insist on the universality of these elements and thereby have a way of comparing, assessing, and evaluating the multiplying visions, stands, and protests that surround us. Such a position finds its most compelling explanation in Weber, who believed that in modern culture "there [are] no perfect answers, but by accepting the historical world as it has become and striving to understand it, and by resisting the temptations of inwardness and subjectivism, one may make possible the emergence of 'contingently hopeful futures.'"[58]

As we approach the twenty-first century, and as the constraints of the post–World War II settlement vanish, Turkey once again comes into focus as both a pivot of the new world order and a successful example of modernization. *The Economist* calls it "the Star of Islam"; Samuel Huntington sees it as a torn country and hence potentially a decisive case in the coming clash "between the west and the rest":

> Having rejected Mecca, and then being rejected by Brussels, where does Turkey look? Tashkent may be the answer. The end of the Soviet Union gives Turkey the opportunity to become the leader of a revived Turkic civilization involving seven countries from the borders of Greece to those of China.[59]

Robert Kaplan, in a devastating prognosis of the possible place of the Third World in the coming century, admires the "formidable fabric of which

Turkish Muslim culture is made." He continues: "A culture this strong has the potential to dominate the Middle East once again. . . . Those people whose cultures can harbor extensive slum life without decomposing will be, relatively speaking, the future's winners."[60]

It might be comforting to some that Huntington situates Turkey in a gray zone in his "clash of civilizations," or that Kaplan is impressed by Turks because they are able to live in slums without decomposing. But it would be wrong to give credence to such confusing and disorienting generalizations. Above all, we should not conclude that in the 1980s and 1990s, the "modern public has shattered into a multitude of fragments speaking incommensurable private languages and modernity has lost its power to give meaning to people's lives."[61] Equating the collapse of state-centered models of modernization with the collapse of modernity itself would mean that we are still reading history through the lens of a very restrictive model. Far from extinguishing the promise of modernity, the ongoing eclipse of these models releases, in theory and in practice, the liberating and enabling dynamics of modernization. Stripped of the artificial certainties and uniformities of yesteryear, the world appears not chaotic and insecure but full of possibilities.

In Lerner's well-known ethnography, the grocer of Balgat says he prefers American movies because they are exciting; they make people "ask what is going to happen next."[62] Perhaps the film is still running, and we don't know what will happen next.

Notes

1. Hasan Cemal, *12 Eylül Günlüğü: Demokrasi Korkusu,* Ankara: Bilgi, 1986, 267.

2. On 1925 and its aftermath, see Erik J. Zürcher, *Turkey: A Modern History,* London: I. B. Tauris, 1993, 180–92.

3. A. Taner Kışlalı, *Atatürk'e Saldırmanın Dayanılmaz Hafifliği,* Ankara: İmge, 1993.

4. A. Bulaç, *Din ve Modernizm,* Istanbul: Beyan, 1992. See also Michael Meeker, "The New Muslim Intellectuals in the Republic of Turkey," in Richard Tapper, ed., *Islam in Modern Turkey,* London: I. B. Tauris, 1991, 189–222.

5. See, for example, Amir Hassanpour, "The Kurdish Experience," *Middle East Report,* vol. 189, 1994, 2–7.

6. Ernest Gellner, *Postmodernism, Reason and Religion,* London: Routledge, 1992, 3.

7. For an optimistic assessment of the 1980s, see M. Heper and A. Evin, eds., *Politics in the Third Turkish Republic,* Boulder, Colorado: Westview Press, 1994.

8. The discussion and definitions in this section are based largely on the following works: Karl Polanyi, *The Great Transformation,* New York: Beacon Press, 1956; Reinhard Bendix, *Nation Building and Citizenship,* Berkeley: University of California Press, 1977; Dean Tipps, "Modernization Theory and the Comparative Study of Societies: A Critical Perspective," *Comparative Studies in Society and History,* vol. 15, March 1973, 196–226; Liah Greenfeld, *Nationalism: Five Routes to Modernity,* Cambridge, Massachusetts: Harvard University Press, 1992; Marshall Berman, *All That Is Solid Melts into Air: The Experience of Modernity,* London: Penguin, 1982; Chantal Mouffe, ed., *Dimensions of Radical Democracy,* London: Verso, 1992.

9. Karl Polanyi, *The Great Transformation,* Boston: Beacon Press, 1957, 76.

10. Tipps, "Modernization Theory and the Comparative Study of Societies," 204. See also S. N. Eisenstadt, "The Kemalist Regime and Modernization: Some Comparative and Analytical Remarks," in J. Landau, ed., *Atatürk and the Modernization of Turkey,* Boulder, Colorado: Westview Press, 1984, 3–16.

11. C. Wright Mills, *The Sociological Imagination,* Oxford: Oxford University Press, 1959.

12. Bernard Lewis, *The Emergence of Modern Turkey,* 2d ed. New York: Oxford University Press, 1968, 17.

13. It is interesting to note that in a recent essay Bülent Ecevit makes the same point. See his "Prospects and Difficulties of Democratization in the Middle East," in E. Goldberg, R. Kasaba, and J. Migdal, eds., *Rules and Rights in the Middle East,* Seattle: University of Washington Press, 1993, 141–63.

14. Lewis, *Emergence,* 353.

15. Lewis, *Emergence,* 409.

16. Lewis, *Emergence,* 404–12.

17. Lewis, *Emergence,* 57. See also Bernard Lewis, "The Impact of the French Revolution on Turkey," *Journal of World History,* vol. 1, 1953, 105–25.

18. Lewis, *Emergence,* 23.

19. Lewis, *Emergence,* 154.

20. Lewis, *Emergence,* 220.

21. Lewis, *Emergence,* 125–26.

22. Lewis, *Emergence,* 416n32.

23. Daniel Lerner, *The Passing of Traditional Society,* New York: Free Press, 1958.

24. Lerner, *The Passing of Traditional Society,* 77.

25. Lerner, *The Passing of Traditional Society,* 101. To be sure, Turkey was not the only country to exhibit conflicting evidence that did not quite fit into the dichotomous ideal types of tradition and modernity. In response to growing evidence for complexity, the modernization literature began to elaborate theories of "post-traditional" (yet premodern) societies. See, for example, the essays in *Daedalus,* vol. 120, no. 1, 1973. This was a significant step in recognizing the difficulties of simplified schemes. But in some of its versions, this step ended up creating yet another ideal type, leaving the reader wondering how a society moves from a traditional to a post-traditional or transitional stage. See, for example, Joseph Gusfield, "Tradition and Modernity: Misplaced Polarities in the Study of Social Change," in J. Finkle and R. Gable, eds., *Political Development and Social Change,* New York: John Wiley, 1966, 15–26.

26. Greenfeld, *Nationalism*, 235.

27. Robert Darnton, *The Kiss of the Lamourette*, New York: Norton, 1990, 9.

28. Lewis, *Emergence*, 102.

29. Lewis, *Emergence*, 268.

30. Lewis, *Emergence*, 269.

31. Lewis, *Emergence*, 414.

32. *Cumhuriyet*, 25 July 1961.

33. See the chapters by Bozdoğan, Nalbantoğlu, and Özbek in this volume.

34. Hilmi Ziya Ülken, *Turkiye'de Çağdaş Düşünce Tarihi*, Istanbul: Ülken, 1966, 40.

35. Quoted in Lewis, *Emergence*, 133–34.

36. Cited in Lerner, *The Passing of Traditional Society*, 136.

37. *Atatürk'ün Söylev ve Demeçleri*, II, Ankara: Türk Tarih Kurumu, 1959, 277.

38. *Atatürk'ün Söylev ve Demeçleri*, II, 212.

39. In *The Decline and Fall of the Roman Empire*, Gibbon wrote that "it may safely be presumed that no people, unless the face of nature is changed, will relapse into their original barbarism." Cited in Peter Gay, *The Enlightenment: An Interpretation. The Science of Freedom*, New York, Norton, 1969, 98.

40. On this point, see Daniel Chirot, "Modernism without Liberalism: The Ideological Roots of Modern Tyranny," *Contention*, vol. 13, 1995, 141–66; Greenfeld, *Nationalism*, 1–26, 189–274, 222–34; Benedict Anderson, *Imagined Communities: Reflections on the Origin and Spread of Nationalism*, London: Verso, 1991 [1983].

41. Anderson, *Imagined Communities*, 26.

42. It is important to note that a parallel development was taking place in the former provinces of the Ottoman Empire, especially in the Balkans. See Fikret Adanır, "The National Question and the Genesis and Development of Socialism in the Ottoman Empire: The Case of Macedonia," in M. Tunçay and E. Zürcher, eds., *Socialism and Nationalism in the Ottoman Empire, 1876–1923*, London: British Academic Press, 1994, 27–48.

43. Interestingly, Abdülhak Adnan Adıvar found the republican norms of education as dogmatic as the Islamic ones they replaced. He paraphrased H. Gibb in saying that, with the reforms of the new regime, "Turkey became a positivistic mausoleum." A. Adıvar, "Interaction of Islamic and Western Thought in Turkey," in T. C. Young, ed., *Near Eastern Culture and Society*, Princeton, New Jersey: Princeton University Press, 1951, 128.

44. *Atatürk'ün Söylev ve Demeçleri*, II, 207.

45. See Zürcher, *Turkey: A Modern History*, 115–16, 175–76.

46. Şerif Mardin, "Just and Unjust," *Daedalus*, vol. 120, no. 3, 1991, 117–29. See also Ergun Özbudun, "State Elites and Democratic Political Culture in Turkey," in L. Diamond, ed., *Political Culture and Democracy in Developing Countries*, Boulder, Colorado: Lynne Reiner, 1993, 247–68.

47. The full texts of some of the papers presented and discussions held at this conference were published in T. C. Maarif Vekâleti, *Birinci Türk Tarih Kongresi*, Istanbul: Matbaacılık ve Neşriyat Anonim Şirketi, 1932.

48. Lewis, *Emergence*, 369.

49. Lewis, *Emergence*, 228.

50. For a number of insightful essays that probe the link between state forces and nonstate actors, see A. Finkel and N. Sirman, eds., *Turkish State, Turkish Society*, London: Routledge, 1990.

51. The epic poem *Memleketimden İnsan Manzaraları*, by Nazım Hikmet, contains a series of sharply drawn characters in Anatolia who exhibit many of these characteristics.

52. Cyril Black, *The Dynamics of Modernization*, New York: Harper and Row, 1966, 121. See also Robert Ward and Dankwart Rustow, *Political Modernization in Japan and Turkey*, Princeton, New Jersey: Princeton University Press, 1964, 456.

53. Lerner, *The Passing of Traditional Society*, 41.

54. Berman, *All That Is Solid*, 16.

55. Lerner, *The Passing of Traditional Society*, 23.

56. Lerner, *The Passing of Traditional Society*, 134.

57. Gellner, *Postmodernism, Reason and Religion*, 40–72.

58. As paraphrased by Gordon Craig, "Demonic Democracy," *New York Review of Books*, 13 February 1992, 41. See also David Harvey, "Class Relations, Social Justice and the Politics of Difference," in M. Keith and S. Pile, eds., *Place and Politics of Identity*, New York: Routledge, 1993, 41–66.

59. Samuel Huntington, "The Clash of Civilizations," *Foreign Affairs*, Summer 1993, 22–49.

60. Robert Kaplan, "The Coming Anarchy," *Atlantic Monthly*, February 1994, 44–76.

61. Berman, *All That Is Solid*, 17.

62. Lerner, *The Passing of Traditional Society*, 28.

3/ Whither the Project of Modernity?

Turkey in the 1990s

ÇAĞLAR KEYDER

In the last decade of the twentieth century, a deep sense of malaise gripped Turkish society. While the elites and the intelligentsia asked themselves where things had gone wrong—or rather, where they had gone wrong—the people strived to accommodate themselves to a lack of direction, growing anomie, the decaying of institutions, and lawlessness. Observing the demise of the developmentalist ideal, they responded to the promises of the nation-state with growing incredulity. In a context where modernity was a conscious imposition by modernizers whose arsenal was the exercise of state power, the crisis of the state seemed to forebode the bankruptcy of the entire project. The pessimism inspired by Turkish reality was compounded by the fear that the global project of modernity was exhausted: that it was no longer possible to emulate the cultural achievements of the West, and that the geo-cultural choice in favor of Europe, which had always been an integral component of the Turkish project, would also have to be abandoned.

Turkish modernizers had readily identified modernization with Westernization—with taking a place in the civilization of Europe.[1] Modernity, in their conception, was a total project: one of embracing and internalizing all the cultural dimensions that made Europe modern. They were not satisfied simply with increasing rationality, bureaucratization, and organizational efficiency; they also professed a need for social transformation in order to achieve secularization, autonomy for the individual, and the equality of men and women. This project permitted local culture no greater space than that of the folkloric; it accepted no adulteration of modernity with a qualifying adjective such as Islamic or Turkish.[2]

It was this conception of modernity, with its strict identification of modernization with Westernization, that led to the pessimism I mentioned. There is, however, another conception in which modernization is taken to mean the process of actual transformations toward organizational efficiency and rationality, which implies no normative commitment to the Enlightenment project. This perspective of non-Western modernization has gained in popularity in the Turkish context. Its proponents, taking a stance similar to the postmodernist celebration of the hybrid, see in the apparent crumbling of social cohesion and the rise of credos actively challenging the aspirations of modernity a welcome sign that some negotiation might occur between the Westernizers and their erstwhile objects. They observe in this challenge a search for cultural identity, the assertion of a claim over life-worlds whose definition had been denied to their inhabitors.

In contrast to the Westernizers, who deplore deviations from the blueprint, what the optimists would like to commend is the possibility of a combination of the local with the modern. Although the terms of the amalgam are not specified, the rubric "Islamic and modern" is usually employed to describe the desired combination.[3] Proponents of this conception announce the death of the modernization project identified with the normative importation of Enlightenment ideals, and they celebrate the possibility of a local (and, some would argue, therefore authentic) appropriation of the modern.

Normatively, I share the Westernizers' position that the project of modernity cannot but be a total one and should seek to realize the Enlightenment ideals. Although it may be correct to diagnose an exhaustion of the momentum represented by modernization-from-above and by the achievements of the nation-state, it is not necessarily the case that the project of modernity will henceforth be permanently stalled. The social engineering associated with modernization-from-above was badly flawed from its inception, and it has to be superseded if the ideal of a society of free and equal individuals is to be achieved. This may only be possible if the locus of modernization shifts to the society itself, with a renewed political and legal framework allowing individuals to attain the status of citizens. Hence, for those with a normative commitment to the project, it is critically important to diagnose the situation correctly: Is there any way of recovering the modernizing momentum that used to be provided by the state? If the modernizing dynamic is henceforth to be located in the society, who will be its principal agents, and what are the political conditions necessary for their success? We do need radical surgery, but it is premature to arrange for an inquest into the death of the project.

Modernization from Above

Of all the words derivative of the radical "modern," that which applies most readily to Turkish experience is "modernization"—defined as a project. The agency behind the project was the modernizing elite, and what they sought to achieve was the imposition of institutions, beliefs, and behavior consonant with their understanding of modernity on the chosen object: the people of Turkey.

The crucial difference between modernization-from-above and modernization as a self-generating societal process is that the modernizers wield state power and are agents with their own interests. For this reason, even if they profess a project of Westernization, they are not necessarily committed to all the dimensions of modernity. It is this potential conflict between the full unfolding of modernity and the circumscribed version that the modernizers would like to see realized which defines the principal problem implicit in the formula "modernization-from-above." That modernity is an indivisible project whose artificial truncation by modernizers generally leads to crisis has been recognized, most famously by Barrington Moore.[4] Moore showed that aspects of modernity could not be picked and chosen at will, as if one were selecting dishes from a menu. In his account, the lack of political modernization (owing to the abiding power of the ruling class of the ancien régime) determined a crisis-ridden trajectory toward fascism. In what follows, I argue that the historical genesis of the state tradition in Turkey determined the choices made by the modernizers in their attempt to delimit the scope of modernity, thus undermining their avowed goal of Westernization.

Most students of the Turkish case agree that there was continuity between Ottoman modernizers and the founders of the Turkish state.[5] There was no overthrow of the Ottoman state structure after World War I; the new Turkish state took over with only slightly different personnel. Furthermore, owing to the ethnic structure of the empire and to the civil war, as a result of which the Christian populations were expelled, the state elite did not have to worry about the cooperation or reluctance of a strong bourgeois class. Most of the merchants, bankers, and industrialists of the empire were no longer there when the Republic of Turkey came into being.[6] Indeed, a new bourgeoisie was created through the policies of the state during the project of nationalist modernization.

These propositions concerning the continuity between imperial and nationalist elites are premised upon a fundamental feature of Ottoman social structure: the absence of large landlords (or, equivalently, the relative independence of the bureaucracy).[7] Because of this absence, the guardians of the ancien régime were simply the nonreformist wing of the bureaucracy; the nationalist intelligentsia did not have to confront any serious opposition. Without a strong landlord class that might have demanded economic liberalism and civil and political rights for its narrow constituency (for example, Latin American oligarchies, or the interests around the Wafd party in Egypt during the 1920s), no group in the society found it possible to challenge the absolutism of the state.

Absent a revolutionary break in the class basis of the state, the fundamental division between the state class and the masses was perpetuated. A factor strengthening the status of the republican state was the material resources it had acquired during the civil wars leading to its establishment. As non-Muslims were eliminated and driven away throughout World War I and the war with Greece, their property, as well as the positions they vacated, became part of the dowry of the new state that could be distributed to the rest of the population. What this distribution achieved was both to expedite the creation of a native bourgeoisie and to make it beholden to the state. Shortly after the establishment of the new state, world economic conditions and the ideological zeitgeist shifted to favor antiliberalism and a state-directed economy. During the 1930s and World War II, the course of capitalist accumulation came under the full control of the state.

After the war, the Turkish state elites were prevailed upon (abetted by their own effort to locate themselves within the bloc of United States hegemony) to adopt liberalism in the economy. Within a few years, however, it became apparent to Americans as well as the Turkish state elite that instead of economic liberalism, a program of planned, import-substituting industrialization would be the proper prescription for development. Hence, the state was invested with expanded prerogatives employing new administrative capacities. In this newly created context, in which the stakes increased as economic development proceeded, it became extremely costly for businessmen to challenge the state.[8] Bureaucrats were in a position to make substantive decisions with virtual impunity, and they evaded accountability in the name of developmentalist efficiency. The social and economic policy of the state also contributed to its ability to effectively prevent challenges originating in the society.[9] This was the period of national developmentalism, when prevailing world conditions allowed the state to regulate the economy under relatively closed circumstances. First, etatism during the Great Depression, and later, import substitution as befit American policies and world economic conditions of the time, had supplied the necessary policy packages.

National developmentalism was successful in its economic promises. There has been in Turkey, as in the majority of peripheral economies until the 1980s, considerable development, national economic integration, urbanization, and increase in levels of welfare. These gains have been transmitted to the populace through social entitlements, feeding into the populist rhetoric. Material progress, however, has not led to the development of individual autonomy or legal rights. On the contrary, it can be argued that the success of the social entitlement programs contributed to an emasculation of the concept of citizenship. Populism emerged as the modality for successfully perpetuating the claims and the status of a strong state, and as long as the state remained strong, full citizenship could be suspended.

Social rights became a means for the state to extend its legitimacy into the population, thus dividing, creating clientelistic networks, and colonizing. The beneficiaries of social programs were defined according to their group attributes—not as individuals.[10] The state's largesse was addressed to corporatized bodies whose very existence derived from the state's need to identify and control a freshly segmented society. When politics was reduced to a bargain over the distribution of material rewards, a strategic and procedural conception of political rights, oriented toward participation in the structure of patronage, seemed normal and sufficient.

A similar account of the isolation and imperiousness of the state elite may be given in terms of nationalist ideology and the culture it propagated. In the transition from empire to nation-state, there had been a change in the legitimating discourse of state authority. The imperial Ottomanist ideology, a blend of Islamism and elite cohesion at the top, had to be abandoned. What took its place was a delayed reaction to and appropriation of what had led to the dissolution of the empire: nationalism. While they battled separatists and irredentists, Ottoman state elites had been slow to concoct their own brand of nationalism, which, of course, would have been self-defeating since their attempt was to preserve the empire. Later, however, when the likelihood of a narrower territorial sovereignty arose after World War I, they had to opt for Turkish nationalism.

Since the mid-nineteenth century, in cases as diverse as Germany and China, nationalism had provided the vocabulary for defensive modernization. The question of modernity in the context of the Third World had become inextricably bound up with the question of constructing the nation-state.[11] It was such nationalism-from-above that constituted the founding ideology of the new Turkish republic. In this construct, the state could demarcate the boundaries of the nation and determine the margins beyond which the necessary unity of the collective body would be threatened. Such an organicist and societal perspective provided the justification for rejecting the possibility of fashioning a civic identity around which the population, as an aggregate of individuals, might find cohesion. In other words, a citizenship constituted foundationally around universally applicable civil rights never developed.[12] Instead, authoritarian nationalism emphasized unity and collective purpose. The nation was supposed to express a homogeneity deriving from ethnic unity, and this unity would be expressed in a single voice. Hence, the collectivist vision implied its authoritarian implementation because it called for a cadre of interpreters and expressers to know and represent the unique voice of the nation. It was this cadre that was inducted as agents of the project of modernity.

It was the elites' perception of underdevelopment that ushered in nationalisms in the periphery. Concurrent with this perception there frequently came a surge of popular resentment stemming from the dislocating, differentiating, and polarizing tide of contact with the West. Such resentment led to a questioning of the customary legitimation of the social order and to a popular resistance against colonialism or incorporation into the world market. The success of the anticolonial and nationalist movement could well depend on how this resistance was contained and channeled by the elites toward the sought-after mobilization for national construction. In other words, in order to strengthen and mobilize the forces for construction of the nation, the elites had to appropriate popular resentment into their own *ressentiment*.[13]

Partha Chatterjee argues that nationalist elites are in a position to articulate the resentment of the masses, yet they feel the necessity of embracing the "modern" if their society is to survive in the new world.[14] Nationalist imagery and historiography will reflect this dilemma and the ambivalence with which the elites embrace modernity. As nationalism faces the problem of seizing the past in order to confront the future, its accompanying texts will reflect the similarly problematic nature of peripheral modernization. A nationalist discourse that does not resonate positively with indigenous culture and its resistance when confronted with Western expansion risks failure and alienation from the masses. If the new construct is designed by the elites solely to be consonant with the perceived requirements of modernity and fails to find a popular echo, problems of legitimation will plague the new regime.

The elites must thus translate and domesticate the transcendent logic of the modern in order to utilize it in their resistance. This domestication is pragmatic and for heuristic purposes, because the nationalist elites already are cosmopolitan; they know how to exist in both worlds and are comfortable in universal and local idioms alike.[15] The masses must be spared such acrobatics, however. The ambivalence of belonging to two worlds is a luxury the intelligentsia may be able to afford; for the masses, something more readily ingestible should be on offer. The imperative to translate becomes the more pressing when popular resentment is palpable, and especially when it has a voice of its own. The very attempt to translate, however, brings the intelligentsia to an accommodation with the popular idiom, to a comprehension of the dimensions of popular anxiety and resentment and of people's willingness to resist. Unless this accommodation is worked out, elite discourse will remain isolated, only to find a greater challenge down the road.

Turkish nationalism is an extreme example of a situation in which the masses remained silent partners and the modernizing elite did not attempt to accommodate popular resentment. The degree of popular sentiment that could be mobilized toward nationalist movements varied widely in the Third World, and Anatolian peasants were at the passive end of the spectrum. The masses in Turkey generally remained passive recipients of the nationalist message propounded by the elites. The continuity between Ottoman reformers and republican nationalists is one factor explaining the lack of popular fervor. Even with such continuity, participation in the nationalist movement could have provided the unifying experience required for allegiance to the new regime. But here, too, there were problems: the struggle with Greece was widely perceived as a war against an outside aggressor rather than as a struggle against a colonial presence. As such, it was yet another military campaign to be endured by the already mobilized Anatolian youth. Once again, for the masses, the high drama of making history could be accessed only through their role as draftees in the army.

What touched the masses directly during the Turkish nationalist movement was the expulsion, deportation, massacre, and exchange of the Greek and Armenian subjects of the empire. Indeed, the presence of the Christian population was the only medium through which Muslim Anatolians had experienced the otherwise abstract notion of peripheralization in their daily lives. Rather than being popular, however, the events culminating in the expulsion and disappearance of some nine-tenths of the Christian population (around one-sixth of the total population in Anatolia) were laden with embarrassment and shame, covered up in official discourse as much as in the national psyche.[16] This is not to argue that there had been no Muslim resentment against the rapid rise in both social and economic status of the Christian subjects of the empire during the nineteenth century. Nonetheless, there was much daily intercourse among the different millets, and prevailing norms of behavior prescribed cordiality and mutual respect.

Given this background, what transpired was way out of proportion to the degree of hostility that might have existed. Even if the war years had aggrandized sentiments against Greeks in the western parts of Anatolia, this was not the case for Armenians in the east in 1915, or for the Karamani or the Pontus Greeks in the interior and on the Black Sea coast, respectively. Rather than rallying the population around the nationalist cause and leading to popular participation, the hostilities created a situation in which the principal event of the nationalist struggle was repressed in the collective memory of all participants. This repression was all the more effective because of the material rewards associated with the physical removal of ethnic minorities.

The degree of participation by the masses not only was important in fashioning the course of the struggle but also determined the content of nationalist historiography and the identity that was created as a basis of legitimation for the new regime. While the aim of the nationalist mobilization was formulated as appropriation of the transcendent logic of the West, it was at the same time imperative that popular sentiments be satisfied through a glorification of something local. This is part of what is regarded as imagining the nation. The main problem with Turkish nationalist historiography was that it did not result from a negotiation between what the nationalist elites were trying to achieve and what could have motivated the masses to participate, nor did it come to terms with the events that loomed largest in the experience of the participants. Consequently, the story propagated through official discourse suffered from the all-too-obvious concealment of a crucial episode and instead gained in pure artifice. There were no grounds in this history for a negotiation because the shared elements of the experience had been eliminated. Thus it became possible for the nationalist elites to treat the construction of history and national identity in an entirely instrumental fashion; the version they eventually settled on was woefully deficient in its accommodation of popular elements. The masses remained passive during the process and apparently accepted the implicit pact for mutual silence.[17]

The silence of the masses also permitted the construction of an imaginary "popular" by the elite. Redefinition of the "popular" (via folklore and history) is a common feature of all nationalisms and is expected to proceed from the assimilation of various decontextualized elements of mass culture to the totalizing semiotics of the national project.[18] In the Turkish case, this redefinition could take place with more than the usual liberty because the freshly constituted elements of a popular "tradition" were represented to the masses as the authentic (and official) version, without much concern for preexisting versions. The defining vector of this reconstitution was an unsullied ethnic heritage endowed with all the positive virtues of might, unity, state-building acumen, and self-confidence. This trope, designed to boost self-esteem, established a matrix through which all the national symbols—from heroic sculptures to ethnographic detail, from folk music, legends, and heroes to public ceremonies—were defined.[19] Henceforth, popular culture would be yet another realm amenable to social engineering.

The gap between the modernizing elites, whose discourse diverged radically from what could be popularly appropriated, and the voiceless masses gradually emerged as the axis around which the subsequent history of Turkish society was played out. No mediations developed between the modernizing discourse of the elites and the practice of the masses. Consequently, the Westernist ideal came to be identified with the statist and authoritarian stance of the modernizers. In response, a resistance culture, packaged as authentic, evolved to challenge the modernizing imposition. Modernization dictated from above necessarily politicizes its object—those who adhere to the already existing indigenous culture—and turns their culture into a residual discourse.[20] In this case, as the confrontation between elites and masses unfolded, this residual discourse animated populist projects of various hues, all of which stemmed from the particular forms in which the potential dialogues had been truncated, had atrophied, or had not been allowed to evolve.

Nationalism, of course, attempts to redefine a collectivity as a community. Turkish nationalism placed special emphasis on the vulnerability of the new community, on its precarious viability in the face of hostile external forces. The state had to be intrepid in protecting it. Predictably, such a defense required the interdiction of internal dissent as well. Authoritarianism became the necessary corollary to reliance on collectivist nationalism as the legitimating principle of the state. In other words, modernization-from-above came to mean modernization of the solidary nation but not of its individual members, who were expected to continue living in their *gemeinschaftlich* universe newly constructed under state auspices. This project did not permit the individuation of the component parts of the national unity. There thus emerged a widening gap between the declared intent of Westernization and the actual practice of limited modernization.

This is why, in cases of elite-directed transformation in which nationalism is the ideological environment of modernization, it is the state elites who have to be defeated in order for modernization-from-above to be transcended by a full project of modernity.[21] The momentum of modernity has to be allowed to overcome the local culture and gradually to dominate the life-worlds of the masses. First, however, imposition has to stop, and along with it the biases imposed on the conception of modernity by the state elite. This can be accomplished only when the legal and political conditions for a popular appropriation of modernity are created—in other words, when the legal basis for citizenship rights and the foundational requirements for individual autonomy are established.[22]

The Crisis of the Project

In world-historical terms, the period of national developmentalism is over.[23] The collapse of the nationalist modernizing state cannot be averted through the injection of a new dose of jingoistic fervor. That scenario would ensure a marginalized involution—an outcome that current world conditions seem not to exclude. It is impossible to believe anymore that capitalism will eventually batter all walls and incorporate all packets of humanity into its purview. Even if it did, however, there is a growing suspicion that capitalism no longer requires its own expansion to be accompanied by cultural transformation toward the modern.[24] Hence, a passive faith in the transformatory capacity of capitalist development is untenable.

Alternatively, the successful advance of the modernizationist momentum without a return to national developmentalism may also be imagined—a new order based on a civic, nonethnic, and nonpopulist principle of citizenship, in which the state will recognize basic civil rights of individuals and in which political liberalism will be accepted as the guiding principle. The proponents of this alternative derive their optimism from the collapse of state-centered developmentalism. It has become clear that national economies cannot be managed and that the policies of nurturing the bourgeoisie and of populist incorporation cannot continue. Consequently, the state is in serious crisis: the legitimacy it once enjoyed has been withdrawn.

One source from which demands for a citizenship-based order may originate is the bourgeoisie, which was successfully nurtured during the authoritarian period yet now finds this political order constraining and its economic orientation archaic. Until recently, the Turkish bourgeoisie had remained weak and diffident. Now, among its ranks is found a faction for whom the costs of the developmentalist state, in its arbitrariness and increasingly self-serving behavior, have become onerous.[25] Businessmen strong enough to compete with and become part of the international corporate bourgeoisie opt for the rule of law and a generally predictable framework for major policies of the state.[26] In their quest for calculability, they want the bureaucracy to become accountable.

The choice in favor of "globalization" made by a part of the Turkish bourgeoisie also requires an acceptance of norms associated with the West. Indeed, this requirement has been instrumental in creating a divide among the state cadres—the erstwhile defenders of modernization-from-above. Turkey's relations with various international organs in Europe, particularly with the European Union, reached a turning point in the 1990s that required a clear enunciation of the goals of Westernization. These fora were no longer willing to accept excuses about how conditions were not ripe for the implementation of reforms in civil and political rights. It became clear that refusal to institute the legal foundations of individual autonomy would be tantamount to giving up the geo-cultural claim of "Europeanness."[27] Hence, one wing of the political elite allied itself with the bourgeoisie (and some intellectuals) to defend the view that rule of law and civil rights are the indispensable foundation for any politics.

Another impetus to the defense of political liberalism has been the attempt to understand and respond to ethnic separatism and Islamic fundamentalism. Although these movements, especially the Islamist, target goals that may be difficult to recuperate under a liberal order, an argument could be made that they would lose a good deal of their fervor if citizenship based on political liberalism and genuine secularism were instituted. For ethnic separatism, this promise is clear: if the ideology of

collectivist nationalism were abandoned in favor of some form of constitutional citizenship, if a credible legal and administrative order enabling
the creation of a public space in which cultural identity could be expressed
were established, then separatist demands would probably be tamed toward the exercise of newly gained rights. Although a "modernist" strand
is harder to find within the religious movement, it is still true that political Islam derives ammunition from the authoritarian conceptions of the
state that pass for secularism. With genuine secularism, the Islamic communitarian movement could well be reduced to an ordinary millenari-
anism and a constituency of the marginalized.

Alternatively, the Islamic social movement may be transformed into a
genuinely Islamic-democratic political party. This is not to say that the
Kurdish and Islamic movements do not currently express demands in the
direction of basic rights and political liberalism. On the contrary, their
public stance and the manner in which they link with international loci
of influence over the Turkish state foreground their democratizing platform. Combined with the universalistic demands of the heretofore silent
religious minority, the Alevis, this makes for an important common front
against the authoritarian state elite. Whether this objective potential for
alliance will be realized in political practice remains to be seen.

Thus, the current struggle in Turkey seems to be between the old
authoritarian-modernizationist, paternalistic state, with its crumbling nationalist and populist legitimation, and a modernist conception of political liberalism and citizenship. It is apparent that the transition from
a modernizationist state that sees itself as the guardian of social change
to a modern state based on political liberalism and citizenship is neither
automatic nor readily attainable. The various practitioners and supporters of the old state conception, interests articulated around authoritarianism, are aware of their weakness and will not concede without a fight.
Indeed, they seem to have opted for rear-guard action designed to extend
the life of the authoritarian ideal. Since the material conditions of state-
centered modernization can no longer be re-created, they may be right
in thinking that this particular choice is the only alternative to a more
rapid exit from the historical stage. As Barrington Moore pointed out, the
trajectory of modernization-from-above could culminate in a strategy by
the ruling class in which reaction is made popular. The ravages wrought
by the collapse of the redistributive economy, as well as the sentiment
that there is growing polarization on a global scale, help make ultrana-
tionalism (and, perhaps, sectarian intolerance) popular in the eyes of the

newly marginalized. If the erstwhile modernizers, the state class, pursue their interests in self-perpetuation, the reactionary path promises to be the most effective barrier to impending political liberalization.

If the project of modernity is to divest itself of its modernizationist encumbrance, then political liberalization, ushering in civil rights and the rule of law, is the next step. For the promises of modernization to be fulfilled in all spheres of life, for Enlightenment ideals of emancipation to be realized, and for individual autonomy to be attained, full citizenship rights have to be instituted. Only then may it be possible to predict the overcoming of the inertia of indigenous culture and its communitarian predilection and to avoid the slide toward a diluted form of hyphenated modernity. But first it is necessary to perform radical surgery on the moribund state tradition—in order to prepare the legal and political coordinates within which the public space of autonomous individuals may flourish.

Notes

1. For a fuller treatment of this point, see Çağlar Keyder, "The Dilemma of Cultural Identity on the Margin of Europe," *Review,* vol. 16, no. 1, 1993, 19–33.

2. For a discussion of these conceptions of modernization, see Dean Tipps, "Modernization Theory and the Comparative Study of Societies: A Critical Perspective," *Comparative Studies in Society and History,* vol. 15, March 1973, 196–226. See also Charles Taylor, "Inwardness and the Culture of Modernity," in Alex Honneth, Thomas McCarthy, Claus Offe, and Albrecht Wellmer, eds., *Philosophical Interventions in the Unfinished Project of Enlightenment,* Cambridge, Massachusetts: MIT Press, 1992.

3. Reinhard Bendix's seminal article would seem to be the initial inspiration for this view: "Tradition and Modernity Reconsidered," *Comparative Studies in Society and History,* vol. 9, no. 3, 1967, 292–346.

4. Barrington Moore, Jr., *Social Origins of Dictatorship and Democracy,* Boston: Beacon Press, 1966.

5. For a forceful historical argument in this vein, see Erik J. Zürcher, *Turkey: A Modern History,* London: I. B. Tauris, 1993.

6. For a fuller account of this period, see Çağlar Keyder, *State and Class in Turkey: A Study in Capitalist Development,* London: Verso, 1987.

7. See Ellen Kay Trimberger, *Revolution from Above: Military Bureaucrats and Development in Egypt, Peru, Turkey, and Japan,* New Brunswick, New Jersey: Transaction Books, 1977.

8. See Ayşe Buğra, *State and Business in Modern Turkey: A Comparative Study,* Albany: State University of New York Press, 1994.

9. On political culture, see Ergun Özbudun, "State Elites and Democratic Culture in Turkey," in Larry Diamond, ed., *Political Culture and Democracy in Developing Countries*, Boulder, Colorado: Lynne Rienner, 1993, 247–68.

10. Lisa Anderson, in "Liberalism, Islam and the Arab State," *Dissent*, Fall 1994, 439–44, makes the same argument in the context of rentier states.

11. There is, of course, a vast literature on nationalism in the Third World. For my purposes in this article, the essential points are covered by Ernest Gellner, *Nationalism*, Ithaca, New York: Cornell University Press, 1983; Eric J. Hobsbawm, *Nations and Nationalism since 1780*, Cambridge: Cambridge University Press, 1990; and Partha Chatterjee, *Nationalist Thought and the Colonial World: A Derivative Discourse*, London: Zed Press, 1986.

12. See T. H. Marshall, *Citizenship and Social Class and Other Essays*, Cambridge: Cambridge University Press, 1950. There is a growing literature devoted to arguing citizenship as a radical concept. For a representative sample, see Chantal Mouffe, ed., *Dimensions of Radical Democracy*, London: Verso, 1992. For an argument linking different conceptions of nationalism and citizenship, see Liah Greenfeld, *Nationalism: Five Roads to Modernity*, Cambridge, Massachusetts: Harvard University Press, 1992.

13. The notion of elite *ressentiment* is discussed by Greenfeld in *Nationalism*, passim.

14. Chatterjee, *Nationalist Thought*, passim.

15. See Alvin Gouldner, "Prologue to a Theory of Revolutionary Intellectuals," *Telos*, vol. 26, 1976, 3–36.

16. This situation has yet to change. One significant study that confronts the silence and underlines the importance of the event for the history of the Turkish republic has, curiously, not received the attention it richly deserves. See Taner Akçam, *Türk Ulusal Kimliği ve Ermeni Meselesi*, Istanbul: İletişim, 1993.

17. The social removal of ethnies considered alien also had the effect of purging the ambivalence that the nationalist elites would otherwise have had to wrestle with. This removal of the material anchoring of Western practices and lifestyles made it possible to imagine a fictional West with no immediate material reference. It could, therefore, be represented in rhetoric in an idealized version with no damaging or dislocating effects. Once the negative dimension was eliminated, modernization could be presented as an entirely positive project against which no defensive posturing was necessary. The elites did not feel any colonial resentment; they did not see themselves as belonging to a world different from the one they sought to emulate.

18. See Michael Herzfeld, *Ours Once More: Folklore, Ideology, and the Making of Modern Greece*, Austin: University of Texas Press, 1982.

19. See James M. Orr, "Nationalism in a Local Setting," *Anthropological Quarterly*, vol. 64, no. 3, 1991, 142–51; and Martin Stokes, "Hazelnuts and Lutes, Perceptions of Change in a Black Sea Valley," in Paul Stirling, ed., *Culture and Economy: Changes in Turkish Villages*, London: Eothen, 1993.

20. For a discussion of this point, see Bobby Sayyid, "Sign O'Times: Kaffirs and Infidels Fighting the Ninth Crusade," in Ernesto Laclau, ed., *The Making of Political Identities*, London: Verso, 1994, 264–86. Sayyid identifies a generic "Kemalism" with such an imposition.

21. See Metin Heper, "The Strong State as a Problem for the Consolidation of Democracy: Turkey and Germany Compared," *Comparative Political Studies,* vol. 25, no. 2, 1992, 169–94.

22. It is true that after World War II, Turkish modernizers had to relinquish their single-party hold on political power and accept limited contestation within the procedures of representative democracy. In retrospect, however, the inception of competitive party politics under the pressure of American hegemony seems less to have signaled the advent of political liberalism than to have opened a narrow arena for elite competition. When the single party lost the elections in 1950, this change was not followed by a legal reform attempting to dismantle the privileges of the state or to define and safeguard the rights of the citizens. The state continued to enjoy its prerogatives, and a legal framework instituting freedom of expression and association for individuals, or even a state of rule-of-law where bureaucratic prerogatives could be challenged in autonomous courts, never materialized. Associations that emerged in this environment never acquired sufficient autonomy from the state to be able to advocate civil rights for individuals.

23. See Immanuel Wallerstein, "The Concept of National Development, 1917–1989, Elegy and Requiem," *American Behavioral Scientist,* vol. 35, no. 3–4, 1992, 517–29.

24. Cultural relativism legitimates this possibility, and a few remaining proponents of Enlightenment ideals in Third World studies struggle against such a conception of capitalist transformation. Compare Arif Dirlik, "The Postcolonial Aura: Third World Criticism in the Age of Global Capitalism," *Critical Inquiry,* vol. 20, no. 2, 1994, 328–56.

25. For a clear statement of this stagist view, see Nigel Harris, "New Bourgeoisies?" *Journal of Development Studies,* vol. 24, no. 2, 1988, 237–49.

26. See David G. Becker, "Beyond Dependency: Development and Democracy in the Era of International Capitalism," in Dankwart A. Rustow and Kenneth P. Ericson, eds., *Comparative Global Dynamics: Global Research Perspectives,* New York: HarperCollins, 1991.

27. I have argued this point in "The Dilemma of Cultural Identity."

4/ Modernization Policies
and Islamist Politics in Turkey

HALDUN GÜLALP

The rise and rapid growth of political Islamism remains an enigma. The legacies of two long-standing traditions are still manifest in the field. One is the Orientalist perspective, which maintains that Islam and the West are fundamentally opposed. Its implication is that the recent rise of Islamism is but a continuation of the age-old conflict between the two civilizations.[1] The other perspective is that of modernization, which contends that Islamic nations will become secular as a result of the modernizing impact of the West. The literature on Islamism in Turkey, in particular, has heretofore been dominated by adherents of modernization theory, who characterize Islamism as a conservative phenomenon and argue that social changes such as industrialization and urbanization will eventually weaken its social bases.[2]

Yet neither theoretical perspective is tenable, considering that the rise of what is called "fundamentalism" is hardly unique to the Islamic world and that Islamism, like other fundamentalisms, is a late-twentieth-century phenomenon.[3] As the case in point, religion-based politics in Turkey has made a comeback in the most recent phase of the country's development. This phase, which began in the 1980s, has been characterized by deepened integration with global capitalism, and it accompanied an erosion of confidence in the nation-state. Defying in particular the predictions of modernization theory, Islamism in Turkey has found new social bases among the dispossessed in the rapidly growing urban centers and among middle-class professionals.[4]

Critics of modernization theory point out that modernization has not displaced religion.[5] That modernization did not displace religion, however, is one thing; that religious politics has been revived in recent years is quite another. The most interesting question remains, what is the specific historical conjuncture in which religion has returned?

Islam versus Political Islamism

Islamism in Turkey, as elsewhere in the region, is a recent and historically distinct phenomenon that arose after a period of dominance of secular nationalism and as a response to its crisis. Thus, even if religion (as "meaning" and "value") were to be considered inexplicable in terms of sociological models, the return of religion-based *politics* should still be explainable in terms of social change. Regarding Muslim societies, Bassam Tibi points out that

> Islam, in the course of [modernization and Westernization] . . . was abandoned as a political ideology in many countries in the Middle East. It has not, however, been replaced as a belief system: Islam continues to prevail as a normative system. The renewed role of Islam, since the 1970s, merely refers to the process of *political* revival of Islam, to its reemergence as a political ideology legitimizing political action.[6]

Thus, we may distinguish between Islam as faith and Islamism as political ideology. The modernization of a number of Middle Eastern countries during the twentieth century led to the displacement of Islamism by secular nationalism and variants of socialism, although Islam always remained as faith. At the end of the same century, Islamist politics is coming back, this time as a postnationalist phenomenon.

This brand of Islamism should be distinguished from Islamic reformism as epitomized by Young Ottoman thought.[7] During the second half of the nineteenth century, the Ottoman Empire was undergoing "modernizing reforms," partly under western European pressure. As the first intelligentsia in Ottoman history, the Young Ottomans contributed to the ideological legitimation of that process. Critical of the "secularism" of the Tanzimat reformers but inspired by the same Western ideas as that group, the Young Ottomans attempted to interpret (and ultimately justify) Ottoman modernization and Westernization in terms of the principles of Islam.[8] Reformist Islamism was an ideological attempt to reconcile Islamic principles with Westernization. *Radical* Islamism of the late twentieth century, by contrast, "is a politico-cultural movement that postulates a qualitative contradiction between Western civilization and the religion of Islam."[9]

In this essay I address the rise of radical Islamism and propose an explanatory framework within which to examine the Turkish experience in terms of social and political change. For this purpose, I make use of a theoretical model that was previously proposed to examine the collapse of democracies in the Third World. Modernization theory in the 1950s and 1960s assumed an inherent association between the modernization of society and the growth of democracy. In a pathbreaking critique of this view, Guillermo O'Donnell contended that although democratization was observed in the early stages of Third World development (thus seemingly confirming modernization theory's predictions), it collapsed in later stages, giving rise to "bureaucratic-authoritarian regimes."[10]

A similar observation can be made about the effects of modernization on secularism. Although early stages of modernization resulted in relative secularization, later stages seem to have led to a revival of religious politics. In order to interpret this situation, I argue that Islamism is a product of the frustration of the promises of Westernist modernization and represents a critique of modernism. This argument not only challenges the received wisdom of portraying Islamism as backward-looking premodernism but also explains its rise in terms of social and political change.

The point of departure for this alternative framework is the following observation: the rise of Islamism in Turkey followed a period of state-led developmentalism that resulted in a crisis. A central concept here is "import-substituting industrialization" (ISI), a common model of Third World modernization in the twentieth century. This model is based on the notion that a country can develop by substituting its own manufactures for items it previously imported, with the help of state interventionism. As a first approximation, ISI can be regarded as the Third World variant of the welfare state of the advanced capitalist world. It is an attempt to combine, around a nationalist ideology, the basic principles of the welfare state with an emphasis on rapid industrialization and economic development. The notion of import substitution is an implicit expression of the desire to "catch up." Thus, if the promise of development that ISI represented has failed—and together with it, faith in modernization—then the crisis of development and the rise of Islamism must be connected.

Nationalist Developmentalism

Nationalist, statist developmentalism in Turkey was identified with "Kemalism." The trajectory of the Kemalist project was part and parcel of a universal pattern. In many underdeveloped countries, developmentalism started in the 1930s, under conditions of relative isolation from the world economy owing to the Great Depression, and continued after World War II. In the postwar period, productive capital originating in the core economies of global capitalism began to make direct industrial investments in the underdeveloped countries. Thus, Turkey was reintegrated into the networks of global capitalism through the international circulation of productive capital. There began a process of ISI in which technology, capital goods, and inputs were imported and the final product was produced domestically to cater to the protected domestic market.[11]

ISI allowed for further industrial development, but on the basis of a specific international division of labor. Turkey produced manufactured goods for its own domestic market, but it depended on imports of capital goods from advanced countries to sustain industrial growth and on world demand for its traditional exports to finance those imports. These two characteristics also brought about the crisis tendencies inherent in ISI. In a situation where sustained industrial development required growing imports while the export base remained stagnant, further industrialization relied on a constantly expanding foreign debt. Under these conditions, ISI necessarily led to a crisis of development.[12]

In many Third World countries, the economic structure of ISI also contained political and ideological dimensions. The state was actively engaged in economic development and protected the domestic market both by regulating imports and by expanding the market through redistributionist policies. The developmentalist and protectionist role of the state bolstered the ideology of nationalism, and its role in promoting the welfare of low-income groups fostered an image of "populism."[13]

In its early stages of rapid growth in Turkey, ISI was successful in combining the interests of various classes around the project of inward-oriented national development. In its later stages, the bottlenecks inherent in ISI led to a crisis and the fragmentation of class coalitions. Throughout the 1960s, Turkey was able to sustain high rates of industrial growth and distribute its fruits in a relatively egalitarian fashion.[14] During this period, the ISI model of development allowed for a populist set of class alliances and supported the conditions for a democratic regime. Various segments of society could benefit from the inward-oriented industrial development, and their common interests led them to coalesce around that process. The ideological elements of ISI—that is, nationalism and developmentalism—allowed for popular participation and supported the structures of democratic populism.[15]

ISI-based development in Turkey was in crisis by the late 1970s. In 1980 Turkey launched a radical shift in developmental trajectory from a statist-nationalist strategy to a market-oriented transnationalist one. This transformation was carried out by a military regime installed later in the same year. The new orientation included the expansion of market forces in the economy as well as the expansion of competitive, individualist ideologies in the cultural realm. Previously, the nation-state had a progressive appearance and often played a politically populist and socially redistributionist role. By contrast, the restructuring in the 1980s entailed an economic model in which benefits accrued to a limited segment of society, a political model that was authoritarian and exclusionary, and an ideological outlook that emphasized competitive individualism. The dominant sentiment was no longer one of trust in, and reliance on, the nation-state. Now the so-called "rising values" included belief in the supremacy of the global market and in the virtues of individual entrepreneurship. The profound restructuring of the Turkish economy, politics, and culture in the 1980s ended the ideological hegemony of nationalist-statist developmentalism.[16]

The Crisis of Development and the Rise of Islamism

The dominant ideology in Turkey between the 1930s and 1970s was nationalist-statist developmentalism. But despite the continued predominance of nationalist pretensions in the post–World War II period, actual development took place in the context of full participation in the world economy. Ideology contradicted reality with respect to (1) the nationalist promise versus the deepening integration into, and dependency on, the world economy, and (2) the populist legitimation of the nationalist-statist project versus the class differentiation brought about by the creation of a domestic bourgeoisie and the collaboration of that bourgeoisie with Western interests. The promises of the developmentalist project could not be delivered.

A prominent assertion of Eurocentrism was that only the West was rational and capable of modernity; the Third World, by contrast, was spiritual, traditional, and stagnant.[17] The nationalists' response to this assertion was to set out to refute the existence of such an essential difference and demonstrate that their own nation was perfectly capable of replicating the Western experience. Nationalism in the Third World expressed its anti-imperialist intentions by adopting Westernization. All those virtues identified by Eurocentrism as markers of Western superiority, such as rationalism, the nation-state, and economic development, were un-questioningly accepted by the nationalists. They could not transcend the Eurocentric problematic because they took Western values and claims as universal truths.[18] Westernization, in this framework, was embraced in the name of "universalism."

Nationalism was internally contradictory. While seemingly asserting a negation of the Western world, it also aimed to replicate the Western ex-perience of economic and political development.[19] The nationalist desire to emulate the West did not result in a successful replication. This fail-ure laid the groundwork for the emergence of radical Islamism. The Is-lamist movement now builds on the failure of the internally contradic-tory promises of nationalism. Islamists condemn nationalism as a project of imitation and accuse the nationalists of aping the West.

Nationalism, as the legitimizing ideology of the modern nation-state, has characteristics originating from modernism—it derives from a belief in human intervention to straighten out worldly matters. Thus, the Is-lamist critique is particularly effective within the context of the global crisis of modernism and the challenges raised against the universalist mythologies of the West. Although Westernization was previously a more or less unquestioned ideal in the name of universalism, the "condition of postmodernity" has begun to cast doubt on the "universal truths" of modernism.[20] This has created an opportune environment for Islamism to mount an offensive against modernism.

At the global level, the crisis of ideologies based on modernist assump-tions has given rise to a proliferation of postmodernist politics of iden-tity. Yet postmodernism, although it is effective as a critique of modernism, does not constitute an alternative social and political project, owing to its inherent cynicism and nihilism.[21] Islamism, however, not only shares many significant themes with the postmodernist critique of modernism but also goes beyond merely pointing out the failures of nationalism and modernism to actually propose an alternative ideology.[22] This, I believe, makes Islamism particularly potent.

The crisis of nationalist-statist developmentalism, too, is part and par-cel of a global trend. A growing literature now recognizes that we have entered a period of crisis of the nation-state.[23] Although early in the twen-tieth century states had begun to regulate national economies and pro-tect the welfare of their citizens, at the end of the same century trends toward "globalization" have undermined the power of individual nation-states. They can no longer independently maintain full employment, sustain economic growth, and preserve reformist welfare policies.[24] In the same vein, "Third World national revolutions as projects of economic and social modernization have proved failures."[25]

Kemalism, as Turkey's project of nationalist-statist modernization, embraced Western-inspired models of development. In opposition, Islamism advances a wholesale critique of the *notion* of development. Turkish Islamists regard "developmentalism" as a Western affliction and link it with the fundamental but discredited modernist assumptions about "progress."[26] Islamists' views on development are directly germane to their critique of Kemalism. Kemalists define progress and catching up with Western civilization precisely in terms of economic and technological development. Islamists, on the other hand, reject both Western civilization and its local adoption through Kemalism. This rejection can be observed most clearly in the Islamist reversal of Kemalist assumptions regarding development.

The Islamist Critique of Development

In Islamist intellectual discourse, devotion to economic growth and development originates in the post-Enlightenment belief in linear "progress" that was born in Europe and then spread to the rest of the globe. "By the 19th century, the notion of progress had become a new religion in all of Europe," and "in Turkey, too, 'progress' was taken as a given from the beginning."[27] Islamists point out that this belief in unlimited progress is the most significant component of "modernism," which they charge with promising paradise on earth and failing to deliver it.[28]

Islamist writers criticize Western civilization for its unflinching devotion to economic growth: "Incessant growth, belief in the virtue of growth, embracing growth with absolute conviction have brought the entire world, starting with the Western countries, face to face with a whole host of economic and social problems."[29] They condemn economic growth as the greatest addiction and as a new idol.[30] They argue that the social consequences of economic growth, where the primary concern is increasing the quantity of goods produced, are one-dimensional societies and one-dimensional humans, consequences that obliterate the mind, the intellect, culture, and creativity.[31]

In a reversal of the nationalist emphasis on economic development, the Islamist critique maintains that "in a civilization where reason alone is dominant . . . it is nearly impossible for technology to be friendly to the environment or to humans," and thus, "in order to save human beings from captivity to production, we must shift our values from money and things to virtue."[32] Paralleling the environmentalist critique of materialism, the Islamist perspective emphasizes unity with nature as an antidote to consumerism: "The source of human happiness can be found not in money or the consumption of material objects, but in living in harmony with nature and the universe."[33] The cause of environmental pollution, in this view, is the irresponsible fixation on production and productivity.[34]

Islamists emphasize that the Islamic person does not regard material gratification as the sole aim in life, and they contend that excessive spending would be ended in the Islamic way of life.[35] The policy proposal originating from this perspective is the following: "If our expenditures do not exceed our subsistence needs such as food, clothing and shelter, then we can lead a serene and productive life free of anxiety." Thus, "the solution is very simple. Just reduce consumption."[36]

All of this represents a complete reversal of the assumptions of nationalist developmentalism, where success in the anti-imperialist struggle was measured in terms of economic growth and industrialization. By contrast, the Islamist position frames the rejection of the West in civilizational terms: "It is no longer indisputable that industrialization should be pursued whatever the cost," because "the issue for Islamic countries is not industrialization; it is the struggle for [authentic] civilization."[37] In an implicit critique of Kemalism, the Islamist view contends that "no civilization can be defeated by its own weapons."[38]

This shift in intellectual discourse from developmentalist to "postdevelopmentalist" concerns can be seen perhaps most starkly in the program of the Islamist political party. In its earlier incarnation as Milli Selamet Partisi (National Salvation Party) in the 1970s, the Islamist party led by Professor Necmettin Erbakan articulated its Islamic themes in accord with the dominant economic and political theme of that era, that is, industrial development. Erbakan's party championed "heavy industrialization" as the surest route to Turkey's independence from the West.[39] Twenty years later, in its present reincarnation as Refah Partisi (Welfare Party), also led by Erbakan, the Islamist party no longer emphasizes the need for industrialization but rather focuses on such "postindustrial" themes as protecting the environment, building civil society, and withdrawing the state from all economic activities.[40]

A prominent Islamist author who has also acted as an ideologue of Refah expresses the shift from developmental to moral themes by condemning single-minded devotion to economic growth for its destructive effects on the human soul as well as on the natural environment: "Humankind has lost its conscience. A new kind of monster has been created, a monster with no heart, a dried-up brain, and a big stomach. . . . We have polluted the air . . . and made a hole in the sky."[41] The guilty party is self-evident: "That magnificient Western civilization! That West which became wealthy by plundering the historical heritage of humankind."[42] Although in the past it was embraced uncritically, "everyone can now see that Western civilization is coming to an end. All that rationality, all the technological trinkets and gadgetry could not fulfill the hopes and promises of happiness."[43] He goes on to explain that despite all efforts to dominate nature by machinery, humankind has been unsuccessful. The solution, therefore, lies in "being at peace with ourselves, with other humans, with nature, and ultimately with God."[44] He points out that the Islamic solution should be carefully distinguished from the Western one: "The Islamic state does not promise wealth and prosperity to the Muslim community. . . . [To expect such a thing] would be to mistakenly expect that a goal promised by capitalism could be reached via the Islamic route."[45]

Conclusion

In his examination of Third World historiographies, Gyan Prakash identifies a "postnationalist" literature that is distinctive for its "repudiation of the post-Enlightenment ideology of Reason and Progress" and thus is different "from the anti-Orientalism of nationalism."[46] This, he argues, constitutes "a challenge to the hegemony of those modernization schemes and ideologies that post-Enlightenment Europe projected as the raison d'etre of history." The Islamist literature in Turkey is, in this sense, clearly postnationalist, although, paradoxically, it is not "post-Orientalist." Whereas the nationalists rejected the Eurocentrism of the West by attempting to demonstrate that they, too, were capable of modernization, the Islamists accept the Eurocentric assertion of an essential difference between the West and the East. In its rejection of the West, Islamism reproduces the essentialist assumptions of Orientalism.

Islamism stems from the failure of the nationalist promises of Westernist modernization. Going beyond all those currents that share the theme of "global modernity"—that is, according to Gyan Prakash, modernization, nationalism, and Marxism—Islamism reasserts the specificity and distinctiveness of Islamic culture. Within the national developmentalist ideology, liberation from imperialist oppression and assertion of national identity were defined primarily within the framework of economic growth and industrialization. Throughout the nationalist period in Turkey, the 1930s through the 1970s, rejecting industrialization would have been considered equivalent to treason. In the 1980s and 1990s, however, the Islamist challenge to the notion of industrialization implies a reversal of the assumptions of national developmentalism. In the Islamist view, the unquestioning acceptance of industrialization is equivalent to submission to imperialism.

Kemalism in Turkey was a paradigmatic model of Third World nationalism in that it perceived and defined Westernization as the attainment of "universal" civilization. The essence of the Kemalist project was the attempt to defeat Western imperialism by adopting Westernization.[47] By contrast, in its plea for authenticity, Islamism accepts the essential opposition between Islam and the West but rejects the Western assertion of superiority. It rejects the nationalist assumptions and asserts the superiority of the spiritual values of Islam over the material wealth of the West.

Notes

1. See, for example, Michael Youssef, *Revolt against Modernity: Muslim Zealots and the West,* Leiden: E. J. Brill, 1985; Bernard Lewis, *Islam and the West,* New York: Oxford University Press, 1993.

2. See, for example, Binnaz Toprak, "The Religious Right," in Irvin C. Schick and E. Ahmet Tonak, eds., *Turkey in Transition,* New York: Oxford University Press, 1987, 218–35; and several chapters in Richard Tapper, ed., *Islam in Modern Turkey,* London: I. B. Tauris, 1991 (with the notable exception of the chapter by Şerif Mardin).

3. For a comparative assessment of fundamentalisms, see Martin Marty and Scott Appleby, eds., *Fundamentalisms Observed,* Chicago: Chicago University Press, 1991. On fundamentalism as a late-twentieth-century phenomenon, see Nikki R. Keddie, "The Revolt of Islam and Its Roots," in Dankwart A. Rustow and Kenneth P. Erickson, eds., *Comparative Political Dynamics: Global Research Perspectives,* New York: HarperCollins, 1991, 292–308.

4. Mehmet Ali Soydan, ed., *Türkiye'nin Refah Gerçeği,* Erzurum: Birey Yayıncılık, 1994. See also Nilüfer Göle, *Modern Mahrem,* Istanbul: Metis Yayınları, 1991.

5. Mary Douglas, "The Effects of Modernization on Religious Change," *Daedalus,* vol. 111, no. 1, 1982, 1–20; Robert Wuthnow, "Understanding Religion and Politics," *Daedalus,* vol. 120, no. 3, 1991, 1–19.

6. Bassam Tibi, "The Renewed Role of Islam in the Political and Social Development of the Middle East," *Middle East Journal,* vol. 37, no. 1, 1983, 3–13.

7. Youssef Choueiri, *Islamic Fundamentalism*, Boston: Twayne Publishers, 1990; Keddie, "The Revolt of Islam."

8. Şerif Mardin, *The Genesis of Young Ottoman Thought*, Princeton, New Jersey: Princeton University Press, 1962.

9. Choueiri, *Islamic Fundamentalism*, 120.

10. Guillermo O'Donnell, *Modernization and Bureaucratic-Authoritarianism*, Berkeley: Institute of International Studies, University of California–Berkeley, Politics of Modernization Series, 1973.

11. Çağlar Keyder, *State and Class in Turkey*, London: Verso, 1987.

12. For the comparable Latin American experience, see the classic work by Albert O. Hirschman, "The Political Economy of Import-Substituting Industrialization in Latin America," *Quarterly Journal of Economics*, vol. 82, 1968, 1–32.

13. Ian Roxborough, *Theories of Underdevelopment*, London: Macmillan, 1979.

14. Korkut Boratav, *Türkiye İktisat Tarihi, 1908–1985*, Istanbul: Gerçek Yayınları, 1988.

15. Haldun Gülalp, "Patterns of Capital Accumulation and State-Society Relations in Turkey," *Journal of Contemporary Asia*, vol. 15, no. 3, 1985, 329–48.

16. Çağlar Keyder, *Ulusal Kalkınmacılığın İflası*, Istanbul: Metis Yayınları, 1993.

17. Samir Amin, *Eurocentrism*, New York: Monthly Review Press, 1989.

18. Gyan Prakash, "Writing Post-Orientalist Histories of the Third World: Perspectives from Indian Historiography," *Comparative Studies in Society and History*, vol. 32, no. 2, 1990, 383–408.

19. Partha Chatterjee, *Nationalist Thought and the Colonial World: A Derivative Discourse?* London: Zed Press, 1986.

20. David Harvey, *The Condition of Postmodernity*, Oxford: Basil Blackwell, 1989; Bryan S. Turner, ed., *Theories of Modernity and Postmodernity*, London: Sage Publications, 1990; Pauline Marie Rosenau, *Post-Modernism and the Social Sciences*, Princeton, New Jersey: Princeton University Press, 1992.

21. Stanley Aronowitz, "Postmodernism and Politics," in Stanley Aronowitz, *The Politics of Identity*, New York: Routledge, 1992, 253–71. See also Robert J. Antonio, "Postmodern Storytelling versus Pragmatic Truth-Seeking: The Discursive Bases of Social Theory," *Sociological Theory*, vol. 9, no. 2, 1991, 154–63.

22. Haldun Gülalp, "Islamism and Postmodernism," *Contention*, vol. 4, no. 2, 1995, 59–73.

23. For a critical review of this literature, see Paul Hirst and Grahame Thompson, "Globalization and the Future of the Nation-State," *Economy and Society*, vol. 24, no. 3, 1995, 408–42.

24. Hirst and Thompson, "Globalization," 413–15.

25. Hirst and Thompson, "Globalization," 421.

26. For a parallel phenomenon in Iran, see Afsaneh Najmabadi, "Iran's Turn to Islam: From Modernism to a Moral Order," *Middle East Journal*, vol. 41, no. 2, 1987, 202–17. According to Najmabadi, for Iranian Islamists, "'development,' 'modernity,' 'modernization,' and 'catching up with the West' are all concerns of the past; the search for a singular 'moral order' is the order of the day" (217).

27. İsmet Özel, "Kalkınma? İlerleme? Varolma?" in Ahmet Tabakoğlu and İsmail Kurt, eds., *İktisadi Kalkınma ve İslam*, Istanbul: İslami İlimler Araştırma Vakfı

Yayınları, 1987, 232. See also Ahmet Tabakoğlu, "İslam İktisadı Açısından 'Kalkınma,'" in Tabakoğlu and Kurt, *İktisadi Kalkınma ve İslam*, 241–43.

28. Ali Bulaç, *Din ve Modernizm*, Istanbul: Endülüs Yayınları, 1991, 27; İsmet Özel, *Üç Mesele: Teknik, Medeniyet ve Yabancılaşma*, Istanbul: Çıdam Yayınları, 1992, 151ff.

29. Ersin Gündoğan, *Teknolojinin Ötesi*, Istanbul: İz Yayıncılık, 1991, 125.

30. Tabakoğlu, "İslam İktisadı," 244.

31. Beşir Hamitoğulları, "İktisadi Vahşi Büyümenin Bunalımları ve İslam Kalkınma Modelinin Vaadettikleri," in Tabakoğlu and Kurt, *İktisadi Kalkınma ve İslam*, 10–12.

32. Gündoğan, *Teknolojinin*, 16–17, 20.

33. Gündoğan, *Teknolojinin*, 25–26.

34. Gündoğan, *Teknolojinin*, 48.

35. Hamitoğulları, "İktisadi Vahşi Büyümenin," 33.

36. Gündoğan, *Teknolojinin*, 154, 158. See also Tabakoğlu, "İslam İktisadı," 247–48.

37. Gündoğan, *Teknolojinin*, 23, 31.

38. Gündoğan, *Teknolojinin*, 31.

39. See Türker Alkan, "The National Salvation Party in Turkey," in Metin Heper and Raphael Israeli, eds., *Islam and Politics in the Modern Middle East*, New York: St. Martin's Press, 1984, 79–102; Binnaz Toprak, "Politicisation of Islam in a Secular State: The National Salvation Party in Turkey," in Said Amir Arjomand, ed., *From Nationalism to Revolutionary Islam*, Albany: State University of New York Press, 1984, 119–33; Ali Yasar Sarıbay, *Türkiye'de Modernleşme, Din ve Parti Politikası: MSP Örnek Olayı*, Istanbul: Alan Yayınları.

40. On the politics of Refah, see Ruşen Çakır, *Ne Şeriat Ne Demokrasi: Refah Partisini Anlamak*, Istanbul: Metis Yayınları, 1994; Serdar Sen, *Refah Partisi'nin Teori ve Pratiği*, Istanbul: Sarmal Yayınları, 1995; and Soydan, *Türkiye'nin Refah Gerçeği*. For a brief analysis of Refah's platform, see Haldun Gülalp, "Islamist Party Poised for National Power in Turkey," *Middle East Report*, vol. 25, no. 3–4, 1995.

41. Abdurrahman Dilipak, *Savaş, Barış, İktidar*, Istanbul: İşaret/Ferşat Yayınları, 1991, 12.

42. Dilipak, *Savaş, Barış, İktidar*, 13.

43. Dilipak, *Savaş, Barış, İktidar*, 39.

44. Dilipak, *Savaş, Barış, İktidar*, 15.

45. Dilipak, *Savaş, Barış, İktidar*, 20.

46. Prakash, "Writing Post-Orientalist Histories," 404.

47. Enver Ziya Karal, "The Principles of Kemalism," in Ergun Özbudun and Ali Kazancıgıl, eds., *Atatürk: Founder of a Modern State*, London: C. Hurst and Company, 1981, 11–36.

5/ Projects as Methodology

Some Thoughts on Modern Turkish Social Science

ŞERİF MARDİN

J'étais convaincu qu'a leur insu ils avaient retenu de l'Ancien Régime la plupart des sentiments, des habitudes, des idées même a l'aide desquels ils avaient construits la révolution qui le détruisit, et que sans le vouloir, ils s'étaient servis de ces débris pour construire l'édifice de la société nouvelle.

—Alexis de Tocqueville

The following is an attempt to study the influence of a perceptual frame inherited by a prominent group of modern Turkish scholars whose analysis of Turkish society it has continued to characterize. In a country like Turkey, where a burning concern with foundational principles is part of a pervasive discourse in which scholarly studies overlap with journalistic work, it is difficult to draw the exact boundaries of the group I have in mind. Its membership consists of "Kemalists," that is, promoters of the ideology of the secular Turkish republic established in 1923, secularists, or persons determined to maintain the principle of laicism introduced by the republic, and "Marxisant" scholars who have pioneered critical studies of society in Turkey.[1] Its worldview may be followed in the writings of contributors to an otherwise solid journal of social studies, *Toplum ve Bilim* (Society and Science), which has gathered the best talent in Turkish social science. A source in English in which the same attitude toward the study of society may be detected is *Turkey in Transition,* edited by Irvin C. Schick and E. Ahmet Tonak.[2] A prominent work with similar earmarks is Mübeccel Kıray's *Ereğli.*[3] The polished and sophisticated studies of Çağlar Keyder reflect similar characteristics.[4]

I claim that the parent ideology of the mind-set I attempt to analyze was the political formula professed by members of the Ottoman bureaucracy, the governing elite of pre-republican times, who promoted an Ottoman version of *raison d'état.*[5] Interestingly, the founding father of the

64

Turkish republic, Mustafa Kemal Atatürk, gave the republican elite—the intelligentsia—the similar task of functioning as wardens of the republic. That much is fairly well known, but not quite so well recognized is the vein in which this assignment was made, reminiscent as it was of the re-creation of the role of these earlier bureaucratic gatekeepers of the *ci-devant* Ottoman regime. This transmission may be conceptualized as the perpetuation by the founding fathers of the republic of key positions in society, as well as definitions of the role of the state. Furthermore, it may be seen as the perpetuation of a tendency to conceptualize social change as promoted by *projects*, that is, plans for change originating among a cohesive group of social "engineers," as we can detect even in some of the essays in this book. Social change, seen as a self-propelling movement with an internal spring, has no place in the approach that underlies "projects," and neither does the concept of an Aristotelian or Hegelian "unfolding."

The secularizing policy of the Turkish republic having unraveled its Islamic moorings, after Atatürk the new wardens of the state functioned without the earlier Ottoman tacit "methodology of the social sciences," an approach that has often been characterized as the "social engineering" bent of Ottoman statesmen. The Western, foreign source of republican reforms—that is, imitation—impeded deeper cultural moorings for the new methodology, a foundation that, in the past, had been provided by Islam as ideation. The reform movement had no identifiable philosophical foundation. Its Jacobinism, possibly its deepest root, was pragmatic and practical, that is, fleshed out as a "project." The republic took over educational institutions and cultural practices (museums, painting and sculpture, secularism) from the West without realizing that these were just the tip of an iceberg of meanings, perceptions, and ontological positions.

An aside about Gramsci may be relevant at this point: If Gramsci had a total, three-tiered "iceberg" in mind in his definitions of organic intellectuals and culture, then his ideas may have had some universal validity.[6] My own perception is that this is not what he had to say, that he was very cavalier about his theory of culture (which seems to have been concerned primarily with reproduction through sometimes narrowly or vaguely defined mechanisms), that Turkish modernization can be used to show that his theories have a basic flaw, and that the whole noise about the revival of his ideas is one about which political scientists (who, in any case, have a somewhat jejeune understanding of culture) should have some reservations.

Recent research seems to indicate that hegemonic class-society link-
ages in fact consist of three "communication loops": first, the state machine; second, cultural institutions; and third, the complex scheme of
language as discourse, sources of self, identity markers, and tacit understandings that underlie both of the other loops and have a structuring
force of their own. I study what happens when loop one is constant, loop
two is taken over from a foreign culture, and loop three is missing. The
extraordinary range, immense complexity, and real "hegemony" of this
third loop is emerging from contemporary studies of semiotics and communication and from the "new" intellectual and social history.[7]

In this essay, I attempt to deconstruct the ideological patterning I impute to the scholars I have in mind by addressing their inability to acknowledge a "micro" component of social dynamics, an inability stemming from the fact that projects are by their very nature "macro" in form.
More precisely, I dwell on their systematic neglect of one of the two main
facets of social life. If those facets are characterized as, on the one hand,
"people in face-to-face interaction" and, on the other, "the wider social
relations . . . in which these activities are embedded,"[8] then my target
group considers the second facet to be the only "truly" significant one.
Their approach may be described as one of selective attention to the macro
dimension of social analysis, and it takes as primordial the constraints of
domination, power, and coercion. These scholars offer no account of a
necessary dimension of domination—the resources of the dominated, or
their "discourse."[9] In a more general sense, they give short shrift to the
whole range of microsociology. The thinkers I have in mind thus dismiss
identity processes, the noninstitutional basis of religion, and personal histories as "colorings" of social processes, frothy surface events without substantive content. They would categorize many of these features as individual performances, bypassing the modern view that "performance" is
itself a category for social analysis.

This approach is particularly puzzling in the Turkish setting, in which
Muslims make up 98 percent of the local population: Muslims are particularly linked in their behavior to the social discourse of Islam and thus
to a dimension of social dynamics that brings into focus micro-level
processes such as the formation of the self.[10] One could speculate that
the progressivism of the group has oriented it in a positivistic direction,
but this uncovers only one aspect of their methodology. Looking at the
problem from the perspective of unacknowledged transmission enables
further elements to emerge. These scholars have been on the lookout for

the latest twists in Western social analysis and have quickly adopted them, yet they have totally neglected the pervasive concern of Western social theory for the linkage between macro and micro elements of society.[11] It is this discrepancy that has to be explained.

The disempowerment resulting from such an inability to focus on micro-level analysis not only results in insensitivity to the complexity of major social processes but also, and more importantly, promotes the use of conspiracy theories where explanations focused on root-level dynamics would be more appropriate. A good example is the recent attribution by a prominent Turkish political scientist—not necessarily part of the group I have in mind but representative of its attitudes—who imputed "cheating" to the Istanbul electorate who carried the conservative religious party to victory in the Turkish municipal elections of March 1994. The citizens, this person claimed, "lied" to pollsters before the elections, thus "willfully disrupting" the predictive apparatus. A more fundamental gap in the analytical apparatus of the prevalent type of Turkish social science has been its inability to understand the power of Islam, which has caused unnecessary consternation among secular intellectuals upon the revival of Islam in Turkey.

In what follows, I approach the problem as a process of personal discovery that allowed me, in time, to focus on the lacunae I have described and that revealed the importance of micro processes for my own research.

Beginnings

My earliest conceptual frame for the study of society was simple: it consisted of a suspicion that the official Kemalist ideology propagated by my Turkish schoolteachers disguised an authoritarianism that contradicted their ubiquitous libertarian discourse. Somewhat later, I undertook a research project on origins of Kemalism, looking at it from the vantage point of the nineteenth-century Ottoman reform movement known as the Tanzimat.[12] I also attempted to understand the background of the Tanzimat. The driving force behind my project was the attempt to clear up the roots of the disparity I had noticed and kept in mind.

The research yielded some interesting findings. Whether promoting their own interests or not, Ottoman officials, at various stages in the development of the empire, seemed uniformly locked into the preservation of a political principle best translated as "stateness" or "the priority of the state," a principle known in Turkish as *devlet*.

It is true that without the ideology of *devlet* and the practice linked to it, the Ottoman Empire would never have survived the impact of nineteenth-century imperialism, and modern Turkey would hardly have achieved the successes it has scored in modernizing its institutions. The present essay is not about this successful dimension of Turkish history but about some of its negative legacies.

The ideology of *devlet,* which antedated the Tanzimat, provides clues to the fundamental thrust even of this early reform movement. It explains why the architects of the Tanzimat conceived of their reform scheme on the model of cameralism, a theory of government developed by professors and publicists in western Europe in the eighteenth century. Cameralists, who saw government as a science of the state to be applied by technicians and managers, included such figures as Seckendorf (1629–1692) and Schlözer (1733–1817), but also Quesnay (1694–1774).[13] They represented the theoretical version of enlightened despotism and had little sympathy for democracy or representative institutions. They were planners, not revolutionaries.

Nineteenth-century Ottoman officials, regardless of their generation or specific worldview, seem to have had the salvation of *devlet* as a uniform goal and bent their minds to this ideal. Cameralism fitted well with this worldview. The centrality of *devlet* in their political ideology promoted a pervasive patriotism that can be traced in the proclamations of Sultan Mahmud II (1808–1839), in the ideas of the reformist grand vizier Mustafa Reşid (circa 1840–1856), and in the ideas of the libertarian theorists of the Tanzimat, known as the Young Ottomans (circa 1865), the ideas of the sworn enemy, Sultan Abdülhamid II (1876–1908), those of Sultan Abdülhamid's own sworn enemies, the Young Turks (1895–1908, 1908–1918), and those of the person the Young Turks had once groomed but who would become their sworn enemy, the founder of the Turkish republic, Mustafa Kemal.[14] Indeed, the flow of Ottoman reform from Mustafa Reşid to Mustafa Kemal followed the convolutions of the western European concept of a science of society from Auguste Comte's positivism to the late-nineteenth-century European disillusionment with parliamentary government, and from there to Emile Durkheim's solidarism.

Throughout, the main task as seen by Ottoman Turks—that is, by the ruling bureaucratic class—was that of improving the administration of the realm and the power of the state rather than promoting democracy. The constitutionalist Young Ottomans (1865–1876) had publicized the idea of representation as the means of saving the empire from disintegration; their eulogies of freedom were directly connected with their patriotism, which appeared even more clearly in the ideas of the less romantic Young Turks of the 1890s. The final step in this progression was the implementation by the single party in power between 1924 and 1950 of ideas—adumbrated in the Turkish Constitution of 1924—that stayed in tune with the earlier ideology of *devlet* but radicalized it by bringing into play a Rousseauist-Jacobin conception of the "general will."[15] This enabled the founders of the Turkish republic to promote an authoritarian theory Rousseau himself had voiced: "Every act of sovereignty, that is every authentic act of the general will, binds or favors equally all citizens so that the sovereign knows only the body of the nation and distinguishes none of those who compose it."[16]

This was the latent but somewhat diffuse and unsystematic premise of the ideology of the single party that ruled the Turkish republic between 1924 and 1950. So far, so good. I had been able to trace one of the elements of Turkish history that I had set out to reconstruct. But new problems kept cropping up. What did I really mean by "radicalism"? And was there really no change from the Ottoman Empire to the republic? Impelled by a sense of fairness, I tried to answer the second question first. That was when I somewhat belatedly came across the ideas of Max Weber.

Patrimonialism-Sultanism

For Turks of my generation in the United States, Weber's term "patrimonialism-sultanism" had a compelling appeal.[17] In it we recognized the distinguishing characteristics our Kemalist mentors imputed to the Ottoman Empire. In the generation of Turkish intellectuals that succeeded us around 1960, Marx filled a similar function, fleshing out a déjà vu deriving from Kemalism. The causes of these divergences between generations need to be examined separately, but the difference between the intellectual scaffold provided by Marx—an increasingly influential model in Turkey after 1965—and that derived from Weber was important. Weber allowed one to go onto an aspect of structure that operated outside the state, the bureaucratic-rational sphere, or the economy.

For me, Weber's concepts concerning patrimonialism-sultanism, when placed against the somewhat wooden ideological prose of Turkish textbooks, seemed a revelation, a more explicit and sophisticated explanation than my Kemalist teachers' simplistic reconstruction of the Ottoman past. Weber did link up with what my generation had heard in school about our sultans and their empire: the land as part of the sultan's *oikos*, the inability of the sultan to extend the organizational reach of the cen-

ter, the slovenliness and inefficacy of the Ottoman administrator. This
view was reinforced by what we remembered of Turkish literature—for
instance, Refik Halit Karay's "Peach Garden," the story of a modernizing
Ottoman bureaucrat who, on stifling summer days, abandoned starched
collar, cravat, riding coat, and intolerant legalism for the delights of night-
gowns worn at dusk in the peach garden of the small town to which he
was assigned.[18] This cultural retrogression, this backward step into the
delights of an enchanted world, was chronicled by more than one modernist Ottoman writer of the early twentieth century.

Weber enabled me to take a first look at the inner spring of *devlet*—its
nonstructural propellant beliefs, ideologies, and ideas. A second finding
using Weberian lenses was the absence in the Ottoman Empire of social
forces that could compare in vigor with the complex developments described by Weber in *The City*.[19] Early Western patrimonialism had been
undermined—and eventually eroded—by the necessity of monarchs to
face up to the forces for change that resided in urban communities. A
projection of this finding was that an autonomous civil society in the
form that had taken root in the West probably did not exist in the Ottoman Empire.[20] This confirmed and equilibrated my conclusions regarding *devlet* and the perpetuation of its ideology; *devlet* now seemed
better understood as having been made up of three "faces": its structure,
its limitations when one looked at its patrimonial-sultanic operations,
and the absence of an organized, rationally and legally legitimated, self-
referential, countervailing urban movement. Underlying these, however,
existed another foundation, that of religion.

The new Turkish republican regime retained elements of *devlet* as a political ideology while it promoted new values. Whereas the Ottoman
patrimonial-sultanic scheme had defined government as underscored by
the duties of rulers to provide good government *for* the people, the Turkish republic conceptualized its ideal of government—even though it was
an ideal—as government *of* the people and *by* the people. This was a plus
for the republic. Although it did not spell it outright, the new principle
intimated an even more radical conceptual change: people not only made
their own personal history but also were not prisoners of recurring cycles of history. This was the final version of a scheme of world history
one could already find among nineteenth-century Ottoman intellectuals, but it was also a principle now asserted with much more conviction
and optimism.

On the negative side, and something that was critically underscored for anyone who read Weber on religion, the new republican system broke with the old Ottoman practice of establishing bridges that linked elite and mass through the recognition of religion as discourse—as *foundational* of society. The new republican ideology, by denying the place of Islam as a discourse and its role as a "cement" of society, increased the distance between the educated and the uneducated. The old system tolerated social heterogeneity because it accepted the necessity of social symbiosis as premise. The new system was built on the (ultimately) Jacobin principle of a republic "une et indivisible" and had as policy the assimilation of deviant groups, who were characterized by republican ideologues as "feudal remnants."[21] The old system took existential questions seriously; the new considered these issues to be "metaphysical" and a residue of scholasticism. This latter attitude was again well illustrated by the thinking of our lycée teachers, who were imbued with the notion of irresistible progress toward a "positive" system relying on a reductionist dialectic made up of two antagonistic postulates, "science" and "reaction."

From Sultanism to the Ottoman "Life-World"

In time it became clear to me that the old system could be understood only in the light of the function that religion had played in it. In that system, Islam made for symbiosis because it promoted a form of solidarity and sociopolitical identity known as *asabiyya,* even though it had no place for the type of solidarity that is emphasized in modern nationalism.[22] With considerable prescience, Islam held the projection of national difference to be a form of tribalism. Islam established bridges between social groups because it functioned as a common language shared by upper and lower classes. Islam, by its very nature, answered existential questions.

Altogether, then, Islam was an important component of the old system before its gradual demise during the republican era, when secular reforms abolished the caliphate, established a state monopoly over education, disestablished the institution of the ulama (doctors of Islamic law), rejected Islamic law and adopted a modified version of the Swiss Civil Code, latinized the alphabet, and, in 1928, struck out the sentence in the Constitution of 1924 which stated that Turks were of the Islamic faith.[23] This extraordinarily pervasive cultural change demanded to be explored for its social consequences, despite the outcries of my colleagues that I was wasting my time with antiquarian concerns (although they imputed most of Turkey's ills to Islamic clerics). These colleagues were implicitly denying the role of the most important of micro structures—religion as belief and "life-world"—a further discovery, but one in which Weber and history seemed more relevant than Schutz's critique of Weber.[24]

But once I began to look at Islam as a social datum, I noticed that I myself had been concentrating primarily on *devlet* in my studies. What emerged from this awareness and the explorations it promoted was that religion not only functioned as an *institution* (i.e., the corps of ulamas, *medreses* [seminaries], *vakıfs* [pious foundations], and sufi orders) but also established noninstitutional links as discourse between *devlet* and the common folk. The nineteenth-century conservative historian Cevdet Paşa gave us a clue about how this system worked in his detailed description of the operation of Islamic public opinion on the occasion of funerals of Muslim officials.[25]

What I was discovering in looking at Islam as discourse was a sphere of social activity covered neither by institution nor by exercise of the power of *devlet*. That is, there existed, embedded in Ottoman social arrangements, a number of levels allowing for surreptitious "operativities" that took their force from the many layers of an Islamic cultural funnel. This conception of daily life as operativities has been promoted by Michel de Certeau, whose concern for the "life-world" overlaps with that of scholars such as the "later" Wittgenstein, Jürgen Habermas, Norbert Elias, and Anthony Giddens.[26] All of them have been interested in finding out how the life-world and its cultural foundations acted as agent in the constitution of society.

Giddens, in particular, has signaled that the complex skills actors use in coordinating their day-to-day behavior assumed increasing importance during modernization.[27] This insight is crucial for an understanding of modern Turkish society. The advent of universal education and mass media, the introduction of multiparty politics, and the enlarging of the sphere of public opinion have brought the Turkish public into a setting in which it has a more extensive "monitoring" role than it had fifty years ago. Where once religion was mediated "through a specialized domain of religious institutions or through other primary public institutions,"[28] it has now become an organic part of highly mobilized Turkish society and works through the interstices of the "everyday." It is this transformation the Kemalist and Marxisant intellectuals have difficulty following, and here the overwhelming stamp of *devlet* as a mode of thinking seems to be at fault.

In short, one of the advantages of this new "micro" view of social relations was that it enabled me to concentrate on the life activities of citizens. None of the items falling under the rubric of microsociology that went back to phenomenological analysis had been picked up by the Turkish group I study here. And yet the end of single-party rule and the greater participation of the common folk in politics made the analytical tool of *devlet,* already stale in the 1950s, even feebler for understanding the many-layered texture of social forces at work in Turkey after the 1950s.[29]

An interesting projection of this continued use of a modified avatar of the ideology of *devlet* is that in Turkey even modern Muslim conservative leaders and their followers conceive of Islam as centralist and hegemonic, that is, as another form of *devlet* that obfuscates the subtle arrangements between elite and folk culture that one observes in Islamic societies. I believe, therefore, that the concept "life-world," which enables one to recapture the many dimensions of a subtler social analysis, sheds more light on the functioning of the Ottoman Empire and on present-day Turkish society than does a concern with macro structures. I am convinced that such an understanding will provide the lenses enabling Turkish secularists to live their daily lives without being bemused by the newly emerging religious forces in their society.

I can present what I have in mind about a new approach to the study of Turkey by drawing a rough sketch of what it would mean for Ottoman studies. One should begin to look at the way in which structures of understanding that existed in the minds of the Ottoman elites were reflected in state practice, the world of *devlet,* and how that world was linked to a homologous, corresponding world of folk practices—another level of the life-world operating in conjunction with Islam. The folk were buoyed by this layer of popular culture, and Ottoman bureaucrats, although they lived in a separate elite layer of culture, were nevertheless suffused with the ambient popular culture, manifestations of which they had names for, such as "janissary behavior," "sufi extremism," "sect formation," and "Ottoman (i.e., strong) women." Such a vocabulary made the ruling class sensitive to the microsociology of the Ottoman Empire.

This organic link disappeared in the republic together with its "reform" of language. The new social vocabulary relied on terms of social analysis introduced in France by proponents of solidarism in the late nineteenth century. Language, then, we are reminded, was a key component of the total set of Islamic "influences," and the new regime was correct in revolutionizing the use of Turkish as one of its props.[30] This revolution, however, created a second-order popular culture in which some of the old concepts lingered as residues unintegrated with an overarching Islamic culture, while the new republican ideology suffered from a similar lack of closure.

The extent to which Turkish society as seen from the perspective of the life-world can be revealing for modern Turkish history is illustrated by the problems faced by one segment of modern Turkey—Turkish intellectuals of republican times—as a consequence of their clean break with the past. There were two areas in which intellectuals felt disoriented in the first years of the republic. One was their role in the new *devlet,* the republican state, but there the difficulties encountered were not insuperable because the new *devlet* had taken over the earlier ideology of *devlet,* maintaining its broad outlines. The other was the shattering of the "everyday" world of the Ottoman intellectual, which seems to have presented more serious problems. This area involved questions relating to the severing of moorings to the Islamic cultural universe and the elaboration of the self linked to it. Questions about the social identity of the intellectual also arose in this context. I propose to examine these problems in connection with the life of Necip Fazıl Kısakürek, an outstanding modernist Turkish poet.

I suggest, as a summary of what follows, that although Necip Fazıl could fit himself into the frame of the new *devlet,* he was thrown off balance by the secular republic's abrogation of what a modified Gramscian scheme would call the cultural *organism* underlying Ottoman state practice—that is, not only the educational and cultural institutions but also the deeper cultural process. The old Ottoman class of guardians and literati was integrated with both the machine and the organism. The new transitional intellectual of the 1930s and 1940s functioned with only one of these frames, the *devlet.* Eventually, the new intellectuals did acquire some confidence, but they never made up for the loss of the less salient cultural elements in the functioning of Ottoman intellectuals. This caused anxiety at the personal level and shallowness in their conceptual apparatus. Some of the quandaries may be followed in the life of Kısakürek.

Necip Fazıl Kısakürek (1905–1983) is one of the puzzles of modern Turkish literature. Although his style is thoroughly modern, he has been an icon for religious conservatives, and he himself assumed the position of someone who systematically attacked Turkey's modern secular culture.[31]

Necip Fazıl did not receive his education in *medrese*s but in a series of modern schools including the naval academy in Heybeliada (Istanbul). He studied literature in Paris; he was one of the rare Turkish litterateurs to have understood Western theories of poetics. His language was consciously the direct, unadorned "modern" Turkish of the twentieth century. Yet in 1934, a Nakshibendi sheikh, Abdulhakim Arvasi, changed his life. Under Arvasi's influence, Kısakürek began the publication of *Great East,* a periodical that took up the defense of the "East" in general and of Ottoman Islamic culture in particular, a stance for which he was jailed a number of times between 1943 and the year of his death.

One explanation of Kısakürek's popularity with conservative Muslims might be that his stance was a lever for acquiring a wide audience, and with it, power, in a country with rising literacy. But the usefulness of such an explanation disintegrates when one remembers that he was popular enough among the secular intelligentsia in his early years to have been asked to rewrite the republic's national anthem (1938). Neither does it explain his attempt to "convert" at a time when it alienated his friends and brought the wrath of the Turkish state upon him. There was no organized Islamic movement at the time he took the plunge. A detailed study of his case shows that a number of subtler microprocesses were involved in his alienation from the mainstream ideology of the Turkish republic. Rather than explaining his conversion as caused by opportunism, we should focus on the pervasive angst that his writings show from the earliest time onward.

Conceptualized in terms of tiers, for the sake of brevity, we can distinguish two levels of Kısakürek's disenchantment and re-Islamization. The first, that of the elaboration of the self, shows two dimensions in turn: on the one hand, an attempt to recapture the "embeddedness" of certain values from his childhood, and on the other, an attempt to elaborate a narrative background for his personal and social memory. The second level was his frustration with the fragility and diffuseness of the available space for intellectuals in Turkey. Elsewhere I have attempted to relate the ways in which these gaps were filled by our poet.[32] A summary would cover the following points.

Kısakürek's work shows the pervasive changes in the "places," the spatial arrangements, of modern Turkey. (One of his most famous poems is titled "Sidewalks.") These spaces are empty for him because they lack the values—sympathy, affection—that prevailed in his foundational space, the mansion (*konak*) where he spent his childhood. Even there, these values were on the wane; his grandmother, a main influence in his childhood, was thoroughly modernist. Consequently, he could perceive only the shadow of a more complete set of "Ottoman" relations. One may notice in his later life a constant effort to reconstruct a whole of which only wisps have been apprehended. The loss of *konak* life, with its intricate interconnections, meant loss not only of the affective background but also of the way in which this affective element was linked by intricate layers of perception related to Turkish society in its functioning both inside and outside the *konak*.

Another element in Kısakürek's alienation was his inability to construct a coherent personal narrative that would integrate the history of the growth of his own self with the history of his family and its glorious feats in the town of Maraş, as well as with the history of the Ottoman Empire. The absence of such a remembered frame of knowledge was, according to him, what had created the superficiality of all modern Turkish literature, a literature that imitated Western *form* but had never been able to fill it with *content*. To me, Kısakürek's explanation does make more intelligible some of the remarks made by Muslim fundamentalists of the Arab sphere, such as Sayyid Qutb, concerning the diffuseness of the self of modern Muslims.[33] Jerome Bruner's (and the narrativists') conception of the "narrative construction of reality" seems to explain more of Necip Fazıl's Baudelarian "spleen."[34] The absence of a narrative canon impeded the use of a time-frame and the construction of a coherent memory, leaving him anguished and lost.

Finally, Necip Fazıl encountered difficulties in his self-positioning as an intellectual. During the Renaissance, such a frame for intellectuals had been elaborated in the West in the form of the Republic of Letters, a network of intellectuals linked not only to each other but also to an imagined audience, the European book-and-pamphlet-reading public. The ideational frame of this social network was what Ernest Gellner has named a common intellectual currency,[35] which increasingly took the form of mechanistic atomism, the Hobbesian equivalent of Newton's physics. It also toyed with the idea that cultures across the globe were on a footing of equality. This last feature, already observable in Montaigne, gained further salience in Europe during the eighteenth century.

This was a far cry from the group identity of the literati of the Ottoman Empire. For them, printed books became widely available only in the nineteenth century, traditional cultural forms prevailed until the 1850s, and philosophy was primarily centered in the mystical tradition. As to the variety of cultures, for Muslims, cultures were arranged in a hierarchical scale with Islam on top. The attempts of the Jesuits to legitimate Chinese culture as a superior one would have seemed quite inappropriate to Ottomans. Furthermore, Ottoman intellectuals and their modern Turkish successors sat comfortably in the ideology of *devlet* and were tied to it by their purse strings. As a result, in the majority they were unable to "float free," something even the earliest members of the Republic of Letters had been able to do because of the real clientele of book readers that arose with the enormous diffusion of the book in Europe. This had not happened yet in Turkey.

Walter Andrews's description of Ottoman literature of all levels as suffused by an ideology of closeness and familiarity is an additional element one must bring into play to understand the inability of the modern Turkish intellectual to fit into the new frame of anonymity.[36] By rejecting Islam as an element of social life, the Turkish republic created a void in the setting and practice of intellectual production, and it also undermined aspects of micro-layers of self-definition and intersubjectivity. In short, a class of literati secure in its group identity was replaced by a class of persons confused about their identity as intellectuals and also as persons. This may well be the reason why many modern Turkish intellectuals adopted a crude sycophantic attitude toward the new *devlet,* an attitude quite different from that of the prominent ulamas in the Ottoman Empire. Marxism was one frame that, in the 1960s, resolved this structural dilemma of the place of Turkish intellectuals by openly making their role a conflictual one. But Islam was a more natural venue in which to dissipate one's fears as a human being and as an intellectual, and that was the road chosen by Necip Fazıl Kısakürek.

The methodological lesson to draw from my explorations is that the exclusively Western mechanistic-positivistic or functionalist view of society used by the inheritors of the tradition of *devlet* can be enriched by an approach that takes the life-world and the "everyday" into account. Today, for studies of Turkey, Mikhail Bakhtin seems more appropriate than Durkheim or Marx in his description of the components of dialogics or in his view of ritual inversions of hierarchy—but it will take some time before the level of Bakhtin's cultural history is tapped by Turkish researchers.[37]

While the Turkish intellectuals of the 1980s and 1990s have mastered a superficial social analysis lacking the many layered depths of earlier Ottoman conceptualizations of society, they are stymied in their analysis of the dynamics of a society where cultural givens—that is, Islam—have acquired a new force.

Notes

1. On Kemalism, see Erik J. Zürcher, *Turkey: A Modern History,* London: I. B. Tauris, 1993, 189ff. On laicism in Turkey, see Zürcher, *Turkey,* and *Cogito* (Istanbul), vol. 1, no. 1, 1994, an issue on laicism that promotes the republican view. Regarding Marxisant scholars, it is interesting to note that for all their attempts to keep up with more fashionable versions of Marxism in the 1970s and 1980s, Turkish Marxians have been unaware of the contributions of Soviet social scientists such as Vygotsky and Bakhtin. See L. S. Vygotsky, *Mind in Society,* Cambridge, Massachusetts: Harvard University Press, 1978; and Katerina Clarke and Michael Holquist, *Mikhail Bakhtin,* Cambridge, Massachusetts: Belknap Press, 1984.

2. Irvin C. Schick and E. Ahmet Tonak, eds., *Turkey in Transition,* New York: Oxford University Press, 1987.

3. Mübeccel Kıray, *Ereğli: Ağır Sanyiden önce Bir Sahil Kasabası,* Ankara: T. C. Başbakanlık Devlet Planlama Teşkilatı, 1964.

4. Çağlar Keyder, *State and Class in Turkey: A Study in Capitalist Development,* London: Verso, 1987.

5. For which see Metin Heper, "Extremely Strong State and Democracy: The Turkish Case in Comparative and Historical Perspective," in S. N. Eisenstadt, ed., *Democracy and Modernity,* Leiden: E. J. Brill, 1992.

6. See Antonio Gramsci, *Selections from the Prison Notebooks,* London: Lawrence & Wishart, 1971; and N. Babbio, "Gramsci and the Concept of Civil Society," in John Keane, ed., *Civil Society and the State,* London: Verso, 1988, 73–99.

7. For these approaches, see Anthony Giddens, *The Constitution of Society,* Berkeley and Los Angeles, University of California Press, 1986. And for cultural history, see Dominick LaCapra and Steven L. Kaplan, eds., *Modern European Intellectual History,* Ithaca, New York: Cornell University Press, 1982; and Lynn Hunt, ed., *The New Cultural History,* Berkeley: University of California Press, 1989.

8. Derek Layder, *Understanding Social Theory,* London: Sage, 1994, 5.

9. For which see James C. Scott, *Domination and the Arts of Resistance,* New Haven, Connecticut: Yale University Press, 1990.

10. For which seen Anthony Giddens, *Modernity and Self-Identity,* Stanford, California: Stanford University Press, 1991.

11. For this problem, see George Ritzer, *Contemporary Sociological Theory,* New York: McGraw-Hill, 1992, 81–82, 397–98, 428–29.

12. For works covering the Tanzimat and the era, see Roderic H. Davison, "Western Publications on the Tanzimat," in Hakkı Dursun Yıldız, ed., *150. Yılında Tanzimat,* Ankara: Türk Tarih Kurumu, 1992, 511–32.

13. On cameralism, see William Doyle, *The Old European Order, 1660–1800,* Oxford: Oxford University Press, 1990, 235.

14. On Sultan Mahmud II, see Ahmet Cevdet, *Tarih . . . Tertib-i Cedid,* Istanbul: Matba-i Osmaniye, 1309AH/1893–94, 300. On Mustafa Reşid, see Bayram Kodaman, "Mustafa Reşid Paşanın Paris Sefirlikleri Esnasında Takip Ettiği Genel Politika," in *Mustafa Reşid Paşa ve Dönemi Semineri: Bildiriler,* Ankara: Türk Tarih Kurumu, 1927, 73. On the Young Ottomans and the Young Turks, see my *Genesis of Young Ottoman*

Thought, Princeton, New Jersey: Princeton University Press, 1962, passim; and my *Jön Türklerin Siyasi Fikirleri,* Istanbul: İletişim, 1985. On Mustafa Kemal, see Şevket Süreyya Aydemir, *Tek Adam: Mustafa Kemal, 1881–1919,* 3 vols., Istanbul: Remzi, 1976.

15. On the link between these ideas and the ideology of *devlet,* see Levent Köker, *Modernleşme, Kemalizm ve Demokrasi,* Istanbul: İletişim, 1990, 71, 81, 96.

16. Jean Jacques Rousseau, *The Social Contract and the Discourses on the Origin of Inequality,* edited by Lester G. Crocker, New York: Pocket Books, 1967, 167.

17. Weber used "patrimonialism" to refer to any type of government organized as a direct extension of the royal household, and "sultanism" to describe extreme forms of personal despotism. According to Weber, "patrimonialism/sultanism," coupled, described best the type of government that developed in the "Orient," whereas "patrimonialism/feudalism" was appropriate for the West. See Reinhard Bendix, *Max Weber: An Intellectual Portrait,* Berkeley: University of California Press, 1977, 100, 344–60.

18. Refik Halit Karay, *Memleket Hikâyeleri,* Istanbul: Semih Lutfi Kitabevi, 1939.

19. Max Weber, *The City,* New York: The Free Press, 1958.

20. See my "Civil Society and Islam," in John A. Hall, ed., *Civil Society: Theory, History, Comparison,* Cambridge: Polity Press, 1995, 278–300.

21. Naşit Hakkı (Uluğ), *Derebeyi ve Dersim,* Ankara: Hakimiyeti Milliye Matbaasi, 1932.

22. On *asabiyya,* see Ira H. Lapidus, *A History of Islamic Societies,* Cambridge: Cambridge University Press, 1988, 14. I was reminded of the importance of the term by my colleague Faruk Birtek of Boğaziçi University.

23. Zürcher, *Turkey: A Modern History,* 194.

24. A. Schutz, *The Phenomology of the Social World,* Evanston, Illinois: Northwestern University Press, 1967.

25. Ahmet-Cevdet, *Tezakir 40-Tetimme,* edited by Cavid Baysun, Ankara: Türk Tarih Kurumu, 1967, 212.

26. Michel de Certeau, *The Practice of Everyday Life,* Berkeley: University of California Press, 1984. Also see Layder, *Understanding Social Theory:* for Habermas, 186ff., for Elias, 114–26, and for Giddens, 125–49.

27. Anthony Giddens, *The Constitution of Society,* Berkeley: University of California Press, 1984, 285.

28. Thomas Luckmann, *The Invisible Religion,* New York: Macmillan, 1967, 103.

29. Turkish Marxists, for instance, have never risen to E. P. Thompson's richer analysis of social texture.

30. For a reminder of the complex and reciprocal relations between language and social tiers, see Emile Benveniste, *Indo-European Language and Society,* Coral Gables, Florida: University of Miami Press, 1969, 225–39. This is a subject that still needs study in the context of modern Turkey.

31. For a biography, see M. Orhan Okay, *Necip Fazıl Kısakürek,* Ankara: Kültür ve Turizm Bakanlığı, 1987.

32. Şerif Mardin, "Culture Change and the Intellectual, a Study of the Effects of Secularization in Turkey: Necip Fazıl and the Nakşıbendi," in Şerif Mardin, ed., *Cultural Transitions in the Middle East,* Leiden: Brill, 1994, 190–213.

33. On Sayyid Qutb, see William E. Shepard, "Islam as a 'System' in the Later Writings of Sayyid Qutb," *Middle Eastern Studies,* vol. 25, 1989, 31–50.

34. See Jerome Bruner, "The Narrative Construction of Reality," *Critical Inquiry,* vol. 18, 1990, 1–21.

35. See Ernest Gellner, *Nations and Nationalism,* Ithaca, New York: Cornell University Press, 1983, 21.

36. Walter Andrews, *Poetry's Voice, Society's Song: Ottoman Lyric Poetry,* Seattle: University of Washington Press, 1985.

37. A rare exception is the work of Ayşe Saktanber in the Department of Sociology of the Middle East Technical University, Ankara. See her "Islamic Revitalization in Turkey: An Urban Model of a 'Counter Society,'" unpublished Ph.D. dissertation, Ankara: METU, 1995.

6/ The Quest for the Islamic Self within the Context of Modernity

NİLÜFER GÖLE

Modernization theories have forced us to look for symmetrical and linear lines of development, sometimes to the exclusion of historical and geographical context. According to these theories, there are universally defined variables and causal sequences between variables (for instance, education and urbanization, economic development and democracy) that create modernization quite independently of time and space. Now, the epistemological pendulum has swung from causal reasoning and methodological positivism toward the question of agency and the analysis of specific, context-bound interpretations of modernity. This shift has had an undeniably liberating effect on the study of non-Western countries. Distancing oneself from universalistic approaches to modernization permits one to examine the subjective construction of meaning and cultural identity—the construction of specific articulations between the local fabric and modernity.

Yet as Anthony Giddens has pointed out, "a rethinking of the nature of modernity must go hand in hand with a reworking of basic premises of sociological analysis."[1] As we move toward an understanding of new forms of hybridization between the particular and the universal, and between local and global realities, we traverse a terrain that has not been explored or explained in the language of the social sciences. This creates, at the outset, a problem of conceptualization. A common approach is to consider all sorts of puzzling hybrids and paradoxes as either parochial signs of a "pathology of backwardness" or simply as postmodern relativisms.

There are two ways in which the study of Islamic movements is related to this intellectual shift from universalistic conceptions to a particularistic analysis of modernization.[2] First, by excluding Islamic identity and culture, the totalizing nature of modernization reveals itself. The reassertion and reelaboration of an Islamic self via political empowerment implicitly addresses the impact of modernization, which has penetrated into the most intimate spheres of everyday life, from definitions of self to gender relations and ethical and aesthetic values. Second, the study of contemporary Islamic movements challenges the assumed binary opposition between tradition and modernity. In doing so, it focuses particular attention on the connections between faith and rationality, morality and modernity, individualism and community, and intimacy and transparency.

Thus, the reconstruction of Western modernity in a Muslim context can help us comprehend competing legitimacies and the Islamic perspective on modernity. Such a cross-reading will assist in integrating what otherwise might be considered the oppositional notions of "the East" and "the West," or "Islam" and "modernity." Instead, the emphasis will fall on the critical interaction between these concepts.

The Civilizing Project and the Turkish Self

Current scholarship explains Islamic movements by assigning priority either to sociopolitical factors or to some part of the religion itself that is presumed to be alien to a series of transformations such as reformism and secularism that occurred in the West. If the research follows the first course, it develops causal reasons—economic stagnation, political authoritarianism, rural exodus—to explain the rise of radical Islam. This type of approach describes the social environment within which oppositional movements are rooted, but it fails to address the reasons why Islam appeals so strongly to the need for cultural and political empowerment. Lines of research that focus on the essence of Islam as a religion, on the other hand, suppose an immutable quality in Islam and thereby take it out of its historical and political context. Scholarship of this sort simply expresses the politico-religious nature of Islamic movements as a summing up of the two different phenomena.

There is no denying that a sphere of tension exists that is sharpened by Islamic movements. This sphere is situated at the crossroads of religion and politics. The debate is defined by different conceptualizations and normative values assigned to such terms as self, gender relations, and modes of life. On the one hand, Muslims define themselves through religious belief, but on the other hand, it is radical politics that empowers and conveys this meaning. Through Alain Touraine's framework of analysis, this sphere of tension can be approached.[3] Touraine sees social movements as struggles for control of cultural models, struggles that are not separate from class conflict. In his formulation, Islamic movements do not express solely a politico-religious opposition but also present a countercultural model of modernization.

To make this realm or sphere of conflict more explicit, one needs to explore the mode of modernization undertaken in Turkey and in the majority of Muslim countries. The study of contemporary Islamic movements, therefore, necessitates a reevaluation of the recent history of Turkish modernization. This period spans the second half of the nineteenth century, when modernization began under the tutelage of Ottoman elites, and most of the twentieth, with the formation and growth of the republican Kemalist elite. One can better understand the problematic relations between Islam and modernity if one takes into account the constructions of "Western modernity" at the local, cultural, and historical levels. Rather than studying relations between Islam and the West, where the West is taken to be an external and physical entity, it is more productive to focus on indigenous forms of modernity. This means examining how the Western ideal of modernity is reconstructed and internalized locally, and how the power relations between Islamic movements and modernist elites take shape.

Often, the transforming impact of Western modernity is studied at the level of state structures, political institutions, and the industrial economy. Its less tangible but more penetrating effects, however, are on the cultural level, in lifestyles, gender identities, and self-definition of identity. The modernization project takes a very different turn in a non-Western context, for it imposes a political will to "Westernize." The terms "Westernization" and "Europeanization," which were widely used by nineteenth- and twentieth-century reformers, overtly express the willing participation that underlies the borrowing of institutions, ideas, and manners from the West. The history of modernization in Turkey can be considered the most radical example of such a voluntary cultural shift. Kemalist reformers' efforts went far beyond modernizing the state apparatus as the country changed from a multiethnic Ottoman empire to a secular republican nation-state; they also attempted to penetrate into the lifestyles, manners, behavior, and daily customs of the people. With the renewal of the Islamist movements during the 1980s, a historical return—a reconsideration of this "civilizing" shift—became crucial to understanding the emotional, personal, and symbolic levels that defined the conflicts and tensions between Islamists and modernists.[4]

The Turkish mode of modernization is an unusual example of how indigenous ruling elites have imposed their notions of a Western cultural model, resulting in conversion almost on a civilizational scale. By building up a strong tradition of ideological positivism, Turkish modernist elites have aimed toward secularization, rationalization, and nation building. The premises of positivist ideology are crucial in the realization of this project.[5] First, positivism holds universalistic claims for the Western model. By not considering Western modernity an outcome of a particular Christian religious culture, positivism focuses on scientific rationality. It represents this model of change as universal, rational, and applicable everywhere and at any time. It is Comte's ultimate positivist stage, which all societies will one day achieve.

Second, the French positivists' motto, "order and progress" (instead of the market anarchy of the British liberals), gives Turkish nationalists powerful encouragement in their attempts at social control. For the ruling Kemalist elites, the unity of society achieved through "progress" of a Western sort is the ultimate goal. Thus, throughout republican history, all kinds of differentiation—ethnic, ideological, religious, and economic—have been viewed not as natural components of a pluralistic democracy but as sources of instability and as threats to unity and progress. Such a perspective permits Turkish modernist elites to legislate and legitimate their essentially antiliberal platform.

The all-encompassing nature of the Turkish "civilizing" project can better be apprehended in reference to Norbert Elias's work.[6] Although the concept of civilization refers to a wide variety of factors, from technology to manners and religious ideas and customs, it actually expresses, as Elias points out, the "self-consciousness" and "superiority" of the West. Technology, rules of conduct, worldview, and everything else that makes the West distinctive and sets it apart from more "primitive" societies impart to Western civilization a superiority that lends a presumption of universality to its cultural model.

Attempts at modernization in Muslim countries become a matter of "civilization" when they are defined essentially by Western experience and culture. Western history has reached a number of peaks, from the Renaissance through the Enlightenment and into the industrial era. It continues to maintain its dominance in the information age. In doing so, it has created its own terrain for innovation and has become the reference mark for modernity. Non-Western experiences no longer make history and are defined as residual, granted an identity only in their difference from the West, namely, as non-Western. As Daryush Shayegan notes, societies on the periphery of Western civilization are excluded from the sphere of history and knowledge, for they can no longer participate in the "carnival of change" and therefore have entered into "cultural schizophrenia."[7] These societies have a "weak historicity," that is, a feeble capacity to innovate or create in their own environment. As a result, their history becomes a continuous effort to imitate, to modernize, and to position themselves in relation to presumed Western superiority. In this cycle, encounters between East and West result not in reciprocal exchanges but in the decline of the weaker, typified in the Middle East by the decline of the Islamic identity.

The term "civilization," then, does not refer in a historically relative way to each culture—French, Islamic, Arabic, African—but instead designates the historical superiority of the West as the producer of modernity. The concept of civilization refers to something that is constantly in motion, moving forward, encompassing the idea of progress. Therefore, it not only refers to a given state of development but also carries with it an ideal to be attained. Contrary to the German notion of *kultur*, which stresses national differences, civilization has a universal claim—it plays down national differences and emphasizes what is common among peoples.[8] It expresses the self-image of the European upper classes, who see themselves as the "standard-bearers of expanding civilization," and it is the antithesis of barbarism.[9] As Turkish modernists have repeatedly stated, the main objective of reforms is to "reach the level of contemporary civilization" (*muassır medeniyet seviyesine erişmek*), that is, of Western civilization. An irony of history is that the Turks, who for centuries symbolized to Europeans the barbarian, Muslim other, are now trying to enter the arena of the "civilized" in part by inventing their own "barbarians" in the form of, first, the Muslims, and second, the Kurds.

The Kemalist Woman and Western Civility

The concept of civilization is by no means value-free or neutral. It is, instead, a concept that refers to power relations between those who appropriate civilized manners and all others, who are, by default, barbarians. Consequently, in the Turkish process of modernization, the distinction between what is considered civilized and what is considered uncivilized comes under scrutiny. Everything that is *alafranka* (the European way) is deemed proper and valuable; anything *alaturka* (the Turkish way) acquires a negative connotation and is somehow inferior. It is interesting to note that Turks now use the foreign word *alaturka* to describe their own habits.[10] Wearing neckties, eating with forks, shaving, attending the theater, shaking hands, dancing and wearing hats in public, and writing from left to right are some of the behaviors that characterize a progressive and civilized person.

This individual ideal is transmitted most vividly through the image of the emancipated—that is, Westernized—woman. Every revolution defines an ideal man, but for the Kemalist revolution, it is the image of an ideal woman that has become the symbol of the reforms. In the Turkish case, the project of modernization equates the nation's progress with the emancipation of women. Even more than the strengthening of judicial and human rights, it is the status of women as public citizens and women's rights in general that are the backbone of the Kemalist reforms.[11] The participation of women in the public sphere necessitates, in the opinion of the modernists, taking off the veil, establishing compensatory coeducation, granting women's suffrage, and the social mixing of men and women.

Kemalist feminism, with its sights set on public visibility and social mixing of the sexes, is creating a radical reappraisal of what are considered the private and public spheres. At the same time, its actions are prompting a reevaluation of Islamic morality, which is based on control of female sexuality and separation of the sexes. The deepest intellectual and emotional chasms between the modern West and Islam exist at the level of gender relations and definitions of the private and the public. Women appear as markers of the frontiers both between the intimate and the public spheres and between the two civilizations. As a result, Kemalist women who participate in public life are liberated from the religious or cultural constraints of the intimate sphere. But they also face a radical choice: culturally, they must be either Western or Muslim.

The Turkish experience is exceptional among its Muslim counterparts in its "epistemological break," its radical discontinuity between traditional self-definitions and Western constructs. The majority of the population can easily create hybrid forms in their daily practice of religion, traditional conservatism, and modern aspirations. But the modernist elites, with their value-references tied to binary oppositions, have clearly sided with the "civilized," the "emancipated," and the "modern." This generates a cognitive dissonance between the value system of the elites and that of the rest of the population, which results in contesting legitimacies.[12] Furthermore, the Kemalists formulate their discourse from the center of power backed by the state, whereas the Islamists formulate theirs through opposition.

"Islam Is Beautiful": A Quest for Legitimacy

The upheavals in lifestyles and in aesthetic and ethical values that occur when an Islamic culture seeks modernization are not independent of social power relations. Western taste as a social marker of "distinction" establishes new social divisions, creates new social status groups (in the Weberian sense), and thus changes the terms of social stratification. Thus, there emerges an arena of struggle, or "habitus," as Bourdieu calls it, that exists beyond will and language and encompasses habits of eating, body language, taste, and so forth.[13]

Contemporary Islamic radicalism reveals this struggle in an exaggerated form. It is critical of the notion that what is "civilized" is "Westernized." The politicizing of Islam empowers and encourages Muslims to return to the historical scene with their own ethics and aesthetics. The politics of the body conveys a distinct sense of self and society in which control (and self-control) of sexuality becomes the central issue.[14] Thus, the veiling of women, the most visible symbol of Islamization, becomes the semiology of Muslim identity. But men's beards, and chastity, and prohibitions against promiscuity, homosexuality, alcohol consumption, and so forth, also define a new consciousness of an Islamic self and an Islamic way of life quite distinct from the "common," "traditional" Muslim identity. What is new here is how, with regard to modernity, Islam is reconstructed and positioned in a new, conflicting, and more confident role.

Traditionally, a woman's status in society parallels the "natural" life cycle as she passes from young girl to married woman and then grandmother. She is denied both individual choice and political power. Women participating in radical Islamic movements not only gain some control over their lives, as they break from traditional roles and develop personal strategies for education and career, but also politicize the entire Islamic way of life.

Islamist female attire, for instance, includes the convention of veiling. But this sort of veiling has little in common with traditional ways of covering the body. It has even less to do with the image of a Muslim woman as docile, devoted to her family and to her traditional roles of mother and spouse (see fig. 6.1). In Turkey, the word *türban* is used to denote the new Islamist head covering, whereas *başörtüsü* ("head scarf") refers to the older, more traditional style. In Iran, the chador is worn both by militant and educated Islamist professional women and by the masses of traditional women. But it is interpreted differently by each group. Islamist profes-

6.1. Istanbul in the 1990s: young girls in head scarves looking at posters of Turkish popular music and film stars. (Photograph by Haluk Özözlü; reproduced from *Istanbul,* 7 October 1993.)

sional women emphasize the Islamic way of dressing. They wear the chador as a powerful statement; it often covers an Islamic dress that completely envelops the body, preventing any possibility that the feminine form might be revealed while the wearer is active. Traditional Muslim women are more practical and pragmatic about wearing a chador. It is simply a covering that can be thrown quickly over their indoor attire and held closed with one hand as they go about their daily chores in the streets.

Such different uses of coverings exemplify the blurring of borders between tradition and modernity. Islamist ways are radically reappropriated by those who have already acquired and are making use of much of modernity. They have been educated, they move about in public urban spaces, and they have influence in the political realm. Thus, Islamism is an expression of the intensifying voice of Muslim identity as that identity, in its search for legitimacy, is radicalized and politicized in the modern world.

In their relationship with enlightened modernity, the Islamic movements exhibit the same critical sensitivity as other contemporary Western social movements. They are not substantially different from black, feminist, environmental, or ethnic movements.[15] All of these movements vividly demonstrate the force that can arise out of repression. A common feature of the postmodern condition is the tension that exists between identity politics, particularism, and localism, on one side, and the uniformity of abstract universalism, on the other. Like feminism, which questions universalistic and emancipatory claims and asserts that women are different and cannot be subsumed under the category "human being" (which is identified with men), Islamism takes issue with the universalism of "civilization" (identified with the West), which does not recognize Islamic differences. Women sharpen their identity by calling themselves feminists; Muslims do the same by labeling themselves Islamists. The sentiments of protest against and rejection of the dominant culture of white, Western men are captured in the phrase "black is beautiful." It is a motto that resonates with pride in that which is different, and it is a source of empowerment in the politics of identity. The motto "Islam is beautiful" is gaining the same sort of potency in Islamic contexts.

Body Politics: The Islamization of Lifestyle

The quest to maintain an identity separate from that of the dominant West—the quest for an "authentic" Islamic way of being—engenders a hypercritical awareness both of traditional, common ways of practicing Islam and of the contemporary forms of Western modernity that homogenize lifestyles through globalization. Islamist intellectuals call for a return to the origins of the faith and for an investigation of Islam's golden age (*asr-ı saadet*), the era of the Prophet, in the hope that there they will find strategies for coping with "westoxication" and for correcting traditional misinterpretations.[16] The radicalism of the Islamic movements stems from this search for the original, fundamental interpretations of Islam. A new definition of the Islamic self is rooted in a religiosity repressed by secularism and is sought in the reinvention of traditions destroyed by modernization.

Body politics is crucial in revealing the new consciousness of the Islamic self as it resists secularism. In the view of Islamist women, veiling has nothing to do with subservience to men or to any other kind of human power. Rather, it expresses the recognition of God's sovereignty over humans and submission to that sovereignty. Readopting the Islamic covering for women, particularly the head scarf, expresses a strong self-assertiveness and constitutes almost a reconversion to Islam.[17] Islamic women consider their religiosity something "natural," "always there," just waiting to be rediscovered. The veil makes Islamization real by an individual act, but it does not admit individualism. It expresses the critical assertiveness of Islamic women with respect to the modern individual who is emancipated from spiritual references and thus secularized.

Secularization and equality, the most significant experiences of Western modernity, are interpreted in the Muslim context as an assault on the most private realms and on social relations. The principle of equality confers legitimacy on a continuous societal effort to overcome social differences that the Muslim accepts as natural and insurmountable. Equality among citizens, races, nations, workers, and sexes defines the historical and progressive itinerary of Western societies. As more realms of social life are delivered from spiritual and natural definitions, the process of secularization deepens. This synergy between secularism and equality is considered the ultimate product of the modern Western individual.

The semiology of body care as manifested by the secularized person and the religious person indicates different conceptions of the body and the self. For the modern individual, the body is being liberated progressively from the hold of natural and transcendental definitions. It enters into the cycle of secularization, eventually penetrating the realm where human rationality exercises its will to master and tame the body through science and knowledge. Genetic engineering and manipulation of reproduction are two examples of such highly scientific interventions. But phobias over cholesterol, taboos on smoking, and an obsession with fitness are more mundane examples of how the notion of health, inspired by scientific rather than by erotic desires, now determines lifestyles. Body sculpting, fitness, and energy are the ideals of the modern individual, who is witnessing the leveling of differences between the sexes and the age groups and the replacement of life cycles with lifestyles.[18]

Through Islamization, specifically the application of Islam to everyday life, differences between the sexes are scrupulously maintained and placed in a clear hierarchy. Any blurring of the border between feminine and masculine roles is considered a transgression, especially the physical masculinization of the female. In this context, veiling becomes a trait of femininity, of feminine modesty and virtue. Furthermore, in the Islamic context, the body has a different semantic: it mediates devotion to religious sacraments, and through ablution, fasting, and praying, it is purified. In addition to the physical body, the spiritual being (*nefs*) is mastered and cleansed through submission to divine will.

But even this comparison is not purely a matter of difference between secular and religious conceptions of self, a difference that exists in almost all religions. Instead, it is a civilizational matter. The notion of body and self explains the almost compulsory resistance of contemporary Islamists to secularism and equality. The Islamic self, which is reconstructed in conflicting power relations with the premises of the modern individual, makes itself different from the latter by seeking its own roots and foundation.[19]

Modern societies are driven to "confess," to "tell the truth about sexuality," as Michel Foucault would put it.[20] According to Foucault, the emergence of modernity can be understood only by taking into account this urge (stemming from earlier religious practices) to confess the most intimate experiences, desires, illnesses, uneasinesses, and guilts in public in the presence of an authority who can judge, punish, forgive, or console. This explains how everything that is difficult to say, that is forbidden and rooted in the personal, private sphere, is confessed, made public and political. Popular talk shows in the United States, which are filled with discussions of sexual harassment, abuse, abortion, rape, and crime, serve as venues in which confessions are made and "truth" sought.

In opposition to the modern West, where the basic presupposition is that absolute truth is a matter not of the collective but of the individual conscience, in Islam this urge is met by submitting oneself to God and letting the community (*cemaat*) serve as one's guide through life.[21] Veiling reminds us that there is a forbidden, intimate sphere that must be confined to the private and never expressed in public. Therefore, by refusing to assimilate Western modernity and by rediscovering religion and a memory repressed by rationalism and universalism, the Islamic subject elaborates and redefines herself. Islam as a lifestyle provides a new anchor for the self and thereby creates an "imagined political community" that reinforces social ties among people who do not know each other but who share the same dreams and spiritual attachments.[22] Islamism is more than a political ideology, for it creates a community forged in the crucible of the sacred.[23]

The Quest for Islamic Identity

One of the most important traits of the Islamic movement that differentiates it from other contemporary social movements is that it retains a holistic strategy of change and the vision of an Islamic utopia. Contemporary Western social movements have become disenchanted with the totalitarian nature of utopian thinking and have been inclined toward a self-limitation in their projects, which admits more pluralism.

The "rise of the oppressed" can be emancipatory only if it is not itself repressive. The quest for "difference," "authenticity," and "morality," necessary as an early elaboration of identity, has its own limitations. It can lead to essentialist definitions and exclusionary stands—Who decides what is Islamic? Who is a real Muslim?—that undermine and subvert the "imagined community" into an oppressive kind of communal authoritarianism. Such totalitarianism is made especially combustible by the search for an all-embracing Islamic identity liberated from the corrupting and domineering effects of Western modernity. As with any utopian philosophy, here, too, there is no place for conflict, for pluralism, or for interaction. The more the relationship between the "pure" self and the "total" community is reinforced, the more Islamic politics becomes that of authoritarian intervention in personal choices.

The relationship between Islamic identity and Western modernity is a crucial one. At the level of discourse, modernity is constantly criticized, but at the levels of individual behavior, political competition, and social practice, the interaction between the two grows deeper and more complex daily. Islamic intellectuals, who are keenly aware of this phenomenon, express their disappointment and address their critique toward the forms of modernity appropriated by Islamists themselves. Islamic pop music and fashion shows are only a few of the indicators of the degree to which modernity has infiltrated the Islamic community. One of the milestones in the quest for Islamic identity within the context of modernity will be the way in which the Welfare Party (Refah Partisi) moves from the periphery to the center of power as it attempts to reconcile its philosophy with the aspirations of the urban lower classes, who are more interested in embracing modernity than in rejecting it.

Notes

1. Anthony Giddens, *Modernity and Self-Identity: Self and Society in the Late Modern Age*, Stanford, California: Stanford University Press, 1991.

2. I use the terms "Islamic movements" and "radical Islamism" interchangeably to designate contemporary Islamic movements as a collective action whose ideology was shaped at the end of the 1970s by Islamist thinkers all over the Muslim world (e.g., Maudoodi, Sayyid Qutb, Ali Shariati, and Ali Bulaç) and by the Iranian revolution. The term "radicalism" is used in the sense that there is a return to

the origins and foundations of Islam in order to realize a systemic change, to create an Islamic society, and to critique Western modernity. Islamic and Islamism are not differentiated, although the latter refers to the project of Islamization of society through political and social empowerment, whereas the former simply denotes Muslim culture and religion in general.

3. Alain Touraine, *The Voice and the Eye: An Analysis of Social Movement,* Cambridge: Cambridge University Press, 1981.

4. Pierre Bourdieu, *Distinction,* Cambridge, Massachusetts: Harvard University Press, 1984.

5. Nilüfer Göle, *Mühendisler ve İdeoloji* (Engineers and Ideology), Istanbul: İletişim, 1986.

6. Norbert Elias, *The History of Manners: The Civilizing Process,* vol. 1, New York: Pantheon Books, 1978, 3.

7. Daryush Shayegan, *Le regard mutilé,* Paris: Albin Michel, 1989.

8. Elias, *The History of Manners,* 5.

9. Elias, *The History of Manners,* 50.

10. The word *alaturka* is still used colloquially by the Turkish elites with a negative connotation, although in recent years there has been an increased appreciation, or perhaps a nostalgia, for things Ottoman and Turkish.

11. This explains why today in Turkey the violation of women's rights and the trampling of secularism upsets the elites even more than does the abuse of human rights or the reneging on principles of democracy.

12. In terms of historical classification and political experience, the legacy of the Democrat Party, which was at the forefront of the transition to political pluralism in Turkey in 1946, is of crucial importance. The Democrat Party, considered too liberal on religious and economic issues, gave voice to those segments of society that were independent of the bureaucratic, Kemalist state. It was a mediating influence and acted as a buffer between the state and society, a role that was filled nowhere else in the Muslim countries of the region. It may even be asserted that it is the Democrat Party legacy that represents Turkish "specificity," rather than radical secularism, which has been imitated to a certain extent in the majority of Muslim countries. In this essay I have omitted a discussion of the Democrat Party's legacy, since I believe it created a political representation of Muslim identity rather than a new intellectual legacy. In terms of initiating new paradigms of legitimacy, the events of 1923 and 1983 are by far the most important.

13. Bourdieu, *Distinction.*

14. Nilüfer Göle, *Musulmanes et Modernes,* Paris: Decourvert, 1993 (English edition *Forbidden Modern,* Ann Arbor: University of Michigan Press, 1997).

15. Craig Calhoun, ed., *Social Theory and the Politics of Identity,* New York: Blackwell, 1994.

16. The term *gharbzadegi* ("westoxication"), first used by the Iranian thinker Jalal Ali Ahmad, became popular among a whole generation of Iranian youths in the 1970s.

17. "Veiling," "covering," and "head scarf" are used interchangeably to designate the Islamic principle of *hijab,* that is, the necessity for women to cover their hair, shoulders, and the form of their body in order to preserve their virtue and

not be a source of disorder (*fitne*). Contemporary Islamic attire is generally a head scarf that completely covers the hair and shoulders. The rest of the body is covered with a long gown that conceals the feminine form.

18. Giddens, *Modernity and Self-Identity*, 80–81.

19. In this respect, although the word "fundamentalism" is widely criticized and frequently rejected, it more accurately describes the situation than does "traditionalism," which supposes a continuity in time and in evolution.

20. Michel Foucault, *The History of Sexuality*, vol. 1, translated by Robert Hurley, New York: Vintage Books, 1990, 61.

21. C. A. O. van Nieuwenhuijze, *The Lifestyles of Islam*, Leiden: E. J. Brill, 1985, 144.

22. Here I am following Benedict Anderson's analysis of nationalism and applying it to Islamism. See his *Imagined Communities: Reflections on the Origin and Spread of Nationalism*, London: Verso, 1983.

23. The French sociologist Emile Durkheim (1858–1917) pointed out almost a century ago the distinct realms of the sacred and the profane, both of which are essential in the establishment and production of social bonds.

7/ The Project of Modernity
and Women in Turkey

YEŞİM ARAT

Professor Nermin Abadan-Unat is Turkey's first female political scientist, an ex-senator, a promoter of women in academia, and a defender of women's rights in Turkey and abroad. She was born in 1921 in Vienna to a German-speaking mother of Baltic origin and a Turkish fruit merchant from Izmir. She lived abroad until her father died, and then, when private education was becoming increasingly difficult for her mother to finance, she migrated—or rather, ran away—to Turkey to continue her education. She had heard that girls as well as boys could be educated for free in Turkey.

After she narrated this life story in her last lecture before retiring from the Faculty of Political Science at the University of Ankara in 1988, Professor Abadan punctuated her story by saying, "I chose my country as well as my nation with my own will. If Mustafa Kemal did not exist, perhaps I would not exist. I suspect now you have understood why I am a Kemalist, why I am a nationalist."[1]

At about the same time, Şirin Tekeli, a leading feminist activist, was publicly criticizing Kemalism.[2] Born in 1944 in Ankara, Şirin was the daughter of prototypical Kemalist intellectuals. Both of her parents were high-school philosophy teachers, and her mother, especially, was a fervent advocate of Kemal. Like Nermin Abadan-Unat, Şirin was a political scientist. After she became an associate professor in the Faculty of Economics at Istanbul University, however, she resigned from the university in protest of the Board of Higher Education established in 1981.[3] She helped organize feminists in Turkey and helped found the Women's Library and Information Center in Istanbul. In an interview for a book on the left's assessment of Kemalism, she explained,

> It is true that the women's revolution was a significant part of Kemalism. Our [feminists'] first question, however, is this: Was this

95

revolution undertaken for women's own rights or was it used in some manner for the other transformation, the transformation Kemalism aimed to accomplish at the level of the state. I solemnly believe there was such an instrumentality. Atatürk was a soldier and an excellent strategist. He was a person who could evaluate what women's rights meant in the context of the transformation of the state. He was a Jacobin and he made use of women's rights as much as he could.[4]

Other feminists are more abrupt. They simply say they are not Kemalists and go on to elaborate why.

In this essay, I explore how women of one generation who, figuratively, owed their existence to Atatürk came to be challenged by a younger generation that radically criticized him. My purpose is to interpret the significance of the modernizing reforms in the context of this new challenge coming from the more radical feminist voices in the contemporary scene. What did the reforms of the 1920s bequeath to the 1980s? Do feminists who oppose the Kemalists undermine or revive the project of modernity the Kemalists initiated? With their demands for autonomy and subsequent criticisms of Kemalism, the feminists, I argue, paradoxically help further the project of modernity in Turkey. Feminist criticisms of Kemalist discourse attempt to free liberalism, democracy, and secularism from a polity that has long repressed those qualities in the name of those very qualities themselves.

Whereas women were essential "actors or pawns" in the republican project of modernity,[5] feminists are a small group in the contemporary scene. Carlos Fuentes, in *The Buried Mirror,* argues that "a constant of Spanish culture, as revealed in the artistic sensibility, is the capacity to make the invisible visible by embracing the marginal, the perverse, the excluded."[6] The feminists are a marginal group, if not the perverse and the excluded, and focusing on their activism makes the invisible threads of the republican project of modernity—its goals, successes, and limits—visible. The emergence of feminism attests to the vigor of the modernist project. The project continues as it is liberated from the monopoly of Kemalist discourse and regenerated by a plurality of voices, including feminisms critical of Kemalist modernism.

I first examine how women helped construct the project of modernity, what Tekeli called "the other transformation at the level of the state." I

7.1. "Turkey of the Future." (Reproduced from *Kalem*, December 1908.)

then try to reconstruct the challenge to that project coming from feminists. Finally, I evaluate the extent to which the feminist challenge un-
dermines or revives the Kemalist project of modernity.

I use the term "feminist" to refer to those who identify themselves as
such in pursuit of women's liberation. During the 1980s, the older generation of Kemalist women identified themselves as egalitarian feminists
or, at times, as Kemalist feminists.[7] When I use the term "feminist," I
mean the younger group who challenged Kemalism, and I call the other
group egalitarian feminists.

The Kemalist Project of Modernity and the Female Cast

The cartoon reproduced as figure 7.1, titled "Turkey of the Future," was
published in the weekly *Kalem* in 1908, before the republic was founded

7.2. The caption for this cartoon reads, "A healthy mind is to be found in a healthy body; therefore, we should do sports." (Reproduced from *Davul*, Jan-

in 1923. It depicts a woman aviator dressed in a traditional *çarsaf,* flying over a hectic urban street to the awed stares of onlookers. The mosques recede in the background, and tall buildings transform the Turkish setting into any "modern" Western one with skyscrapers and department stores.

This 1908 vision was actualized both literally and figuratively in two or three decades in the early republican period. The change was greater than could have been envisioned in the 1900s. Women did not just fly but shed their *çarsaf*s as well. Atatürk's adopted daughter Sabiha Gökçen became the first military aviator in Turkey. The image of Sabiha Gökçen in her air force uniform, with respectful male onlookers, including her proud father, is ingrained in the collective consciousness of at least the educated urbanites in Turkey. Figuratively, if the project of modernity aimed for a Westernizing polity that was liberal, democratic, and secular, then a female aviator could herald all. This was a new image for Turkey, a new role model for the country's women. A female military aviator insinuated nationalism (because the Turkish nationalist myth upheld male-female equality), democratic participation of women in the making of the new polity, and a secular ethos (because the Muslim opposition did not promote public activism of women). Turkey was taking wings to the future, with women playing leading roles.

The cartoon shown as figure 7.2, published in 1909 in the weekly *Davul*, can be read symbolically. The woman riding the bicycle in Western clothes symbolizes the tantalizing modernity that the West represents for the traditional Turkish man, who pursues her earnestly. With a fez on his head, the man in pursuit has the trappings of a gymnast on his legs, but the woman, in her Western-style evening dress, looks physically more fit. What is of the West is sound, fit, and ought to be pursued.

By the 1990s, much has been said about the role women were made to play in the project of modernization in Turkey. Many have pointed to the instrumental nature of the modernizing reforms.[8] The adoption of the Civil Code in 1926 to replace the Shari'a was a severe blow to the Islamic opposition. The extension of suffrage to women in 1934 was an important move underlining the democratic aspirations of the new republic, despite its authoritarian practices. The principle of male-female equality was defended in the new republic with appeals to a golden Turkic past in Central Asia.[9] To the extent that the defense of women's rights involved reference to the mythic Turkish past, they also provided occasion to reinforce that nationalist myth.

The republican fathers who initiated these reforms believed they knew the best interests of their polity, and these corresponded to the best interests of women in the polity. Atatürk could found the republic and claim, "Republic means democracy, and recognition of women's rights is a dictate of democracy; hence women's rights will be recognized."[10] Similarly, he could say that "if knowledge and technology are necessary for our society, both our men and our women have to acquire them equally."[11] Both quotations reveal not merely the instrumental, functional approach to women's rights but also the certainty with which what was good for the other was assumed. What women wanted was not a problematical issue.

Hence, if the dictates of modernization required that women play not merely public roles but also traditional ones—but with a Western ethic— then they were encouraged to play these revised traditional roles. Yael Navaro draws our attention to the adoption of Taylorism in housework in the early republican era.[12] While the state encouraged increasing involvement by a group of elite women in public life, it sent a different message to an increasingly large number of "other" women: they were expected to contribute to the process of modernization not by becoming elite women professionals but by being housewives à la the West, bringing "order," "discipline," and "rationality" to homemaking in the private realm. Girls' institutes founded under the Ministry of Education in 1928 and "evening girls art schools" (Akşam Kız Sanat Okulları) that were later instituted served this purpose.[13] They channeled women to the task of "modernization" at home by applying the methods of Taylorism to housekeeping in Turkey.

While men may have found it expedient to redefine women's roles in their project of modernization, at least a critical number of women did benefit from these changes and endorsed them earnestly. All reforms that helped secularize and Westernize the republic (including the elimination of the caliphate, or religious orders, the introduction of secular education, language reform, and the adoption of the Western calendar and metric system) encouraged women to play new public roles in society. They could now become professionals expected to be equal to men in the public realm, embodying the universal ideals of equality of humankind.

Women assumed their new roles with a vengeance. Theirs was a nationalist mission. They worked in service to the modernizing state, conscious of being women in the public realm and in line with the prevailing populist ethics. Hamide Topçuoglu, a vanguard woman professional, recalled that being a professional "was not 'to earn one's living.' It was to be of use, to fulfill a service, to show success. Atatürk liberated woman by making her responsible."[14] The purpose of the professional work expected of women was service to the modernizing nation. Women internalized this expectation and were proud to carry it out.

These professional women perceived themselves as representatives of Turkish woman, used in the singular without reference to regional or other differences. A disregard and distaste for difference was in harmony with the populist custom of the day, which assumed all existing cleavages to have melted in the nationalist pot. Thus Nakiye Elgün, a woman appointed as a representative to the parliament, could speak from the floor in 1939 to celebrate the annexation of Hatay to Turkey and advise the women of Hatay to remember to be "Turkish woman" and stay faithful to the cause of the Turkish woman.[15] That Hatay was a highly contested piece of land between Turkey and Syria, with a predominantly Arab population, had to be denied in the populist nationalist discourse. Women were doing their share in modernizing and defining the best interests of "other" women.

The Limits to Equality and Autonomy

While women who did their share in the Kemalist project of modernity could seek to be equal to men in the public realm, there were clear limits to women's autonomy. (During the authoritative single-party era, many men, too, could not act autonomously in the public realm.) Women's activism was circumscribed by the dictates of an autocratic Westernizing state. Zafer Toprak has brought to our attention two revealing cases of the way the modernizing state restrained women's activism when it was considered dissonant with the interests of the state. In 1923, when women appealed to the authorities for permission to found a Republican Woman's Party, they were refused.[16] It was argued that a woman's party could detract attention away from the Republican People's Party, soon to be founded. Similarly, in 1935, when the Turkish Woman's Federation collaborated with feminists from around the world to host a Congress of Feminism in Turkey and issued a declaration against the rising Nazi threat, the modernizing elite was displeased. The federation was closed.[17] It was argued that the republic had given women all their rights and there was no more need for women to organize. Women had displayed increasing autonomy from state policies when they collaborated with feminists from around the world, especially when they criticized the Nazis while their government was carefully keeping a low profile on the international scene.

Although there were limitations to women's autonomous public activism, the Kemalist discourse nevertheless provided legitimacy for women's claim to equality with men in the public realm. Those who had access to that realm could benefit from this privileged equality. Yet the Kemalist understanding of equality was based on an assumption of sameness between men and women that could, in the public realm, be created artificially. This particular understanding of equality was transformed into a hierarchical relationship between men and women when their differences had to be acknowledged in the private domain. Durakbaşa's quote from *Yeni Adam,* a popular journal of the day, is revealing of the nature of equality espoused by the Kemalist modernizers.

7.3. A cartoon depicting Mustafa Kemal's divorce as his taking off the Western mask. (Reproduced from *Khayal al-Zill,* August 1925.)

In the land of the Turks, male-female distinction does not exist anymore. Distinctions between masculinity and femininity are not those
that the nation pays attention to, labors over. They belong to the
private existence of a single man; what is it to us? What we need
are people, regardless of whether men or women, who uphold national values, national techniques.[18]

The Kemalist project of modernity legitimized male-female equality as it
denied male-female difference. Equality was conceived of as irreconcilable with difference.[19] Within this discourse, women's equality to men
in the public realm necessitated a denial of difference between men and

women. To the extent that difference was acknowledged in the private realm, it precipitated hierarchy.

The cartoon in figure 7.3 is a telling illustration of how Atatürk himself, the champion of Westernization and women's rights, was (or could be) a traditional patriarch in his private life.[20] Made by an Egyptian cartoonist and published in a Cairo weekly, *Khayal al-Zill* (Shadow Play) in 1925, the cartoon depicts Atatürk in traditional garb divorcing his Western-educated wife, Latife. He has shed his modernist mask, top hat, and evening dress—symbols of his Westernism—as he orders his wife out in a Shari'a-style divorce. In the private realm, Atatürk, the leader of women's rights, is a traditional patriarch. Differences between men and women prevail, to the detriment of women.

Revisionist History: Feminist Assessment of the Project of Modernity

Until the 1980s, there was a consensus in society that Kemalist reforms had emancipated women and that this "fact" could not be contested. Not merely the educated professional women agreed; so did both educated and illiterate housewives who knew their daughters would benefit from opportunities the reforms provided. The consensus broke down when a younger generation of educated women professionals who called themselves feminists challenged the tradition. In search of new cultural identities, feminists criticized the project of modernity as it affected women. Their goal was not to seek equality with men in the public realm but to question the heritage which upheld that equality. They were ready to commit a sacrilege and deny being Atatürkists.[21]

Recalling Nermin Abadan-Unat and Şirin Tekeli, who were introduced at the beginning of this essay, can help us identify the generational changes that have occurred in the polity and that are critical for putting the contemporary feminists into perspective. Both were educated elite intellectuals. Abadan-Unat had to sever her ties with tradition (which assigned homemaking roles to women) in order to get the education she did, and she had to cling to the opportunities the project of modernity provided to carve out her role in the academic world. Tekeli, born to Kemalist parents in Ankara, the heart of the new republic, could take her secular public education for granted. Tradition was set for her to move into the ranks of academia. She severed her ties when she rejected the role model of the successful career woman, which people like Abadan-Unat and her own mother provided for her, and resigned from her academic career. She created her own model for a new type of feminist. The Kemalist project of modernity had provided no special opportunity for her as it had for the earlier generation, and she could distance herself from its architects in a critical manner. In the unique context of the 1980s, when domestic and global factors charted the parameters of its political space, feminism emerged in Turkey. [22]

Feminist criticism of the Kemalist project of modernity, specifically on questions of women, was radical because feminists altered the perspective from which women's issues were addressed. They traced women's problems to the way women were conceived of in the making of the new republic. For the founding fathers, the "woman question" was part of the populist project, which believed in acting "for the people against the people." From this perspective, these men, and later the women who shared their legacy, could address the "woman question" in order to save the women of their country, not themselves.

Feminists, on the other hand, did not address the "woman question" per se. Instead, they addressed, or rather articulated, the problems they themselves experienced because they were women. It was a move from the personal, from what concerned them immediately, to what other women might share. In this approach there was no mission, no explicit goal to save others. In the feminist page of *Somut,* the weekly journal that was the first platform from which women who called themselves feminists raised a feminist voice, Stella Ovadia explained what they were doing:

> We tried to say "I" or "we"; not "those" women, but "we women." Not "woman questions" [*kadın sorunları*], but questions of being women [*kadınlık*], becoming women [*kadın olma*], attempts to become subjects. To tell about ourselves and speak in our name. Finally to have a say. And write, learn to write, go beyond our fears.[23]

This feminist perspective was radically different from the republican modernist one, which assumed that the best interest of society came prior to the best interest of the individual or any group of individuals and that the modernizing elite responsible for guarding the "best interest" also knew what it consisted of. In a private interview, another feminist described Kemalist women or Kemalist feminists as follows, when she explained the differences between the older and younger generations: "These women [the Kemalists] are content with what they are. They are "liberated" women; someone else liberated them for them. And they always want to liberate others. They are somewhere else. They were liberated by Atatürk. How dare a man raise his hand against them?"

This change of perspective that feminists brought precipitated further criticism of the republican project of modernity. When they articulated the problems they had because they were women, feminists discovered that within the republican project of modernity their private lives were smothered under the public expectations they had to live up to. Despite radical changes in the Civil Code, primordial male-female relations and the moralities that regulated gender relations could continue with little interference from the state. When private lives and interpersonal relationships were questioned, hierarchies and controls that had been ignored now surfaced. Sexual liberties and freedoms, once taboo, became articulated issues. Under the critical gaze of the older generation of Kemalist women, who claimed that society would not tolerate the sexual freedoms they demanded,[24] these radical feminists challenged the morality of their mothers and modernizing "fathers" in search of liberation beyond emancipation.[25] Şule Torun wrote of the fears feminists individually tried to conquer:

> I cannot think about sexuality and write because it will be considered a shame [*ayıp olur*]. I can not write beautiful, fluent prose; I should let good writers write. What I write might be too private and individualistic. Then they will accuse me of not being a communalistic person [*toplumcu olmamak*].[26]

The fears feminists had to conquer to be able to write as feminists reveal the parameters of the space created within the project of modernity for women to realize themselves. Repression of sexuality, faith in professionalism (or education), and respect for the community over the individual demarcate women's space in the republican project of modernity.

One target of this introspection and protest was the republican legal framework. The laws, especially the Civil Code, which until the 1980s had been presented by the state (through the educational system or media) and accepted in public consciousness as progressive beyond time and place, were shown to be unegalitarian. In the Civil Code there were articles that designated the husband head of the family (art. 152/1) and representative of the marriage union (art. 154). The husband was allowed the privilege of choosing the place of residence (art. 152/2), and he was expected to provide for the family (art. 152/2). The wife was explicitly made to play a secondary role as helper to the husband for the happiness of the

family. Beyond these articles, as feminists pointed out, the state was patriarchal, endorsing and legitimizing patriarchal institutions such as the
family, the media, and the educational system.

From Individual Demands to Institution Building

Feminist demands for individual autonomy were creatively channeled
toward building institutions. In a society where modernization meant
state activism, women, for a change, were taking the initiative to bring
about transformation. While they sought liberation individually, these
women, who criticized the earlier generation for its "for the people against
the people" populism, helped build institutions that allowed feminists
to reach beyond their immediate circles. Feminist individualism manifested civic responsibility.

One of the two successful institutions established in Istanbul was the
Women's Library and Information Center, founded in 1990. The other
was the Purple Roof Women's Shelter Foundation, established the same
year. Both institutions grew out of feminist activism in Turkey. Şirin Tekeli,
in a speech delivered in April 1990 during the inauguration ceremony
for the library, explained that the library was an outcome of this feminist awakening. Similarly, the brochure published by the Purple Roof
Women's Shelter Foundation explicitly stated that the idea of a women's
shelter was born together with the Campaign Against Domestic Violence.
Perhaps ironically, the project proposal for the women's library, which
needed the support of the Istanbul municipality, referred to the egalitarian values of modernity to legitimize the need for the library.[27] On the
other hand, to explain why the shelter was instituted, the foundation's
brochure appealed to norms of difference, claimed that one woman in
four was beaten by her husband, and cited a survey by a public-opinion
survey company, PIAR.

Feminist attempts at institution building thus channeled demands for
autonomy into generating power from civil society. While these attempts
may have been marginal in terms of the number of people they affected,
they were significant in going beyond the tradition of "for the people
against the people" in Turkey. Women were acting as women for women.
These institutions were created by the women—not by the state for women.
Perhaps ironically, to the extent that women reached out from the private to the political and from personal confrontation in their private lives
to public institution building, which aimed to uphold and support other
women, they were reaching out for universal values the way republican

modernizers had. Although their starting points were very different, male-female equality was still an important goal.

Secularism

The most important tenet of Kemalist modernization that directly affected women had been secularism, including the secularization of the legal and educational system. The Civil Code and suffrage, critical for improving women's status, were passed in opposition to religious groups and as a means of undermining them. In the contemporary scene, the new generation of feminists, as well as the Kemalist feminists, represent pillars of secularism in society.

Perhaps unique in an ultimately Muslim context, the new generation of radical feminists was not deeply threatened by the Islamist revival of the 1980s. Even though the feminists' secular demands ultimately collided with the Islamist deference to a hierarchical God who, at best, circumscribed what women could and could not do, the two groups did not work against each other. In other Muslim contexts, such as Egypt and Pakistan, where Islamic practice and women's activism had their own unique histories, there have been explicit clashes between feminists and Islamists.[28] In Egypt, Margot Badran has argued that Islamist and feminist agendas have been competing since the nineteenth century.[29] Similar competition has existed in other parts of the Muslim Middle East, even when nationalist demands, in places like Algiers or Palestine, have curbed women's demands.[30] In the case of Egypt, the claim has been made that Islamist revival helped account for women's activism in defense of their rights in the 1980s.[31]

Against this background of the Muslim Middle East, the peculiar history of Turkish secularism and the way feminist activism contributed to that history can be better appreciated. In a context where competitions between Islam and secular ideology had long been won by secularists in the public realm, the new generation of feminists was not immediately threatened by the strong, visible Islamic revival. Their feminist activism began independent of Islamic activism. The parameters of this radical feminist activism were defined by Kemalism, the left, and the worldwide revival of feminism. Although they disagreed with women activists in the Islamist ranks and argued that theirs could not be considered "feminist" activism, some feminists, if not all, respected the fight Islamist women gave.[32]

In an essay in which she first declared her atheism, Tekeli addressed women wearing the turban: "While I do not share your thoughts and beliefs and try to persuade other people that what you argue is not correct, I respect your turban and in fact condemn those who pressure you to take it off. What about you? Do you accept me as I am?"[33] For Tekeli, Islamist women were her equals, and she was proposing mutual recognition—the white flag, so to speak. In a reception given to celebrate the anniversary of the Women's Library and Information Center, one could run into Islamist women with head scarves and men with Islamist beards.

In a polemical debate that took place in the journal *Kaktüs* between a group of Islamist women and Sedef Öztürk, a contributor to *Kaktüs*, Öztürk attempted to outline the points of convergence between feminist and Islamist women. She argued:

> Perhaps the only common denominator they [feminists] could have with Islamist women was Islamist women's claim that "being socialist, secular, or Muslim is not a guarantee of being kept under control as women." Perhaps a second could be that as women who live in different class, national, ethnic, or religious groups and adopt different ideologies, we are all in fact in a struggle for ourselves against ourselves—at times challenging the limits of the other ideologies that shape our being, forcing the limits of Islam or socialism.[34]

The feminist argument that underlined the problems women confronted because they were women would thus be the fulcrum of feminist solidarity, independent of other ideological links.

Unlike the younger generation, the Kemalist women perceived the Islamic upsurge more as a threat, and they did organize to counter it. The reaction of Kemalist women to the Islamists differed from that of the younger generation of feminists both in emotional intensity and in adversariness. The transformation of Kemalist women into Kemalist feminists took place as these women organized against the Islamist challenge in the late 1980s. They founded a group called the Association to Promote Contemporary Life (Çağdaş Yaşamı Destekleme Derneği) to fight the Islamists.[35] Aysel Ekşi, its first president, explained their rationale:

> For some time now, we have been confronted by a serious and surreptitious reactionary movement that hides behind the curtain of "freedom of woman to dress as she wishes" but in reality struggles to return our society to the darkness of the Middle Ages. We do not doubt that this reactionary movement, led by a handful of dogmatic,

diehard Islamists who have roots outside [the country] and who deceive many of our well-meaning, innocent people, sees the destruction of the secular republic as its first goal and pursues the establishment of a shariat order. We came together with the awareness of this danger and the authority that Atatürk's reforms have given us in order to protect the Atatürk reforms, the secular republic, and our rights, which are an inalienable part of these [reforms and the secular republic].[36]

The Kemalist women, as the quote reveals, see Islamist activism, as well as their relationship to the republic, in intensely emotional terms. While Islamists are depicted as reactionary, of the Middle Ages, and foreign, Kemalist women's right to oppose them derives from the secular state. These women identify themselves and their power with the state. In an unmistakable sign of their distinctive discourse, one in which they—the educated elite—know the good of the other, they comment on "their" innocent people being deceived by reactionary Islamists.

Conclusion

Şerif Mardin argues that "while the autonomy of the town was the core datum of Western civility, equity and justice in the lineaments of the State were the core values of Ottoman civilisation."[37] The immediate heirs of the Ottomans, the Kemalists, in the context of their project of modernity, sought to make women equal to men. Proclamation of universal rights for men as well as women was both the goal of the modernist project and the means by which to actualize it. Implicitly, women were expected to act like men and be like men. In the 1980s, feminists asserted their differences. They sought autonomy for themselves through an autonomous civil society, "the core datum of Western civility." In the 1980s, the republic was more "Western" and "modern" than it was in the 1920s.

Feminist activism in Turkey attests to the strength of the republican project of modernity in Turkey. Although feminists levy sharp charges against and distance themselves from Kemalists, it would be misleading to see Kemalist reformers and contemporary feminists in oppositional terms. Despite their revolt, feminists, in their search for autonomy, contribute to a liberal, secular, democratizing polity, which is what the Westernizing republic that the Kemalists founded stands for. Despite their criticisms, feminists ultimately believe in universal rights that go beyond local traditions and provincial moralities.

Notes

1. Ahmet Taner Kışlalı, "Niçin Kemalist'im?" in *Yıllık: Nermin Abadan-Unat'a Armağan*, Ankara: Ankara Üniveritesi Basımevi, 1991, ix–x.

2. Şirin Tekeli, "Tek Parti Döneminde Kadın Hareketi de Bastırıldı," in Levent Cinemre and Ruşen Çakır, eds., *Sol Kemalizme Bakıyor*, Istanbul: Metis Yayınları, 1991.

3. The board aimed to centralize and oversee higher education in Turkey. It had deleterious effects on universities and academicians, who resigned in the hundreds.

4. Tekeli, "Tek Parti Döneminde," 93–107.

5. "Actors or pawns" is quoted from Deniz Kandiyoti, "Women and the Turkish State: Political Actors or Symbolic Pawns?" in Nira Yuval-Davis and Floya Anthias, eds., *Woman-Nation-State*, London: Macmillan, 1988.

6. Carlos Fuentes, *The Buried Mirror*, New York: Houghton Mifflin, 1992, 16–17.

7. The term "Kemalist feminist" points to the unique nature of this feminism. As MacKinnon, reacting to Marxist feminism, elaborates, feminism is "a politics authored by those it works in the name of," and naming it after an individual demarcates a unique understanding of feminism. See Catharine MacKinnon, "Feminism, Marxism, Method, and the State: An Agenda for Theory," *Signs: Journal of Women in Culture and Society*, Spring 1982, 516.

8. Tekeli, "Tek Parti Döneminde"; Yeşim Arat, *The Patriarchal Paradox: Women Politicians in Turkey*, Fairleigh-Dickinson University Press, 1989; Kandiyoti, "Women and the Turkish State"; Ayşe Durakbaşa, "Cumhuriyet Döneminde Kemalist Kadın Kimliğinin Oluşumu," *Tarih ve Toplum*, no. 51, March 1988; Nilüfer Göle, *Modern Mahrem*, Istanbul: Metis Yayınları, 1991; Zehra Arat, "Turkish Women and the Republican Reconstruction of Tradition," in Fatma Müge Göçek and Shiva Balaghi, eds., *Reconstructing Gender in the Middle East: Power, Identity, and Tradition*, New York: Columbia University Press, 1994; Ayşe Kadıoğlu, "Birey Olarak Kadın," *Görüş*, May 1993.

9. Kandiyoti, "Women and the Turkish State."

10. Afetinan, *Atatürk Hakkında Hatıralar ve Belgeler*, Ankara: Türk Tarih Kurumu Basımevi, 1959, 257.

11. Zehra Arat, "Turkish Women," 3.

12. Yael Navaro, "'Using the Mind' at Home: The Rationalization of Housewifery in Early Republican Turkey (1928–1940)," honors thesis submitted to the Department of Sociology, Brandeis University, 1991.

13. By 1940, 35 girls institutes existed in 32 different cities, and 65 evening girls art schools in 59 towns. In the school year 1940–41, 16,500 women were enrolled in these schools.

14. Quoted in Durakbaşa, "Cumhuriyet Döneminde," 43.

15. Yeşim Arat, "Türkiye'de Kadın Milletvekillerinin Değişen Siyasal Rolleri, 1934–1980," *Ekonomi ve idari Bilimler Dergisi*, Boğaziçi University, vol. 1, no. 1, 1987, 50.

16. Zafer Toprak, "Cumhuriyet Halk Fırkasından Önce Kurulan Parti: Kadınlar Halk Fırkası," *Tarih ve Toplum*, March 1988, 30–31.

17. Zafer Toprak, "1935 Istanbul Uluslararası 'Feminizm Kongresi' ve Barış," *Düşün,* March 1986, 24–29.

18. Quoted in Durakbaşa, "Cumhuriyet Döneminde," 43.

19. For an eloquent analysis of how equality and difference cannot exist in opposition to each other and how the concept of equality is contingent on an assumption of difference, see Joan Scott, "Deconstructing Equality versus Difference, or the Uses of Poststructuralist Theory for Feminism," *Feminist Studies,* vol. 14, no. 1, 1988, 33–50.

20. I would like to thank Professor Günay Kut of Boğaziçi University, Department of Turkish Language and Literature, for helping me with the translation from the Arabic in this cartoon.

21. To underline the novelty of someone's denying to be a follower of Atatürk, and as a reminder of Atatürk's deification in Turkey before the 1980s, I quote Vamık Volkan and Norman Itzkowitz, *The Immortal Atatürk: A Psycho-biography,* Chicago: University of Chicago Press, 1984, 345–46: "As a national leader, Atatürk became a necessary idealized object of his countrymen, one essential for the maintenance of Turkish pride. . . . [He] has continued to live as a symbol and a concept. His picture continues to be reverenced alongside the national flag and is displayed beside it on days of national celebration or remembrance. He is omnipresent. He is on postage stamps and money, both bills and coins. Statues of Atatürk are everywhere, and his words are chiseled on the stone facades of buildings. His photograph is found in government offices and in the corner grocery store. His name has been bestowed on boulevards, parks, stadiums, concert halls, bridges, and forests. When the Turks seized the northern sector of Cyprus in 1974, busts of Atatürk were brought ashore with the troops and erected in every liberated Turkish village. Mental and physical representations of Atatürk have fused with and are symbolic of the Turkish spirit, and thus he has indeed become immortal."

22. Şirin Tekeli, "Women in the Changing Political Associations of the 1980s," in Andrew Finkel and Nükhet Sirman, eds., *Turkish State, Turkish Society,* London: Routledge, 1990; Nükhet Sirman, "Feminism in Turkey: A Short History," *New Perspectives on Turkey,* vol. 3, no. 1, 1989, 259–88; Yeşim Arat, "1980'ler Türkiyesi'nde Kadın Hareketi: Liberal Kemalizmin Radikal Uzantısı," *Toplum ve Bilim,* no. 53, Spring 1991, 7–20.

23. Stella Ovadia, "Bu Yazı Son Yazı mı Olacak," *Somut,* 27 May 1983.

24. Necla Arat, *Feminizmin ABC'si,* Istanbul: Simavi Yayınları 1991.

25. Deniz Kandiyoti, "Emancipated but Unliberated? Reflections on the Turkish Case," *Feminist Studies,* vol. 13, no. 2, 1987, 317–38.

26. Şule Torun, "Genel Bir Değerlendirme," *Somut,* 27 May 1983.

27. More precisely, the proposal responded to the question "Why the need for the women's library?" as follows: "The modernity of a country is measured by its degree of male-female equality. This process is particularly important for our country. The attainment of this equality requires various endeavors. To reach this aim, institutions that nurture it and help reach it are necessary. In a broad spectrum, these range from a Ministry of Woman's Rights to a Women's Library" (Kadın Eserleri Kütüphanesi ve Bilgi Merkezi Vakfı Kuruluş Taslağı, 3).

28. Nadia Hijab, *Womanpower: The Arab Debate on Women at Work,* Cambridge: Cambridge University Press, 1988, 30–35; Ayesha Jalal, "The Convenience of Subservience: Women and the State of Pakistan," in Deniz Kandiyoti, ed., *Women, Islam, and the State,* Philadelphia: Temple University Press, 1991, 77–114.

29. Margot Badran, "Competing Agenda: Feminists, Islam, and the State in 19th and 20th Century Egypt," in Kandiyoti, ed., *Women, Islam and the State,* 201–36.

30. Hijab, *Womanpower,* 26–29; Rosemary Sayigh, "Palestinian Women and Politics in Lebanon," in Judith E. Tucker, ed., *Arab Women,* Bloomington: Indiana University Press, 1993.

31. Mervat Hatem, "Toward the Development of Post-Islamist and Post-Nationalist Feminist Discourses in the Middle East," in Judith E. Tucker, ed., *Arab Women,* 31.

32. Gül, "Hem Mümine Hem Feminist," *Feminist,* no. 4, 1988.

33. Şirin Tekeli, *Kadınlar için,* Istanbul: Alan Yayıncılık, 1988, 381.

34. Sedef Öztürk, "Eleştiriye Bir Yanıt," *Kaktüs,* no. 4, November 1988, 28–30.

35. The association opened its ranks to men and women but only women responded. There were about six hundred members of the association in the summer of 1993.

36. Aysel Ekşi, "Neden Kurulduk," *Çağdaş Yaşamı Destekleme Derneği Bülten,* no. 1, March–June 1989.

37. Şerif Mardin, "European Culture and the Development of Modern Turkey," in Ahmet Evin and Geoffrey Denton, eds., *Turkey and the European Community,* Opladen, Germany: Leske and Budrich, 1990, 14.

8/ Gendering the Modern

On Missing Dimensions

in the Study of Turkish Modernity

DENİZ KANDİYOTİ

Studies of modernization in Turkey have generally privileged the juridico-political and institutional realms, starting with the Ottoman reform era and continuing through the Kemalist period to more contemporary developments. I argue in this chapter that comparatively little attention has been paid to the less tangible effects of processes of social transformation on the emergence of new identities and forms of subjectivity, and there has been little critical awareness of the specificities of the "modern" in the Turkish context. I develop this contention with reference to a relatively restricted field of inquiry—namely, discourses about the modern family and the construction of gender—in order to make the broader methodological point that "ethnographies" of the modern that deal with the full complexity of the contemporary cultural landscape are long overdue.

The relative impoverishment of this field has not been altogether accidental. The polemical perspectives adopted both by apologists of Turkish modernization—Kemalists in particular—and by its critics have inadvertently limited our conceptual horizons by falling short of interrogating the notion of the "modern" itself and charting its local specificities. Instead, a substantial literature, popular and academic, appears to revolve around two opposed narratives, with their respective demonologies, that could arguably be said to represent two sides of the same discursive coin.

On the one hand, perspectives emanating from official Kemalism equate modernization and nation building with progress and the irresistible forward march of civilization. The heroic figures of the idealist *kaymakam* (district officer) and the village teacher bringing enlightenment where obscurantism and superstition prevailed, the effort to eradicate malaria, and the move toward the emancipation of women all appear as part and parcel of the same ideological package. Critics of modernization, on the other hand, interpret this package as a totalizing and authoritarian project that marginalizes and even destroys the life-worlds of those purported to represent the "traditional." The Western orientation of reformist elites has lent substance to the notion that state-led modernization is an alien and alienating project, inviting local attempts at resistance or subversion. New social movements, including Islamism, could thus be reinterpreted within the framework of a critique of modernity. Doing so, in turn, risks bringing us full circle to positing notions of lost authentic "indigeneity" and inviting forms of neo-Orientalism that are inimical to an understanding of complex historical processes.

There is little doubt that interrogating central tenets of modernity such as science, secularism, nationhood, and individualism has had a salutary effect and has destabilized artificial modern-traditional dichotomies. We are, however, faced with the task of moving beyond this critique and grappling with the actual content and meaning of complex contemporary cultural forms. Some crucial questions need to be raised in this connection. How has the field of meanings and practices designated as "modern" been constituted in Turkey? Have these meanings shifted and altered through time? What sources of legitimacy did discourses about the "modern" seek? How did they construct and define what they sought to displace? What sorts of relationships between the indigenous and the foreign, the local and the global were at stake? Did these relationships coalesce into items of taste and style and into discernible cultural codes?

These questions open up a broad field of investigation within which I confine myself in this essay to analyzing how and why sexuality, family relations, and gender identities came to occupy a central place in discourses about modernity. I pursue three distinct yet interrelated lines of inquiry as a means of mapping out this terrain. First, I examine discourses about the "modern" family with respect to the forms of regulation of interpersonal relations and sexuality that they imply. Second, I attempt to disentangle some of the concrete, everyday practices that go into the making of class, status, and gender codes that, at the same time, denote different insertions into the modern. Finally, I explore the extent to which different expressions of gender and gendered identity have themselves become both products and signifiers of modernity.

The "Modern" Family as a New Regulatory Discourse

The *Dictionary of Turkish Costume and Self-Adornment* features an intriguing entry with accompanying illustrations under the rubric "Young Man's

Veil."[1] Two young men are depicted, one in janissary costume, the other wearing a turban and *shalwar,* each carrying an impressive sword and sporting a face veil. The entry explains that after the popular classes gained access to the Janissary Corps in the later part of the seventeenth century, young men (novices) between the ages of fifteen and eighteen began applying to join in large numbers. At that time, the discipline of the corps had been eroded to the extent that janissaries lived outside of barracks, in rooms, hostels, and coffeehouses, and some befriended and became the "patrons" of young novices who roomed with them as their servants. In order to protect these young men—who, we are told, were of popular extraction and pleasing countenance—from the importunate gazes of ill-intentioned people, they covered them with face veils made of golden or straw threads. This fashion lasted for more than fifty years, only to disappear in 1826 with the abolition of the Janissary Corps.

This tantalizing vignette offers us a glimpse of a by-gone age when social ranking, ethnic particularities, and sexualities merged to create myriad identities, some more permeable and transitory than others: male and female slaves, eunuchs, concubines, and patriarchs and military men who may themselves once have been palace "boys." Was it in the nature of these premodern identities that we should have so little access to them or that they were largely unspoken of and unwritten about except in the necessarily partial testimony of European visitors? The answer must be affirmative in view of the veritable explosion of discourses on marriage, the family, and appropriate gender roles that erupted during the nineteenth century. The unwary observer might be excused for thinking that modernization was primarily about reordering the domestic lives of a new citizenry, which must now include women.

In an impressively detailed study, Alan Duben and Cem Behar opened new vistas on Ottoman modernization by examining demographic data and texts on marriage and the family in the late nineteenth and early twentieth centuries.[2] What their material revealed about the propagandistic emphasis on the companionate, child-centered conjugal family as the epitome of both modernity and nationalistic social responsibility was not unique in itself. Beth Baron has provided strikingly similar evidence from turn-of-the-century Egypt, and the history of bourgeois domesticity in colonial Bengal presents important parallels.[3] I have also argued elsewhere that the "woman question" and, more broadly, the "politicization" of gender arose in contexts of heightened national self-consciousness in which crises of postcolonial (and, in the Ottoman case, postimperial) identity could be articulated as crises of gender and domestic organization.[4]

Duben and Behar's work, however, reveals something further that the authors themselves do not comment on sufficiently, namely, the extent to which such polemics were overlaid by a quasi-scientific discourse on "appropriate" reproductive heterosexuality. During this period of vigorous growth of the print media, advice and information could be obtained from newspapers, magazines, pamphlets, and books on topics ranging from home economics and good child-care practices to marital etiquette.[5] Islamic regulations of the body and social space were increasingly being encroached upon by a new discourse that removed the body from the realm of the sacred to medicalize and secularize it. Early marriages and large age differences between spouses were condemned because they made for an unfavorable milieu, in both psychological and "hygienic" terms, for the healthy conception and rearing of the young. Expert medical opinion was invoked to determine the proper age for marriage. Likewise, arranged marriages and polygyny were assigned to a world of reprehensible and "unhealthy" custom.

In view of demographic evidence pointing to the actual prevalence of the idealized family model (marriage age in Istanbul households was fairly late for both men and women, families were small and mainly of nuclear composition, and polygyny was negligible), Duben and Behar rightly puzzle over this concern about polygyny, adolescent marriages, and joint families, which could be construed only as a misconception on the part of commentators and polemicists. They state:

> The advice and recommendations which appeared in the popular press and in books and magazines during the late nineteenth and early twentieth century corresponded almost exactly to the demographic realities of the time. Most of those who wrote on this topic, however, were somehow convinced that the practice—and the unspoken rule—in Istanbul was teenage marriage. Many of the articles and books we have quoted were written in criticism of teenage marriages, and there is little doubt that, though most of them are anonymous, they were penned by the "modernists" of the time.[6]

It is not in the realm of misconception, however, but in the urge to articulate a new morality that we must look for explanations of such preoccupations. Like all regulatory discourses, the ideal of modern bourgeois domesticity needed its civilizational "others," and the normalization of certain forms of sexuality and gender was predicated upon a critique and stigmatization of others. The "modernists" could formulate their vision of the modern family only with reference to an assumed prior state that was defective and in need of reform, regardless of whether the patterns in question actually obtained in their society. Focusing on the emulation of Western patterns of domesticity as a driving force for family reform conceals from view a more hidden preoccupation with local forms that were destined to become marginal or deviant and, in due course, like the veiled boys, wither away.

The civilizational "others" of the modernists were dual rather than singular: they resided both in an already modern West and in the local customs associated with an ancien régime that became the target of vociferous and sometimes self-denigrating condemnation or of wounded and defensive apologia. The nationalistic moralism of the early modernizers could condemn both the license and freedom associated with the West and what they interpreted as elements of degeneracy in the patriarchy of local tradition. Defining responsible social adulthood in terms of monogamous heterosexuality was not only a matter of proscribing co-wives, concubines, and child brides but also of taming other, unruly forms of male sexuality. The world in which the former palace boy could become a respected patriarch and in which sexualities and life cycles could merge and mingle in fluid ways had passed. A rising nationalist elite was giving voice to and shaping a new normative order. Although a history of Ottoman sexualities remains to be written, we must acknowledge that the emergence of contemporary gender identities cannot be fully grasped without being informed by this history.

It must also be noted that discourses about modernity underwent a series of transformations. During the reform period of the late nineteenth and early twentieth centuries, the West represented both the emancipatory potential of the modern (in contrast to the traditional Ottoman order) and the dangers of excessive individualism, selfishness, and narcissism.[7] After the demise of the Ottoman regime and the establishment of the republic, the modernizing gaze turned inward toward the rural hinterland, which became the repository of immobility, tradition, and backwardness, best represented in the figure of the overfertile and brutalized rural woman. Depictions of rural women contained revealing ambiguities. They were idealized as the bearers of the pre-Islamic Turkish egalitarianism that featured prominently in Republican ideology, but they were also portrayed as victims of local customs that kept them ignorant and downtrodden.[8]

In time, rapid urbanization and the influx of rural populations into the cities created a bewildering array of styles and subcultures. New modes of dress and consumption became complex signifiers of class, gender, place of origin, and, more recently, ideological predilection. The boundaries of the traditional and the modern became open to both multiple interpretations and contestation. These interpretations are constructed through the perspectives of social actors who are differently located with respect to class, status, gender, ethnicity, and residence. Any engagement with the complexities of this new field of meanings must therefore pass inevitably through an examination of tastes and styles.

Habit, Modernization, and Style

Taste classifies, and it classifies the classifier.
—Pierre Bourdieu, *Distinction*

As I reflected about the subtler implications of processes of modernization, a childhood memory suggested itself as a useful starting point. My family and I used to spend our summers on an island about an hour away from Istanbul where women and children could relax by the seaside while the men commuted to work by boat. On weekends, crowds of Istanbul residents who could not afford holidays elsewhere came to the island to escape the summer heat and rest under the pine trees. They came as families equipped with carpets, cushions, pots and pans, cooking stoves, and, sometimes, musical instruments. Once at the picnic site, the carpets and cushions would be laid out and the area would be transformed into a cozy interior. The permanent residents of the island, walking past the picnickers in their tennis or beach outfits, were greeted by sights of men in their pajamas, women cooking, and children playing or being rocked to sleep in makeshift cradles. Sounds of popular music and smells of cooking formed the sensory backdrop of this scene.[9]

Through my child's eyes, the alterity of these day visitors was encapsulated in a single item of clothing—the pajamas worn by the men, garments associated with the intimacy of the bedroom. This was how I formed one of my first, nebulous (and misguided) understandings of the category of "traditional," a category that was vaguely coterminous with certain items of popular taste and style. Yet what could have been more novel than what I was witnessing? A new form of leisure was on display involving open-air, mixed-sex, family entertainment, denoting rhythms of work and rest unknown in the rural areas from which most of these new urbanites came. What, indeed, could be more sensible than wearing pajamas and bringing cooking utensils from home if your budget and personal inclinations did not favor the purchase of specialized leisure wear and picnic equipment? It was easy to mistake a new style of living for an expression of difference that could be articulated in the language of custom and tradition. But where did the stuff out of which I had constructed "difference" come from? Was it in patterns of consumption? Or was it in more complicated notions of propriety and behavior in public places that formed some implicit code of class and gender? Finally, how did the "West," from which most items of fashion and modern material culture emanated, contribute to this construction?

Commenting on changing urban mores at the turn of the century, Duben and Behar draw our attention to the way the "Europeanization" of the Ottoman upper and middle classes created a split between the *alaturka* and the *alafranka* (respectively, the Ottoman-Turkish and European "frankish" styles) that penetrated the inner workings of family life.[10] The appearance of Western implements and items of furniture and clothing clearly had a bearing upon intimate bodily habits. Sitting in high-backed chairs engaged different sets of muscles, eating in the *alafranka* style involved new rules that introduced a certain distance and even formality among family members who previously had dipped into the same bowl of food, mealtimes became more regular, and new rules of etiquette demanded that women be served first, a total reversal of Ottoman proprieties.

Such changes implied not simply a refashioning of tastes but also a hierarchy of worth whereby former habits, such as eating with one's hands, could be redefined as unhygienic or even repulsive and older patterns of deference could be deemed uncivilized. As Bourdieu notes, the redefinition of apparently banal physical practices constitutes an attempt to refashion habit among social groups seeking to shape new subjects.[11] In Turkey, this transformation also involved the creation of new notions of the "private." One source of the obsessive preoccupation with family life referred to earlier resides precisely in the fact that the domestic became the terrain on which this "private" was being both constructed and contested.

In practice, modernization involved a selective appropriation of items of material culture, habit, and taste by different strata of society, creating styles that were also insignia of social status. Ekrem Işın traces this process to changes in the urban landscape of Istanbul in the nineteenth century: the decline of local trades, the appearance of *bon marché* high-street stores in the Pera district displaying imported goods, and the differentiation of tastes, fashions, and leisure in conjunction with changing patterns of stratification.[12] In a recent study, Sencer Ayata offers important insights into how tensions between images of tradition and images of modernity are being lived concretely in Turkish households as a literal split between the styles of formal dress and consumption displayed in the guest room and those adopted in the intimate inner space of the rest of the house, which is a place of informality and closeness.[13] This description also denotes a petit bourgeois style in contrast to that of the more thoroughly Westernized house interiors of the upper and professional middle classes. Incongruous combinations of the local and the foreign can be made into objects of derision, hallmarks of the parvenu or the newly rich—such as drinkers of whisky who also eat the humble *lahmacun,* a local pita bread. Preferences in fashion, food, music, and general aesthetics thus map out a complex topography of status, which is the subject of running social commentary in cartoons and popular satirical magazines.

In short, different constructions of what it means to be modern have come to inform not only the most intimate aspects of daily life but also subtle codes of class and status. I suggest that gender emerged as one of the key arenas in which such differences could be articulated and expressed. Both individual expressions of masculinity and femininity and different norms and styles of cross-gender interaction gained new meanings in a field powerfully defined by these new parameters. I next attempt to show that changing identities for men and women, which had become part and parcel of the modernist project in Turkey, now expressed a substantially transformed reality.

Masculinities: Old and New

The polemical literature of the turn of the century about Ottoman domestic mores appears to single out one main victim, the woman. Her ignorance and seclusion and the indignities of polygyny and repudiation were major objects of criticism. The denunciatory voice was that of the male modernist reformer. Implicit in this critique was also the belief that men were condemned to loveless matches arranged by their kin and inadequate spouses who could not provide intellectual companionship.

My initial interpretation of this apparent male feminism was that men were using women's plight to bemoan their own disenfranchisement in the face of paternal autocracy, a disenfranchisement that was mirrored in the political arena by the absolutism of the Ottoman state.[14] I subsequently became concerned with the added possibility that these generational tensions also corresponded to changes in the expression of hegemonic masculinity in Ottoman society.[15]

The Ottoman patriarch represented central features of the old order: hierarchy, fixity, and absolute authority. The "new" man was aspiring to a domestic setting in which these values were overthrown, in which emotional distance between spouses was replaced by love and companionship, in which both men and women were emotionally involved and close to their children, and in which the conjugal pair could claim some autonomy from their elders. The Ottoman patrician, the paterfamilias of the *konak* (mansion), was being challenged by a younger generation whose aspirations for modernity were expressed partly in a preference for single-family apartment living and Western styles of entertainment.

Yet there is no question that the passing of the Ottoman patriarch elicited profound ambivalence, not to say nostalgia. In an insightful book about the Tanzimat novel, Jale Parla argues that the early Ottoman novelists expressed this nostalgia through the metaphor of the fatherless home, where the novelist himself took on the role of paternal guidance vis-à-vis his disoriented society.[16] Early depictions of Westernized, upper-class men were, indeed, far from flattering; the *züppe* (snob) of the Tanzimat period emerged as effeminate and foppish.[17] He represented simultaneously a departure from solid, sober Ottoman masculinity and a threat to the Ottoman communitarian conservatism that shunned ostentation and mandated that the wealthy take care of the less fortunate.

The figure of the Ottoman patrician had his popular counterpart in the *kabadayı* (literally, "tough uncle," meaning a neighborhood tough). Ref'i Cevat Ulunay describes the phenomenon in colorful detail as a form of urban chivalry whose context was the traditional *mahalle,* or urban quarter.[18] *Mahalle*s were small, well-entrenched units of residence, divided mainly along ethnic rather than class lines, with a strong sense of communal identity and territoriality.[19] Like the household and the family, the *mahalle* had an honor to be defended. The *kabadayı* ensured that the women of the quarter were protected, that there were no importunate visitors from other quarters, that dealings among inhabitants were honest and fair, and that infractions of propriety did not go unpunished. They were mostly uneducated but could be artisans practicing their trade, and they were generally respectable members of the community. (Indeed, Ulu-nay suggests that they were most concerned about being mistaken for *külhanbey*, rakish scamps displaying irresponsible and lumpen styles of masculinity).

Both the patrician and the *kabadayı*, and the masculinities they implied, were the guarantors and protectors of a normative order that was at once stifling and reassuring, constraining yet deeply familiar. It is little wonder that expressions of rage and nostalgia mingled in equal measure in many literary productions of the time.

What, then, were the contours of the new patriarchy—that of the citizen and the modern husband-father—being shaped through the reforms culminating in the republican era? Although the effects of Kemalist reforms on women's identities have received some attention,[20] the masculine ideals of Turkish nationalism have remained somewhat more nebulous. The figure of Mustafa Kemal Atatürk, however, portrayed alternately in military uniform and Western tuxedo, provides some clues to this question.

A fact about the republican dress code that is often overlooked is that Atatürk never actually outlawed the veil (unlike Reza Shah in Iran, who did) but was ruthless when it came to the sorts of headdresses men chose to wear. In the Ottoman empire, rank, origin, and ethnicity could be read clearly in the costumes and even the colors that subject populations were allowed to wear. Similarly, men of religion could be clearly distinguished by their turbans and garments. The Western hat and tie were not merely items of fashion but became the solvent and suppressor of these differences, a uniform of secularism that also signified loyalty to the state. The new cadres of the republic, civil servants and professionals, wore the insignia of their allegiance; conversely, insubordination could be indicated by misplaced facial hair or the wrong hat.

Moreover, this new uniformity among the elite exacerbated the visible differences between urbanites and peasants. While the modern man of the republic appeared at public functions with his bare-faced wife at his side, his rural brother was pictured, and frequently caricatured, in traditional garb with his veiled wife following forty paces behind him (preferably, he rode his donkey while she walked). The unreconstructed masculinity of tradition, the sharp age and gender hierarchies, and the oppression of women were now portrayed through rural mores and interpreted as a deficit in civilization. The civilizing mission of the village teacher and *kaymakam*, alluded to earlier, was portrayed as the struggle of science and enlightenment against ignorance and obscurantism. On the other hand, populist discourse idealized village life and the person of the Turkish peasant as the true repository of folk wisdom and indigenous values. This ambivalence lodged itself at the heart of discourses about modernity in Turkey, where the boundary between the modern and the alien remained alarmingly indistinct.

The paternal role was also redefined for modern men. The remote, authoritarian father figure began giving way to a new intimacy and paternal involvement. The modern father had a special link to his daughters, who were valued, educated, and nurtured—men gave social birth to the new woman of the republic. This new affective tone is captured well in the correspondence of Ziya Gökalp, a major architect of Turkish nationalism, with his daughters from his exile in Malta. Atatürk's choice of daughters as his adopted children, in a society where male child preference was the uncontested norm, was also heavy with symbolic significance.

It should be clear from the foregoing that these new identities reproduced aspects of both gender and social class in a society with a small urban and literate population and a large rural hinterland with varying degrees of integration to national and international centers of trade and culture. Çağlar Keyder points out that the single-party regime (1923–45) was based on an alliance of urban and provincial elites and notables who were invested in state-led development policies and who, in the international climate created by the Great Depression of the 1930s, were able to opt for etatism and an inward-oriented path of industrialization.[21] This populist elite, however, did not modernize the rural masses, despite some efforts at spreading schooling and health services and improving infrastructure. It was only after World War II and the transition to multiparty democracy that rural areas experienced major transformations, which have been extensively documented in the economic and sociological literature. Processes of rural-to-urban migration totally changed the urban landscape. New patterns of social mobility and elite recruitment created diversity and heterogeneity among a previously narrow and relatively homogenous state elite whose cultural hegemony was being challenged.

The contemporary context for social identity formation not only involves local particularities of status, region, and rural or urban extraction but also an increasingly complex network of influences resulting from the globalization of culture.[22] Mass consumption and media images now have their own independent roles to play. To take but one example, some versions of masculinity enacted by youths of popular extraction owe much to kung-fu films and television heroes whose exploits can be emulated in local karate clubs (which have enjoyed a considerable vogue). When coupled with certain patterns of peer group activity and ideological sympathies, these styles can also come to signal particular subcultures on the political right or left.

The lack of detailed studies of emerging subcultures, however, makes it difficult to come to grips with the nature and scope of contemporary transformations. Few existing studies of popular culture, notably on *arabesk* as a style of popular music, give us valuable clues.[23] It is worth noting that the most popular *arabesk* singers enact styles of masculinity that reinstate a modern version of the *kabadayı* in a changing urban landscape and exalt the virtues of loyalty, unselfishness, and moral rectitude, but with a bitter undertone of perpetual betrayal and disappointment.

The extreme diversity of the arenas in which contemporary masculinities may be enacted—from the football stadium to the mosque, from the coffeehouse to the disco, from the school to the street corner, from the sports club to the bazaar—mandates detailed ethnographies. Distinctions of class and taste are mediated through items of consumption and brand names, making it possible to differentiate the jeans of the lumpen youth (the *zonta*) from the expensive ones of his upper-class counterpart. Other badges of identity are also displayed on the body: this mustache indicates left-wing leanings; that beard bespeaks Islamist sympathies. (Significantly, after the coup of 1980, the military rulers ordered government employees, including university lecturers, to remove all facial hair). Even expressions of different sexualities have become more overt; the haunts of male transvestites and transsexuals and some of the locales where homosexuals congregate are more visible.[24] Detailed studies of contemporary expressions of gender remain to be carried out. For the time being, suffice it to say that the male transvestite occupies the same modern space as his bearded brother who displays novel forms of Islamic militancy.

Daughters of the Republic

Compared with the relatively gradual changes in masculine identities, ideological interventions with respect to women in Turkey appear to have been both more abrupt and more hotly contested. Throughout the reform period, debates on women and the family became self-consciously integrated into different ideological recipes for salvaging the threatened empire. From Islamists who advocated a return to the unadulterated application of the Shari'a to Westernists who favored a radical break with Islam, all used the condition of women as an indicator of the moral health of society. Cultural nationalism created a new discursive space by appropriating women's emancipation in the name of pre-Islamic Turkish egalitarianism and condemning certain aspects of Ottoman patriarchy (such as polygyny and the seclusion of women) as a corruption of original Turkish mores. The republic adopted this approach to women's emancipation as an item of official state ideology.[25]

In the first decades of the republic, the modernity of the new state was most eloquently signaled through images of women that became central to the iconography of the regime—parading in shorts and bearing the flag, in school or military uniform, or in evening dress in ballroom dancing scenes. Sarah Graham-Brown remarks that visual images of the 1920s and 1930s exuded a sense of self-confidence which concealed the fact that republican reforms were a remote and unrealized ideal for the vast majority of rural women.[26] Indeed, Yakın Ertürk argues that, paradoxically, rural women of eastern Anatolia may have been even further marginalized by the secular reforms because their access to institutions of the modern state was mediated through men, whose own access was in turn dependent upon the intercession of more powerful men such as tribal leaders, landlords, and leaders of religious sects.[27] Thus, women's encounters with modern or secular structures merely bound them even more tightly to local power holders rather than defining them as equal citizens of the state.

For the first generation of university-educated women, however, who went on to swell the ranks of republican cadres and professionals, there was an unmistakable sense of being in the vanguard. Ayşe Öncü suggests that the entry of Turkish women into the professions was a function of the initial mode of recruitment of cadres under conditions of rapid expansion in the new republic. The growth of elite cadres with specialized and technical education may necessitate the recruitment of people from manual-labor or peasant origins if upper- and middle-class women do not begin to enter professional schools. The favorable climate of opinion about women's education was instrumental in the recruitment of upper- and middle-class women into prestigious and well-remunerated occupations.[28] Thus women's education may initially have acted not so much as a means of mobility as of class consolidation, since recruiting women may have been less threatening than admitting upwardly mobile men from humbler origins.

However class-biased this initial mode of recruitment may have been, it did have long-term effects in establishing the legitimacy of a female presence in the public sphere. Yet, according to Şirin Tekeli, the primary roles of women continued to be defined in nationalist rhetoric as those of enlightened motherhood and child rearing, which provided the ultimate justification for a modern education.[29] Tekeli argues that the "state feminism" which propelled women into the public world of work and put formal equality on the agenda was not matched by significant changes either in domestic divisions of labor or in sexual morality. This created a split between the public and the domestic personas of women professionals, a split that is currently being contested by contemporary Turkish feminists.

There were also serious problems of identity management in a culture where, by and large, women were still perceived as either under the tutelage of a man, and therefore protected and worthy of respect, or unprotected and therefore "loose." It is important to remember that models for "respectable" independent womanhood (spinsterhood, "genteel" occupations, or even monastic orders) were entirely absent in the Ottoman-Turkish context, in which high nuptiality and easy remarriage of widows meant that women were almost always absorbed into a family. I have argued elsewhere that the very fact that women were no longer secluded or veiled might, paradoxically, have mandated new forms of puritanism that could be mobilized as symbolic shields in a society where femininity was incompatible with a public presence.[30] The "modern" woman found herself in the unprecedented position of having to construct a new set of signals and codes that would enable her to function in the public realm without being importuned or molested. Unlike the veil, which, by concealing its wearer, confirms her unquestionable femaleness, the severe suit and bare face of the woman civil servant can emit powerful messages of sexual unavailability by deemphasizing femininity and projecting a "neuter" identity.[31] Thus the management of femininity and sexual modesty became part and parcel of the symbolic armor of the "modern" woman.

The kinship idiom continued to provide an effective vehicle for easing social interaction and defusing tensions in cross-gender interactions among unrelated persons.[32] The common use of terms of address such as *ağabey* (older brother) and *abla* (older sister), or *amca* (uncle) and *teyze* (aunt), in everyday interactions implied respect owing to seniority, while terms such as *oğlum* (son) and *kızım* (daughter) designated a younger person worthy of protection. There were, therefore, a variety of culturally sanctioned ways of signaling the sexually neutral character of interactions, ways that could be mobilized and put to use in novel settings.

In this connection, the theme of the sexually unavailable woman, neither a mother nor a sister but a symbolic sister, the *bacı,* was quite strong in various forms of cultural and literary expression. To choose but one example, the central woman character in the film *Şöför Nebahat* (Nebahat the Driver, a popular production of the 1950s) is portrayed in a highly unconventional role. She drives a cab, wears leather jackets and a cloth cap, and mingles with the boys. But she is pure as the driven snow, and none would dare show her disrespect without incurring the wrath of her cab-driving brothers.

This portrayal corresponds to that of the *erkek kadın,* the "manly" woman, who does not have to be "butch" or unfeminine but simply unremittingly chaste. That is, until she meets her true love, who transforms her into what she was always destined to be—a truly feminine woman, finally dominated by a male who can outman her. This, of course, removes her from her place as one of the boys and restores her to her proper station. I find this a telling parable of modern womanhood in Turkey because it unwittingly reveals the terms under which women may attain a measure of freedom and unconventionality in the social roles they enact. It is against this background that we must evaluate contemporary feminists' attempts to assert themselves as *both* independent beings and sexual beings.

These tensions of identity management were experienced and responded to differently by women in different social locations. For women of the urban upper classes, habits of mixed-sex entertainment and sociality could easily be transposed to the classroom or the office, and a higher level of consumption, such as the ability to travel in private cars, sheltered them from direct exposure to those public spaces still inhabited mainly by men. Women from more modest and conservative backgrounds, who did not go out to work, were also sheltered from such pressures by continuing to lead home- and neighborhood-centered lives that minimized the need for new adaptations. The large group of women of rural and small-town extraction who became mobile through higher education and joined the ranks of office workers and city commuters faced quite a different predicament, as did women factory and service workers who needed to work for wages. Most found themselves thrust upon a world of men whose own backgrounds and habits of interaction did not prepare them to deal with women in anonymous settings such the classroom, the office, the street, or the bus. Ingenious ways had to be devised to deal with the ensuing confusion; these often involved implicit, hidden forms of segregation, such as male and female workers keeping different schedules for tea at the canteen.

The tensions involved are best exemplified by a recent debate over whether the municipality of Istanbul should run women-only buses. This demand, initiated by Islamist women in the name of appropriate Muslim etiquette, found favor among some secular feminists, thus creating a split with secularists who could not condone a return to the old days of segregated public transport. What is interesting to note here is the recognition of a common predicament by women whose lifestyles mandate exposure to public places and daily interaction with unrelated men.

Evaluated in this context, the decision to veil may indeed take on a variety of meanings. I agree with Leila Ahmed when she states that "Islamic dress can be seen as the uniform, not of reaction, but of transition" or as "the uniform of arrival, signalling entrance into, and determination to move forward in, modernity."[33] Yet it is not totally without reason that Islamic dress and deportment are labeled, by some, as traditional. This labeling partly belongs to the world of misapprehension I explored earlier when I referred to my own reaction to men picnicking in their pajamas. To the extent that veiling is not merely expressive of individual tastes, however, but may also signal the presence of an alternative hegemonic political project, it arouses intense anxiety among those secularists who fear that their life-world may be encroached upon and threatened. This anxiety inevitably leads to constructions of veiling as "tradition" in the sense of something that has to be overcome yet is still raising its ugly head. This "politicization" of identities is, arguably, one of the main factors that make subcultural expressions of taste and style in the Middle East distinct from those in the West, where they are easily absorbed into the mainstream and commodified.

In contemporary Turkey, expressions of femininity signaled by modes of dress, makeup, and body posture have become entangled in local idioms of social status and ideological predilection as well as in global media and advertisement images of modern womanhood. Like modern masculinities, feminine identities are subject to mediations through multiple codes articulated through fashion and modes of consumption. The trained eye, however, has little difficulty distinguishing the modestly dressed woman of recent rural origin from her committed Islamist sister, or telling the peroxide blonde from the shanty district from the fashionably underdressed university student. It would be a truism to say that these styles represent distinct modes of insertion into the modern, but the fact remains that attributions of "tradition" and "modernity" continue to be part of a political struggle over different visions of the "good society."

Conclusion

Studies of modernization in Turkey have, by and large, suffered from a lack of critical perspectives on the "modern" as an analytic category and have not adequately or explicitly addressed the local specificities of modernity. Although in the introduction to this essay I attributed these lacunae primarily to the nature of local polemics, the roles of modernization theory and Marxism as leading paradigms during the formative years of Turkish social science must also be acknowledged. The assumed inexorable march of society from traditional, rural, and less developed to modern, urban, industrialized, and more developed, or, alternatively, from feudal to capitalist, meant that complexities on the ground could be dismissed as "transitional" forms.[34]

Studies of the family and gender relations could also mirror the templates of modernization theory by linking extendedness and gender hierarchy with tradition and nuclearity, and conjugality and egalitarianism with modernity. The question of gendered subjectivities and changing feminine and masculine identities did not even appear in treatments of social change, because questions of culture and identity could be accommodated neither in the Parsonian schematisms and aridities of modernization theory nor in the abstractions of Marx-inspired social theory. As a result, the possible links between expressions of gender and other markers of social status and difference, although utterly commonsensical, managed to escape any form of scrutiny. This, as I hope I have demonstrated, deprived us of an important point of entry for both a better understanding of the complexities of the "modern" in Turkish society and the development of a more self-reflexive social science. The analysis of gender by no means exhausts nor remedies these lacunae; it merely highlights the possibilities of a form of cultural analysis that should now find its way into a new agenda for social research.

Notes

A first version of this essay was presented at the Social Science Research Council conference on "Questions of Modernity," held in Cairo, May 28–30, 1993. I am grateful to the other participants for their comments. I also wish to thank Lila Abu-Lughod, Nancy Lindisfarne, Michele Cohen, Ayşe Öncü, Aynur İlyasoğlu, and Reem Saad for their helpful comments on the first draft of this essay.

1. Reşat Ekrem Koçu, *Türk Giyim Kuşam ve Süslenme Sözlüğü,* Istanbul: Sümerbank Kültür Yayınları, 1969.

2. Alan Duben and Cem Behar, *Istanbul Households: Marriage, Family and Fertility, 1880–1940,* Cambridge: Cambridge University Press, 1991.

3. Beth Baron, "The Making and Breaking of Marital Bonds in Modern Egypt," in Nikki Keddie and Beth Baron, eds., *Women in Middle Eastern History,* New Haven, Connecticut: Yale University Press, 1991; Partha Chatterjee, "The Nationalist Resolution of the 'Women's Question,'" in K. Sangari and S. Vaid, eds., *Recasting Women: Essays in Indian Colonial History,* New Brunswick, New Jersey: Rutgers University Press, 1991.

4. Deniz Kandiyoti, ed., *Women, Islam and the State,* London: Macmillan, 1991.

5. For a good overview of the role of the women's press between 1839 and 1908 in disseminating information on health, child care, and home economics, see Zehra Toksa, "Haremden Kadın Partisine Giden Yolda Kadın Dergileri, Gündemleri ve Öncü Kadınlar," *Defter,* Spring 1994, 116–42.

6. Duben and Behar, *Istanbul Households,* 139–40.

7. These negative properties of modernity were frequently linked to the emancipation of women and the anxiety that women would opt out of their traditionally sanctioned roles as mothers and housekeepers. The Westernized (*alafranka*) woman was invariably depicted in literary texts as idle and corrupt. See my "Slave Girls, Temptresses and Comrades: Images of Women in the Turkish Novel," *Feminist Issues,* vol. 8, no. 1, 1988, 35–50.

8. Nükhet Sirman, "Friend and Foe? Forging Alliances with Other Women in a Village of Western Turkey," in Şirin Tekeli, ed., *Women in Modern Turkish Society,* London: Zed Books, 1995.

9. During a visit to the island in the summer of 1994, I noted some important changes. Day-trippers arrived by chartered motorboat in heterogenous age groups. The younger members, male and female, sported trainers, bermuda shorts, and T-shirts. Musical instruments were replaced by portable music sets of the "ghetto-blaster" variety. Older women wore head scarves and long-sleeved, flowered dresses, while men wore nondescript attire, mainly short-sleeved shirts and trousers. A younger woman in head scarf and flowing robe, although not encountered on this occasion, would denote something entirely different now from what it meant during my encounters as a child.

10. Duben and Behar, *Istanbul Households,* 202–14.

11. Pierre Bourdieu, *Outline of a Theory of Practice,* Cambridge: Cambridge University Press, 1977.

12. Ekrem Işın, "19 yyda Modernlesme ve Gündelik Hayat," *Tanzimattan Cumhuriyete Türkiye Ansiklopedisi,* Istanbul: İletişim, 1985, 538–63.

13. Sencer Ayata, "Statü Yarışması ve Salon Kullanımı," *Toplum ve Bilim,* no. 42, 1988, 5–25.

14. Kandiyoti, "Slave Girls, Temptresses and Comrades."

15. Deniz Kandiyoti, "The Paradoxes of Masculinity: Some Thoughts on Segregated Societies," in Andrea Cornwall and Nancy Lindisfarne, eds., *Dislocating Masculinity: Comparative Ethnographies*, London: Routledge, 1994.

16. Jale Parla, *Babalar ve Oğullar*, Istanbul: İletişim Yayınları, 1990.

17. Şerif Mardin, "Super-Westernization in the Ottoman Empire in the Last Quarter of the Nineteenth Century," in Peter Benedict et al., eds., *Turkey: Geographic and Social Perspectives*, Leiden: E. J. Brill, 1974.

18. Ref'i Cevat Ulunay, *Sayılı Fırtınalar*, Istanbul: Yeni Matbaa, 1955.

19. Ekrem Işın traces the dissolution of the *mahalle* structure to the social and demographic changes of the nineteenth century and maintains that it survived as a cohesive unit until then. See Ekrem Işın, "19 yyda Modernleşme," 548.

20. Yeşim Arat, *Patriarchal Paradox: Women Politicians in Turkey*, Princeton, New Jersey: Princeton University Press, 1989; Ayşe Durakbaşa, "Cumhuriyet Döneminde Kemalist Kadın Kimliğinin Oluşumu," *Tarih ve Toplum*, vol. 9, no. 51, 1988, 167–71; Şirin Tekeli, "The Meaning and Limits of Feminist Ideology in Turkey," in Ferhunde Özbay, ed., *Women, Family and Social Change in Turkey*, Bangkok: UNESCO, 1990.

21. Çağlar Keyder, *State and Class in Turkey*, London: Verso, 1987.

22. Arjun Appadurai, "Disjuncture and Difference in the Global Cultural Economy," *Public Culture*, vol. 2, no. 2, 1990, 1–24.

23. Martin Stokes, *The Arabesk Debate: Music and Musicians in Modern Turkey*, Oxford: Clarendon Press, 1990; Meral Özbek, *Popüler Kültür ve Orhan Gencebay Arabeski*, Istanbul: İletişim Yayınları, 1991.

24. Nurdan Gürbilek draws our attention to the fact that the 1980s constituted a watershed in terms of making the "private" something that could be articulated and exposed in public, especially through the media, fueling "private life" industries. For a full analysis of the implications of the valorization of the private, see Nurdan Gürbilek, *Vitrinde Yaşamak: 1980'lerin Kültürel Iklimi*, Istanbul: Metis Yayınları, 1992.

25. See Afet Inan, *The Emancipation of the Turkish Woman*, Paris: UNESCO, 1962. Inan was the leading architect of this official version, noted for her contribution to the Turkish history thesis.

26. Sarah Graham-Brown, *Images of Women*, London: Quartet Books, 1988.

27. Yakın Ertürk, "Rural Women and Modernization in Southeastern Anatolia," in Tekeli, *Women in Modern Turkish Society*, 141–52.

28. Ayşe Öncü, "Turkish Women in the Professions: Why So Many?" in Nermin Abadan-Unat, ed., *Women in Turkish Society*, Leiden: E. J. Brill, 1981.

29. Şirin Tekeli, "The Meaning and Limits."

30. Deniz Kandiyoti, "Patterns of Patriarchy: Notes for an Analysis of Male Dominance in Turkish Society," in Tekeli, *Women in Modern Turkish Society*, 306–18.

31. For similar issues of identity management in the Iranian context, see the discussion of the concepts of *ommol* (too traditional) and *jelf* (too loose) by Afsaneh Najmabadi, "Hazards of Modernity and Morality: Women, State and Ideology in Contemporary Iran," in Kandiyoti, *Women, Islam and the State*, 66.

32. For a more general analysis of the importance of the kinship idiom in the Turkish context, see Alan Duben, "The Significance of Family and Kinship in Urban

Turkey," in Çiğdem Kağitçıbaşı, ed., *Sex Roles, Family, and Community in Turkey,* Bloomington: Indiana University Press, 1982.

33. Leila Ahmed, *Women and Gender in Islam,* New Haven, Connecticut: Yale University Press, 1992, 225.

34. I am indebted to Aynur Ilyasoğlu for reminding me of the influence of the Marxist-inspired social-structural research of the 1940s in establishing base/superstructure models of social change.

9/ The Predicament of Modernism in Turkish Architectural Culture

An Overview

SİBEL BOZDOĞAN

I n 1930, the arrival of the modern movement in Turkey was celebrated in the official republican daily *Hakimiyet-i Milliye:* "In the last few years, the new architecture of the new age has been forming in all parts of the world. Young architects are breaking through old mentalities and traditions and marching toward the truth. We are proudly happy that some of the new construction in Ankara is a manifestation of this new architecture."[1] The basic principles of this *yeni mimari* (new architecture), as the modernist avant-garde was then called, were captured in three words: rationalism, functionalism, and *simenarme* (reinforced concrete), uttered with all the quasi-religious zeal and optimism of Kemalist "nation building," in both the literal and the metaphorical senses of the term.

Today, with no traces of this optimism left, the public and the architectural establishment in Turkey are lamenting the irreversible destruction of cities by reinforced concrete atrocities and by the sheer ugliness of the vast majority of new buildings, compared with the superior aesthetic qualities of the Ottoman heritage. At the same time, faced with its impotence to control the economic, social, and political forces behind this aesthetic degradation, the architectural profession is retreating to its more conventional preoccupation with form making, surrendering any larger mission of transforming society. As a panacea for the havoc wrought by sixty years of modernism, many Turkish architects in the 1980s have replaced the spirit of celebration that accompanied the arrival of the modern movement in the 1930s with an enthusiastic reception of the formalist, historicist, and eclectic experiments of postmodernism.

In this overview, I suggest that a less polemical and more fruitful approach to the predicament of modern architecture in Turkey, and elsewhere, would be to abandon the binary logic of modern versus postmodern altogether and face the historical complexity and ambiguity of the project of modernity in architecture. The central intellectual dilemma in many disciplines today is how to rely on the post-structuralist critique of Enlightenment values (and from that, on the post-Orientalist/postcolonial critique of the "Western canon" in art and culture) and yet invoke some of the same emancipatory and humanist values in order to engage with authoritarian political and cultural structures.[2] This dilemma preoccupies those of us in the discipline of architecture in our own way. We are all critical of the universalistic claims and totalizing discourse of high modernism, yet few of us can deny the initial critical force, democratic potential, and liberating premises of modern architecture as it emerged historically in Europe at the beginning of the twentieth century.

It was, after all, the pioneers of modernism who first installed issues of dwelling, housing, urbanism, and production as the legitimate and primary territory of architecture and who, indeed, wished to replace the preceding "architecture of historical styles" with "a new culture of building."[3] This was hoped to be a new culture in which form would not be stylistically a priori but would result from considerations of program, function, site, practicality, simplicity, economy, materials, and rational construction. It would be, by definition, an architecture appropriate to its cultural and national context, varying in appearance from place to place but universal in the principles of design thinking that informed it. In the famous dictum of the modernist architect Bruno Taut, to whom the education of young Turkish architects was entrusted in 1936, "all nationalist architecture is bad, but all good architecture [read, modern] is national."[4]

It was implicit in this early modernist conception that the modern project in architecture was not only "unfinished" but should have remained so by definition, always resisting self-closure into orthodoxy and continuously rethinking its own premises in the light of new developments and new contexts. By the 1930s, however, the self-closure had already occurred. The modern movement in architecture was "invented" and codified as a unified formal canon (the so-called "international style" of white cubic forms, reinforced concrete, and glass) and as a thoroughly rational doctrine expressing the zeitgeist of the modern age.[5] For some time now, critics and revisionists in the historiography of modern architecture have compellingly argued that the reduction of modernism to a formal or stylistic canon and a scientific doctrine is a contingent *historical* phenomenon that needs to be carefully dissociated from the explicitly antistylistic and critical premises of early modernist thinking. Nonetheless, an uncritically construed and drastically reduced "modernist evil" has long been a convenient straw man for postmodernist attacks in the architectural culture at large, with an especially strong appeal outside the Western world, parallel to a mounting obsession with identity.

I argue in this essay that in Turkey, the truly critical and creative potential of modern architecture was compromised from the beginning because it was introduced to the country from above (and from without) as one aspect of the official program of modernization and was inscribed within the official cultural politics of the nation-state. Indeed, over the years, "modern architecture" has come to be equated exclusively with modern forms, and its legitimacy has been posited less in terms of its critical force to transform the discipline of architecture *from within* than in terms of its status as the bearer of the republican project, often in reference to ideologically charged polarities that are no longer tenable—for example, modern as opposed to traditional, and therefore progressive as opposed to reactionary. Especially after the Second World War, coinciding with the heyday of modernization theories in the social sciences, the notion of "modern architecture" was taken for granted as synonymous with the official high modernism of the West in its most sterile formal manifestations (boxes of glass and concrete), simplistic slogans ("radical break with history"), and universalizing claims (e.g., form as a thoroughly rational consequence of function and technique).

In what follows, I look at the predicament of architectural modernism in Turkey in three periods, each lasting about a decade and each bearing the legacy of a leader under whom the urbanscape and architectural culture of the country were dramatically transformed—namely, the founder of the republic, Kemal Atatürk, in the 1930s, Prime Minister Adnan Menderes in the 1950s, and the late President Turgut Özal in the 1980s. The central argument underlying my historical overview is that if modernism can once again be thought of as a critical, pluralist, inclusive, antistylistic, formally indeterminate discourse grounded in the historical condition of modernity and irreducible to any official style or doctrine, then it will be seen already to have much in common with the recent critique directed at the formal sterility, semantic poverty, and instrumental rationality of high modernism. In other words, it is theoretically possible to hold onto the programatic and democratizing content of modernism in architecture while rejecting its totalizing discourse of universal rationality. A modernist critique of what has been done in the name of modernism is, I believe, still a viable—and perhaps the only meaningful—way out of the current architectural impasse without necessarily endorsing either of the two currently popular options that postmodernism, as a styl-

9.1. "Ankara Construit." (Reproduced from *La Turquie Kemaliste,* Ankara, 1935.)

istic trend in architecture, seems to offer: a "return to tradition" or the "global theme park."

Modernism and Kemalism: The 1930s

Any discussion of modern architecture outside the West has to proceed from the premise that it was typically introduced in the conspicuous absence of all the conditions under which Western modernism flourished—especially the industrial city, capitalist production, and the autonomous bourgeois subject. It was therefore not grounded in a radical rethinking of the discipline of architecture in the context of profound historical, social, and technological transformations. Rather, it was primarily a form of "visible politics" or "civilizing mission" that accompanied official programs of modernization, imposed from above and implemented by the bureaucratic and professional elites of paternalistic nation-states.

It is precisely such historical circumstances that underlie the paradoxical nature of nationalist discourses of modernity outside the West and the inherent ambivalence of architectural modernism as an expression of this paradox.[6] Epitomized by the Kemalist aspiration "to be Western in spite of the West," Turkish architectural culture of the 1930s adopted the formal and scientific precepts of Western modernism and yet posited itself as an anti-imperialist, anti-Orientalist, and anticolonialist expression of independence, identity, and subjecthood by a nation hitherto represented only by the Orientalist cultural paradigms of the West. This profound ambivalence in the Kemalist project of cultural and architectural modernism, frequently overlooked in the postmodern tendency to focus only on its "colonizing" effect upon its own traditional population, is not unlike that of Salman Rushdie's postcolonial immigrant in a Western metropolis, whom the author describes as "a disguise [inventing] his own false descriptions to counter the falsehoods invented about him" and therefore representing heroism as much as pathos.[7] It is this "heroic" aspect that comes across most forcefully in representations of the construction of Ankara as the modern capital of Kemalist Turkey in the 1930s—in one case, an architectural collage showing a futuristic city of abstract, purist buildings reminiscent of the tectonics of the Russian constructivist avant-garde (fig. 9.1).

That modern architecture was instantly identified as "cubic" (*kübik mimari*) when it "arrived" in Turkey alongside the Westernizing institutional reforms of Kemalism bears testimony to the priority of exterior form during this period, a priority to which architectural culture, by its very nature, was among the most vulnerable. The novelty and revolutionary rhetoric of cubic or prismatic forms, reinforced concrete construction, wide terraces, cantilevers, and flat roofs, all without historical references, conveniently complemented the Kemalist "revolution" (*inkilap*), symbolizing the country's emergence from "Oriental malaise" (*şarklılıktan kurtulmak*) and its willingness to participate in "contemporary civilization" (*asrileşmek*).[8] An article in the 1933 issue of *Mimar,* the new professional journal of Turkish architects in the republican period, juxtaposed the caption "Mimarlıkta İnkilap" (revolution in architecture) with the canonic Villa Savoie of Le Corbusier, the brainchild of the modernist avant-garde, thus explicitly associating it with the Kemalist revolution, "in need of its appropriate architectural expression."[9]

9.2. Sergi Evi (Exhibition Hall), Ankara, 1933. (Postcard in the author's personal collection.)

Above all, *yeni mimari,* the new architecture, effectively legitimized the architect as a "cultural leader" or an "agent of civilization" with a passionate sense of mission to dissociate the republic from an Ottoman and Islamic past. Furthermore, the scientific claims of official modernism, grounded in doctrines of rationalism and functionalism, were especially favorable to the espoused positivism of the Kemalist project, lending credibility and authority to the expertise of an emerging architectural profession. In the minds of young Turkish architects there was no doubt that the nation-state was the bearer of modernity, and hence the formal and scientific precepts of official modernism, well established in Europe by the 1930s, were the most appropriate and progressive expressions of this unifying national ideal. The propaganda function of the modernist aesthetic was most conspicuous in buildings designed for national education and public indoctrination, such as schools and "Peoples' Houses" (*Halkevi*), as well as in exhibition spaces such as the Izmir International Exposition buildings and the paradigmatic Sergi Evi, or exhibition hall, in Ankara (fig. 9.2).[10]

The proliferation of images during this period and the formation of what may be seen as a "republican visual culture" (such as paintings depicting scenes of the Kemalist "cultural revolution," posters by the prolific graphic designer İhap Hulusi advertising products of national industry, and the photographs in *La Turquie Kemaliste*) was also instrumental in establishing modernism as primarily an *aesthetic* discourse. In spite of the arbitrariness of associating both the cultural and the scientific agenda of Kemalism with specific modern forms, the net result of this history has been an essentially *formalist* understanding of the term "modern architecture" rather than a deeper awareness of its critical content, and, in turn, a widespread identification of these forms with the secular nationalism of the republic. This tendency to charge architectural forms ideologically and to lose sight of their basic autonomy vis-à-vis politics has unnecessarily politicized and polarized the architectural culture in Turkey, even to this day, between a stubborn and uncritical defense of "modern architecture," equated with defending the republic, and its indiscriminate condemnation as the built legacy of a mistaken era. What is frequently overlooked in this partisan polemic is that the architectural forms condemned as "modern" are merely images of modernism without the substance of modernity.

Most importantly, the inadequate resources of the country, especially the poverty of the construction industry in the 1930s, ruled out any substantial program of housing, urbanism, and rationalized production—the very basis of the democratic vision of the modernist utopia that sought to empower people in the politics of daily life. Unlike the extensive housing programs of the Weimar Republic in Germany, for example, which were an inspirational model for modernist discourse everywhere, including that of Turkish architects, actual building in the specifically and paradigmatically modernist category *mesken mimarisi* (architecture of the house/dwelling) was limited to a handful of villas and urban apartments for the republican elite, reinforcing that category's associations with official culture and its popular perception as "alien" and "imposed." Indeed, by the late 1930s, after a period of fervent controversy over the term *kübik* (cubic),[11] the "coldness and sterility" of such forms were rejected as the expression of an alienated, cosmopolitan society—of modernity in the most negative sense.

On the other hand, the rejection of *kübik* in favor of forms inspired by traditional Turkish houses, and the resulting search for a "national" style under the leadership of the prominent architect Sedad Hakkı Eldem, was not necessarily a rejection of modernism as architectural historians have typically suggested (thereby betraying their own formalist-stylistic understanding of the term "modern architecture"). Eldem's own admission that he "discovered" the Turkish house in Europe, through the principles of Le Corbusier and the drawings of Frank Lloyd Wright's prairie houses in the United States,[12] reveals the essentially modernist spectacles through which he viewed tradition, however passionately he expressed this view in the nationalist rhetoric of the 1930s. What it also reveals is that, in spite of its own slogans and oversimplifications to the contrary, modernism is not a matter of form and is not necessarily antagonistic to tradition.

Finally, it should be noted that the buildings of the 1930s exhibit an architectural quality and care unmatched by subsequent architectural production. So far as the idea of the house is concerned, for example, the irony of modern architecture in Turkey is that the authoritarian and etatist early republican period produced the detached villa and row-house types (following European models of the same period that are still highly desirable environments when maintained and landscaped), whereas the relatively more liberal period after 1950 witnessed the introduction of high-rise slab block construction, the notorious symbol of the sterility, banality, and repetitiveness of high modernism or "international style" as it proliferated in every country after World War II.

"International Style" in Turkey: The 1950s

Marshall Berman's account of twentieth-century modernism as a "flattening of perspective"—as modernity losing sight of its own origins and its own profound ambivalence over a simultaneously liberating and alienating historical possibility—is especially relevant for architectural culture in the 1950s.[13] The hygienic, scientifically controlled, rationally ordered urban utopias that early modernists had projected as reactions to the social and environmental ills of the nineteenth-century industrial city (its congestion, pollution, degradation of workers, etc.) themselves became the established norm in planning. The cosmopolitan messiness, mixed-use patterns, and collective memory of Baudelaire's Paris, the very locus of nineteenth-century modernity and urban life, were radically disrupted by the reductive and sterilizing principles of high modernist urbanism, informed by and operating with a relentless instrumental rationality. Especially after World War II, in an all-encompassing zeal for urban renewal and postwar reconstruction, the principles of modern urbanism—rational planning, functional zoning, the cutting of wide thoroughfares and traffic arteries through historical fabrics, the repetitive boom of high-rise housing blocks, and so forth—were applied on a large scale by Western, socialist, and Third World governments alike, with well-known disastrous results.

In Turkey, the elections of 1950 marked not only the end of the early republican era and the beginning of the more liberal economics and populist politics of the Democrat Party but also the unleashing of high modernism in architecture and urbanism. The extensive urban interventions carried out in Istanbul in the 1950s (fig. 9.3), a major project of political legitimacy and public relations under the personal directive of Adnan Menderes, constitute the closest Turkish counterpart to the modernism of Robert Moses, which Marshall Berman describes. The Beyoglu-Pera district of Istanbul, the city's nearest equivalent to Baudelaire's Paris, declined dramatically during this period, following the exodus of its non-Muslim population. At the same time, the phenomenal urbanization unleashed by massive migration from rural areas and the concomitant growth of squatter settlements around major cities (fig. 9.4) brought a much larger population into the ambivalent experience of modernity—that is, its seemingly endless possibilities, lifestyles, aesthetic norms, and high cultures, as well as people's simultaneous awareness of their own exclusion from these things. One could say that while modernism as a political project reached its epitome in this period, it also became transparent as an irreversible historical condition.

During the 1950s, the flow of foreign aid to Turkey, the arrival of Western experts from various international organizations, and Turkey's aspiration to become "the little America" accelerated the dissemination of precepts of the "international style" in architecture and its wide acceptance by the country's professional establishment. It is enough to note that even an architect like Sedad Hakkı Eldem, who advocated a state-sponsored "national" style in the 1930s and 1940s, later became the local collaborating architect for the Hilton Hotel in Istanbul, the hallmark of "international style" in Turkey designed by the corporate firm of Skidmore, Owings, and Merrill (fig. 9.5). Many examples and variants of this corporate style, with its concrete slabs and glazed skin surfaces, were designed by prominent Turkish architects throughout the 1950s and 1960s.

The high-rise slab block model for housing was introduced to the country during this period, too, under the initiative of the Emlak Kredi bank. The bank was originally established to provide long-term, low-interest credit to alleviate the drastic housing shortage accompanying rapid ur-

9.3. Demolition and urban renewal in Istanbul in the 1950s. (Photograph by Ara Güler; reproduced from *Istanbul,* 6 July 1993.)

9.4. Squatter settlements on the urban fringes of Ankara. (Photograph by M. Pehlivanoğlu, Archives of the Aga Khan Trust for Culture.)

9.5. Hilton Hotel, Istanbul. Architects Skidmore, Owings, and Merrill; local consultant Sedad Hakkı Eldem, 1952. (Reproduced from "Skidmore, Owings, and Merrill," Aga Khan Program at MIT, n.d.)

9.6. Ataköy housing, Istanbul. (Courtesy Ataköy Planning Office, Archives of the Aga Khan Trust for Culture.)

9.7. Proliferation of concrete slab block apartments in Istanbul. (Photograph by the author.)

9.8. Social Security complex, Zeyrek, Istanbul, 1962–64. Architect Sedad Hakkı Eldem. (Photograph by A. Dündar, Archives of the Aga Khan Trust for Culture.)

banization. It ended up financing examples like the Levent and Ataköy housing blocks in Istanbul that were far from being subsidized, low-income housing, turning instead to upper-class apartments. At least these early examples followed the modernist emphasis on rational design, sun angles, ventilation, and greenery (fig. 9.6). In contrast, lesser examples of high-rise slab block construction on narrow urban lots multiplied rapidly during the speculative apartment boom of the following decades, replacing architectural concerns with the priorities of the developer and reaching a level of "visual contamination" that has bred today's reaction (fig. 9.7). What is frequently forgotten in hasty denunciations of modern architecture is that there is no necessary link between the *architectural* precepts of modernism and all the negative consequences of condominium legislation (kat mülkiyeti kanunu), a speculative market in developer-initiated housing, and planning codes that do not lend themselves to experimentation with more appropriate urban alternatives such as low-rise, high-density housing or perimeter block construction.

From the late 1960s onward, however, as the architectural culture at large embarked upon a critique of the environmental and social failures of "high modernism," architectural discourse in Turkey also expressed increasing discontent with the legacy of the 1950s—the overwhelming aesthetic invasion of major cities by concrete-frame, slab block apartment construction and the destruction of historical fabrics by large-scale urban interventions.[14] What is important to note, however, is that none of this critique was yet formulated in explicitly anti- or postmodernist terms, and the word "postmodernism" in architecture, adopted by Charles Jencks in 1977,[15] was not yet in favor or wide circulation among Turkish architects.

Indeed, discontent with the architectural and urban effects of modernization was being voiced precisely at a time when, perhaps for the first time since the republican project of modernization was proclaimed, the liberating promise of modernity was also being felt by masses of people attracted by the richness of life and opportunity in urban centers. The consensus within the professional and educational establishment was toward mitigating the negative consequences of architectural high modernism by fragmenting its boxy aesthetic into modular systems or organic forms, replacing its slick surfaces of glass and plastered concrete with the more textured surfaces of the "new brutalism" of exposed concrete, brick, and wood, and revising its universalistic formulations with regionalist overtones. The Turkish Historical Society building in Ankara, designed by Turgut Cansever, and the Social Security complex in Zeyrek, Istanbul, designed by Sedad Hakkı Eldem, can be cited as successful examples of such unorthodox modernism in the 1960s (fig. 9.8). At that particular point in history, Eldem had dropped the nationalist rhetoric he had attached to his architecture in the 1930s and 1940s, and Cansever had not yet resorted to Islamic cosmology and "return to tradition" to explain the qualities of his work.

Today, by contrast, blaming the contemporary plight of architecture and urbanism on the humanism of the Renaissance and the instrumental rationality of modernism, Turgut Cansever portrays Islam not only as the source of his architecture but also as the only significant basis of resistance to the culture of consumption, instant gratification, and rampant economic injustice in Turkey in the 1980s.[16] What gets lost in his words is that it is essentially from a sensitivity to place, craft, texture, light, site, and topography that his work derives its quality and poetics. His highly acclaimed Demir Holiday Village in Bodrum, constructed in the stone vernacular tradition of the Mediterranean, is frequently portrayed as a symbol of the triumph of tradition over the contentious history of modern forms. Beyond the polemics, however, this building, like many other examples of "critical regionalism" (i.e., context-sensitive modernism) everywhere, is simply good architecture (which is frequently limited to well-crafted individual houses for well-off clients) that cannot be explained by Islam or tradition or, for that matter, region or culture alone.[17] Cansever's case, like that of Sedad Hakkı Eldem before him, bears testimony to the predicament of modernism in Turkey, which is the recurrent habit of enframing architecture within some kind of identity politics —nationalism, or "Turkishness," for Eldem, and Islam and tradition for Cansever—even though there is ample evidence that at its best, modern architecture resists all the essentialist claims to identity that supposedly inform it.

Throughout the 1960s and 1970s, intellectuals and the highly politicized Chamber of Architects leaned toward Third World–ist versions of modernization, looking no longer at the West but at squatter houses and folk architecture and shifting their emphasis from the aesthetics of architecture to the politics of production processes. Thus they also triggered growing academic interest in squatter settlements as an alternative social and architectural process outside the domain of both the state and the profession. Ideas about participatory and democratic design processes in housing, especially the possibilities of self-help schemes (combining the provision of preliminary design, infrastructure, and services at the professional level with the local resources and labor of the squatter populations), began to make their way into the discourse of the discipline and into architectural schools, if not into actually implemented examples.

In contrast, the current sense of the impotence and irrelevance of architecture in engaging with these issues has effectively surrendered the ground to a phenomenally unchecked and unplanned speculative development of cheaply built, substandard housing inhabited by second- and third-generation squatters. It may not be too farfetched to claim that in the late 1960s and early 1970s there was a moment for a critique of high modernism in architecture *from within modernist premises*—a brief moment that was rapidly lost in the political, economic, and cultural climate of the 1980s.

The Panorama of Postmodern Turkey: The 1980s

The defining feature of "postmodern" Turkey in the 1980s can be summed up as a growing reaction to the official ideology, cultural norms, and mental habits of the old republican elite, as well as of the traditional left, by groups ranging from advocates of liberal economy, civil society, popular culture, and feminism to Muslim intellectuals. The austerity and paternalism of official modernism were challenged in all expressions of culture, from literature and music to architecture and cinema.

In economic and political terms, this reaction bore the legacy of figures such as Ronald Reagan, Margaret Thatcher, and the late Turkish president Turgut Özal, and it marked the historical end of nationalist developmentalisms everywhere.[18] In cultural terms, it was marked by a radical departure from the universalistic claims of modernization theories in favor of a new emphasis on cultural identity and difference, prompting even the old guard of well-established modernist architects in Turkey to experiment with historicist and vernacular forms and at times even to pay lip service to Islamic quotations. The embracing of the term "postmodernism" in the 1980s by the architectural establishment throughout the world coincided with the new economic, political, and cultural developments and frequently obscured the crucial distinction between the critical dimension of postmodernity and its co-option into a justificatory stylistic trend in architecture.[19] While the critical dimension prompted everyone to question the assumptions of official culture and high modernism rather than taking them for granted, among architects it also led to a de facto legitimization of the stylistic trend.

The cultural expressions, construction boom, and changing urbanscape of the Özal years in Turkey bore ample witness to this ambivalence of the postmodern moment. On one hand, in a potentially democratic impulse, educated elites became increasingly more aware of the multiplicity of taste cultures, and especially of popular culture as the manifestation of the struggle of marginalized peoples for cultural expression and self-representation. We all began learning to suppress our contempt for *gecekondu* taste, *arabesk* music, *kebab* houses, intercity bus terminals, and cheap little mosques with aluminum domes, if we did not actually begin rather to like them, as we confronted our own ambivalent experiences of modernity.

Today, the elitism, austerity, and paternalism of the official modernism of the republic are increasingly unpopular, and so is the avant-garde theory of false consciousness that gives the traditional elites the right to redeem the masses in their name. Of course, where to draw the line between this democratic impulse and what is essentially an endorsement of *kitsch* just because "it belongs to the people" (often the mark of an elite guilt consciousness) is a formidable question that we constantly confront, especially in an inherently elite discipline like architecture.

The case of the phenomenal increase in the number of badly designed and poorly built new mosques (often a mosque–office block–shopping complex) is a telling example. Treated with contempt by the architectural establishment, they testify to the overall environmental and aesthetic contamination brought about by economic, social, and political forces far beyond the control of the architectural profession. Yet they also bear testimony to the traditional failure or reluctance of the professional elite to treat the mosque as an important architectural type or design problem, thus surrendering it to the domain of the least educated and most populist groups in society.[20]

On the other hand, it should be noted that the architectural establishment is celebrating what is perceived to be a "liberation" from the sterility and facelessness of international modernism, ironically and precisely at a time when the country has opened up to a further internationalized and globalized capitalism.[21] Most significant in architectural and urban terms is the proliferation of five-star hotels (Conrad, Swiss, Mövenpick, and Ramada in Istanbul; Hilton and Sheraton in Ankara), supermarkets and shopping malls (Ataköy Galleria and, more recently, Akmerkez in Istanbul; Karum and Atakule in Ankara) (fig. 9.9), business centers and glazed atria, and holiday villages connected to international chains (Club Med, Robinson, etc.). The latest examples of transnational

9.9. Karum shopping mall, Ankara. (Photograph by the author.)

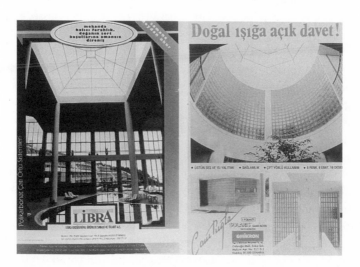

9.10. Advertisements for building materials, components, and fixtures, 1990s. (Reproduced from *Arredemento Dekorasyon*, no. 11, 1994.)

postmodernism and "high-tech" expressionism are replicated by, mostly, a younger generation of architects, often with qualities comparable to those of their Western models. Although there is, admittedly, something refreshing about this reorientation of attention toward the discipline of architecture itself, rather than toward its political and economic context, it manifests itself as experiments in form and image making for private clients who can afford it, at the expense of the larger social agenda of modernism.

Complementing these trends, there is a hitherto unprecedented proliferation of glossy publications, design and decoration magazines, office supplies and professional tools—including sophisticated computer-aided design systems—and imported building materials, components, fixtures, and finishes, as well as their domestic imitations, with ever-improving marketing techniques. Looking at the advertisements in architectural magazines for space frames, precast or lightweight concrete components, or glass blocks (fig. 9.10)—that archetypal material of the early modernist aesthetic in Europe—one cannot help thinking that at the same time modern forms are being rejected, the material basis of a modernist aesthetic (that is, new materials informing the modernist aspiration for lightness, transparency, and standardization) is just emerging in Turkey. Perhaps more phenomenal in the residential patterns of the upper classes and the emerging "yuppies" is the move away from the city to villa-type developments such as Mesa Koru Sitesi in Ankara or Alarko-Alsit in Istanbul (fig. 9.11), or to exclusive new suburbs like Bahçeşehir and Kemer Country outside Istanbul—complete with the cult of nature and health, swimming pools, tennis courts, golf courses, and horseback riding.

The case of Kemer Country, developed on a large site outside metropolitan Istanbul and surrounded by a belt of forest ten kilometers deep, is a particularly significant one. Publicity brochures and occasional newsletters issued since the inception of the enterprise in 1991 openly identify the scheme with the passionately antimodernist architectural discourse of the "traditional neighborhood development" promoted by Prince Charles (and his neoconservative architect Leon Krier) in the West. We are told that "Kemer Country is designed to revitalize an old lifestyle in which neighborhood (*mahalle*) was the keyword and we all belonged to our neighborhoods. The greatest problem of Istanbul today is not noise or pollution or traffic, nor is it congestion or high cost of living, all of which we cope with in one way or other. It is, instead, the loss of our *sense of belonging*, without which we cannot survive."[22] Especially in the

9.11. Advertisement for duplex villas on Anadoluhisarı, Istanbul. The caption reads, "Far from sight, close to your work!" (Reproduced from *Kapris*, 1987.)

9.12. Advertisement for the development project called Kemer Country. The title reads, "We now have a neighborhood." (Reproduced from *Newsletter of the Kemer Construction and Tourism Company*, Winter 1994.)

third phase of the development, the prominent Florida architectural firm of Andres Duany and Elizabeth Plater-Zyberk were employed "to restore this lost sense of neighborhood." The accompanying sketches depict villas inspired by traditional Turkish houses: tile roofs, modular windows, projecting bays on upper floors (*cumba*), courtyards (*avlu*), narrow streets (*sokak*) and small squares (*meydan*), to which the historical Ottoman aqueduct constitutes an appropriate backdrop (fig. 9.12).

Kemer Country claims to represent the pragmatic design approach of "traditional neighborhood development" in which, after certain building codes and stylistic features are fixed as the basis of the "civic identity of the place," the design process involves groups ranging from teams of designers to speculative developers, and from administrators and management consultants to prospective users. Although this in itself is an innovative approach with a democratic potential inconceivable under the authoritative idealism of the heroic modern architect, there is nothing in it that automatically leads to or necessitates the traditional, antimodern forms that Duany and Plater-Zyberk have produced in most of their schemes. In the last analysis, not unlike the modernism it vehemently condemns, the Kemer Country project still sets priority on exterior form, and in its antimodernist rhetoric it is no less ideological than modernism.

When all is said, behind the proudly "traditional" facades of Kemer Country—from Turkish vernacular to Tuscan villas and Georgian mansions —we find straightforward upper-class suburban villas with Jacuzzi bathrooms, basements, yards, and garages. What remains to be seen is whether reconstructing the physical fabric of the traditional neighborhood is indeed a restoration of the relationship between architecture and pluralist democracy, as is claimed by the Turkish developers of the scheme[23] (although who can claim that traditional Ottoman neighborhoods were "democratic"?), or, instead, an inevitably artificial "public realm" that, in claiming to restore a sense of belonging, still excludes many who do not belong there. That the prices of the fourteen different types of villas range from U.S. $350,000 to $2 million, not to mention the prerequisite of car ownership to live there, suggests the latter. Indeed, in many of these recent architectural developments in Turkey, from upper-class shopping malls to suburban villas behind well-guarded enclosures, there is a conspicuous erosion of accessible-to-all public space that is the hallmark of a real urban condition and real cultural and class diversity.[24] Notwithstanding its critique of the self-righteous republican elite, postmodernism in architecture continues to cater primarily to the exclusive lifestyle of a privileged elite—except this time it is an elite of industry, finance, and business that replaces the bureaucrats of the republic.

Conclusion: A Critical (Post)Modernism?

There is no question that in Turkey, as elsewhere, the postmodern critique in architecture has rightly questioned the aesthetic canon of official high modernism as well as the universalistic discourse, elitism, and instrumental rationality of its politics. Contrary to the claims of postmodernists, however, most of this critique is hardly new or, for that matter, incompatible with a critical modernism. The first and perhaps only point we can legitimately make about a critical modernism in architectural culture is that it would be self-defeating to codify it in a priori formal or stylistic terms. It is "radically indeterminate" in its forms, just like the project of democracy to which it is intimately connected.[25] Thus it is theoretically an "empty space" or "utopic void" that needs to be filled historically and contextually, not by ahistorical and essentialist truths, and not arbitrarily in the total absence of any truth. With significant implications for the recent identity consciousness in the architectural culture of non-Western countries, such a critical modernism is radically opposed to making identity politics the centerpiece of design, knowing that identities are always complex, shifting, and contradictory, always contesting the constructs that attempt to fix them.

On the other hand, the contingency of all truth claims and the possibility of alternative modernisms does not make them all equal or eliminate the mandate of educated elites, such as architects, to address problems and offer options, if not impositions. That the profession of architecture is radically challenged by recent developments in the world—on one hand, the computerization of design (the "anybody can design given the right software" argument), and on the other, the appearance of hitherto marginalized groups (the "canons of a discipline laid out by white, male, Western or Western-educated architects cannot respond to a pluralist society" argument)—does not necessarily render the profession obsolete, as some today would argue it does. It only gives the profession all the more reason to engage with these new challenges.

The forms and doctrines of the modernist utopia may no longer be tenable. Yet few would deny that its programmatic content—its preoccupation with issues of housing, urbanism, and building production, revised and enhanced by more recent concerns such as ecology, public space, and cultural diversity—"still matters" as far as the discipline and profession of architecture are concerned.[26] Any recent celebration of post-modernism in architectural culture as "the liberation of the discipline" would be incomplete without the larger picture, which depicts a drastically diminished role, relevance, and significance for architecture in the society at large. As Stuart Hall cogently puts it, "it is perfectly possible to invoke the postmodernist paradigm and not understand how easily post-modernism can become a kind of lament for one's own departure from the center of the world."[27]

To conclude with the post-Enlightenment dilemma that I touched on in the beginning, the best we can hope for is continuously to sharpen our awareness of the inherent ambivalence of the initial modernist project, which was without doubt a *political* project (as postmodern criticism has exposed) but also, I would insist, a *historical condition* that has opened up possibilities far too rich to be reduced to the now-discredited political project. It is neither fair nor theoretically consistent to portray modernity only as an oppressive political project and, in opposition to this, celebrate postmodernity only as a historical condition with democratic and pluralist implications. At least in architecture, the reverse could be argued with equal conviction.

I have tried to suggest in this essay that, at least in my field, a more fruitful premise on which to pose the debate lies first in moving beyond reductionist and simplistic definitions of *both* modernism and postmodernism, dispensing with the notorious binary opposition set up between them largely for polemical purposes. Second, it is important to recognize the disciplinary autonomy of architecture, or of other forms of cultural production for that matter, whereby individual works, overdetermined by a multiplicity of factors both external and internal to the discipline, are as much products or expressions of the culture and politics of an era as they are possible sites of resistance to it.

Notes

1. "Yeni Mimari: Mimarlık Aleminde Yeni Bir Esas" (New Architecture: New Principles in the Architectural World), *Hakimiyet-i Milliye*, 2 January 1930. Also important in the proliferation of the term "new architecture" was Celal Esat Arseven's *Yeni Mimari*, Istanbul: Agah Sabri Kütüphanesi, 1931, which was based on Andre Lurcat's *Architecture*, Paris: sans pareil, 1929.

2. This dilemma is expressed cogently by Tim Mitchell and Lila Abu-Lughod in

"Questions of Modernity," *SSRC Newsletter,* vol. 47, no. 4, 1993, 82. For an acknowledgement of this dilemma by Edward Said, the most prominent critic of the Western canon in art and culture, see his "Politics of Knowledge," *Raritan,* Summer 1991, 17–31.

3. The distinction between the architecture of historical styles and the new antistylistic art/culture of building is captured, for example, by the title of Herman Muthesius's *Style Architecture and Building Art,* translated by Stanford Anderson, Santa Monica, California: Getty Center, 1994 (originally published as *Stilarchitektur und Baukunst,* 1902) and expressed in different ways by many modernist architects of the early twentieth century. The same distinction between style architecture (*üslup mimarisi*) and building art (*yapı sanatı*) permeated the discourse of Turkish architects in the 1930s.

4. Bruno Taut, *Mimarlık Bilgisi* (Lectures on Architecture), Istanbul: Güzel Sanatlar Akademisi, 1938, 333.

5. See Giorgio Cuicci, "The Invention of the Modern Movement," *Oppositions,* no. 24, 1981, 69–89. Particularly instrumental in this construction of an official history for modern architecture was Philip Johnson and Henry-Russel Hitchcock's *The International Style: Architecture since 1922,* New York: W. W. Norton, 1932, accompanying the famous Museum of Modern Art exhibition, and Siegfried Giedion's *Space, Time and Architecture,* Cambridge, Massachusetts: Harvard University Press, 1941.

6. The paradoxical nature of nationalist discourses outside the West is discussed by Partha Chatterjee, *Nationalist Thought and the Colonial World,* London: Zed Books, 1986.

7. Salman Rushdie, *The Satanic Verses,* Dover, U.K.: The Consortium, 1992, 49.

8. See my "Architecture, Modernism and Nation-Building in Kemalist Turkey," *New Perspectives on Turkey,* no. 10, 1994, 37–55.

9. Behçet Bedrettin, "Mimarlıkta İnkilap," *Mimar,* 1933, 245. *Mimar* started its publication in 1931 and was renamed *Arkitekt* three years later.

10. The Sergi Evi building, designed by the Turkish architect Şevki Balmumcu, was later converted by the German architect Paul Bonatz into the State Opera and Ballet. The nature of this conversion, from a modernist aesthetic to a more austere and official building with "Turkish" details, illustrates the idological climate of the 1940s.

11. Best known in the literature of the period are the negative portrayals of a cubic house in Yakup Kadri Karaosmanoğlu's 1934 novel *Ankara* (Istanbul: İletişim Yayınları, 1991 [1934]) and of a certain "cubic palace" in Halide Edip Adıvar's *Tatarcık,* which was serialized in the popular weekly magazine *Yedigün* in 1939. Peyami Safa, in "Bizde ve Avrupa'da Kübik," *Yedigün,* 14 October 1936, no. 8, 7–8, designated "cubic" as a disease "more dangerous than the fires that devastated the traditional houses of Istanbul."

12. See Sibel Bozdoğan et al., *Sedad Eldem: Architect in Turkey,* Singapore: Concept Media, 1987.

13. Marshall Berman, *All That Is Solid Melts into Air,* New York: Simon and Schuster, 1983.

14. The critique of "high modernism" especially followed the impact of Jane Ja-

cobs's seminal *The Death and Life of Great American Cities*, New York: Random House, 1961.

15. See Charles Jencks, *The Language of Post-Modern Architecture*, London: Academy Editions, 1977.

16. Interview with Turgut Cansever in *Dergah*, July 1991.

17. I use the term "critical regionalism" in the sense in which it is articulated by Kenneth Frampton, "Towards a Critical Regionalism: Six Points for an Architecture of Resistance," in Hal Foster, ed., *The Anti-Aesthetic: Essays on Postmodern Culture*, Port Townsend, Washington: Bay Press, 1983, 16–30.

18. On the end of nationalist developmentalism, see Çağlar Keyder, *Ulusal Kalkınmacılığın İflası* (The Bankruptcy of National Developmentalism), Istanbul: Metis Yayınları, 1993, and also his "The Dilemma of Cultural Identity on the Margin of Europe," *Review*, vol. 16, no. 1, 1993, 19–33.

19. On the embracing of the term "postmodernism" by the architectural establishment, see Mary McLeod, "Architecture and Politics in the Reagan Era: From Postmodernism to Deconstructivism," *Assemblage*, no. 8, 1989. See also her chapter "Architecture" in Stanley Trachtenberg, ed., *The Post-Modern Moment*, Westport, Connecticut: Greenwood Press, 1985, 19–52.

20. For these points, and for a recent discussion of contemporary mosque architecture, see the writings by Doğan Kuban and Uğur Tanyeli in a special section titled "Contemporary Mosque Architecture" in *Arredemento Dekorasyon*, no. 11, 1994, 80–91.

21. For the urban and cultural expressions of this new atmosphere, see also Asu Aksoy and Kevin Robins, "Istanbul between Civilization and Discontent," *New Perspectives on Turkey*, no. 10, 1994, 57–74.

22. Kemer Country, publicity brochure for the third phase of development, Istanbul, 1993.

23. "Zaman Ötesi'nin Peşinde Kemer Country" (In Pursuit of the Timeless: Kemer Country), interview with the developer, Esat Edin, and the design coordinator, Talha Gencer, in *Arredemento Dekorasyon*, no. 10, 1993, 121.

24. See Aksoy and Robins, "Istanbul between Civilization and Discontent."

25. Here I am inspired by Chantal Mouffe's discussion of "radical democracy" in her "Democratic Citizenship and the Political Community," in Chantal Mouffe, ed., *Dimensions of Radical Democracy*, London: Verso, 1992, 225–39. The idea of maintaining the democratic and critical potential of modern architecture while rejecting its totalizing and universalistic discourse is analogous to Mouffe's critiquing the epistemological project of the Enlightenment while maintaining its political project of democracy. See her collection of essays, *The Return of the Political*, London: Verso, 1993, especially her introduction, "For an Agonistic Pluralism," 1–8.

26. See Marshall Berman, "Why Modernism Still Matters," in Scott Lasch and Jonathan Friedman, eds., *Modernity and Identity*, Oxford: Blackwell, 1992, 33–58.

27. Stuart Hall, "The Emergence of Cultural Studies and the Crisis of the Humanities," *October*, no. 53, 1990, 11–23.

10/ Once There Was, Once There Wasn't

National Monuments

and Interpersonal Exchange

MICHAEL E. MEEKER

The Atatürk Memorial Tomb and the Kocatepe Mosque in Ankara are arguably the two most important monuments of the Turkish republic. The tomb provides for visitations and observances in memory of the founder of the republic; the mosque provides a great place of worship representative of the republican period. Yet their prominent hilltop locations and extensive physical layouts indicate that both are intended to have a much larger significance than these specific ceremonial purposes. The two sites, one Kemalist and the other Islamist, represent the claims of two different "orders" of meanings and values to a dominant position in the public life of the Turkish republic. In this respect, the architecture and ceremonies of each monument separately compose the Turkish past, present, and future.

Moreover, standing at similar elevations and in open view of one another, the tomb and the mosque can appear to be in a relationship of challenge and response. The completion of the Kocatepe Mosque in 1987, some thirty-four years after the completion of the memorial tomb in 1953, added one to one in order to make *three,* not *two:* a shrine of Kemalism, a shrine of Islamism, and the polemical relationship between the two.

By their visible juxtaposition in the landscape of central Anatolia, both the one and the other can be perceived as an argument against its counterpart as much as an argument for itself. If public perceptions of the two monuments were drawn in this direction—and there are some signs of such a trend—the parallel siting of the two would lend support to a fabled but misleading perception of Turkish society.[1] As the Kemalist site stands opposed to the Islamist site, so it might be reckoned, nationalism is opposed to religion, modernity is opposed to tradition, and state is opposed to society. The very separateness of the two monuments as distinct architectural and ceremonial entities seems to suggest the possibility of two clearly defined but mutually exclusive alternatives. One would be founded on secular reason, the other on religious faith. One would look to the future, the other to the past. One would rely on top-down strategies of institutional organization, the other on bottom-up strategies of popular mobilization. But have the citizens of the Turkish republic, or, for that matter, the citizens of any modern state, ever faced such a clear set of mutually exclusive choices?

In this essay I compare the "alternative" representations of tomb and mosque in order to clarify the common ground that both monuments address. Each of the two sites attempts to compose two horizons of experience closely associated with the nation-state. On the one hand, individuals live within a mass society of anonymous others through the rationalization of public space and time. On the other hand, individuals live among intimate others linked by circuits of interpersonal exchange.[2] Interconnected but not entirely compatible, the two horizons constitute a stimulus for anxiety, if not paranoia, among the citizens of potential and realized nation-states. Are not *our* circles of familiarity and intimacy vulnerable to the order of mass and reason? Is not the order of mass and reason vulnerable to *their* circles of familiarity and intimacy?

The nationalist imagination—so characteristic of the age of mass communication, bureaucratic government, technical knowledge, and rationalized markets—responds directly to these sometimes spoken, sometimes unspoken fears. In the nation-state, the order of mass and reason would become but a projection of homogeneous circles of interpersonal relationships. In accordance with principles of a national order, the relationship of the two horizons would be perfectly composed. The allure of such a projection—its practical realization being another matter altogether—is therefore contingent upon a necessary but not sufficient precondition. The prospects of any nationalist movement would depend upon the preexistence of a certain minimal amount of raw material at the level of social relations: circuits of interpersonal exchange based on a shared language of familiarity and intimacy. Without such a foundation, any imaginative projection of the nation-state would lack credibility, and hence, also, any measure of practicability. That is to say, if the idea of the modern nation is unthinkable apart from a mass of anonymous others, then it is also equally unthinkable apart from a system of face-to-face, person-to-person relationships. The nation is therefore truly imaginable only when the former and the latter come into contact with each other.

To see how the memorial tomb and the Kocatepe Mosque obey this imperative of the contemporary nationalist imagination, we cannot begin straightaway with the monuments themselves. We must first have some understanding of the cultural weight and structural position of circuits of interpersonal exchange in the Turkish republic. In the section that follows, I discuss a shared language of familiarity and intimacy that is widely disseminated in contemporary Turkey.

A Language of Familiarity and Intimacy

In the course of fieldwork in different regions of the Turkish republic, I encountered elaborate vocabularies of personal dignity, intimate exchange, and social relationship. The prominence of such vocabularies, not to mention the large number of conventional greetings, expressions, and proverbs used in everyday conversations, is a direct reflection of the importance of face-to-face, person-to-person association in Turkish society. As an ethnographer, I would have to say that there is not one but many vocabularies of personhood and sociability, such that terms and usages vary from region to region, if not from town to town or even village to village. Yet these differences can also be viewed as local dialects of a common language of familiarity and intimacy.

The common language, I would say, is an artifact of the old regime that has passed over into the new regime. Transformed by and adapted to the environment of the Turkish republic, it is now addressed and claimed by the partisans of both Kemalism and Islamism, even though, strictly speaking, it is neither the one nor the other. Rather, it is an implicit philosophy of social thought and action that serves in its own right as a vehicle of family, kinship, friendship, partnership, and patronage—indeed, of all kinds of unofficial and uncodified associations.[3] It gives rise to a specific form of consciousness that is still associated with face-to-face, person-to-person relationships in salons, coffeehouses, workplaces, and offices. Circuits of interpersonal exchange operate more or less autonomously and independently of public institutions even while influencing their character.

As my notebooks began to fill with glosses on local idioms, I began to press my interlocutors to comment on the principles of social thought and practice. Occasionally I was rewarded with a kind of philosophical discourse in miniature. One of the most intriguing of these responses, which I encountered on more than one occasion, involved what might be called a "theory" of the constitution of personhood in terms of "passion" (*nefs*) and "intellect" (*akıl*). I have repeatedly found this theory to be a remarkably effective tool for understanding the way in which relationships of self and other are linguistically registered and constructed. In the paragraphs that follow, I summarize this commentary more or less in my own words.

Each individual consists of an essence of "passion," as designated by the Turkish word *nefs*. This essence has the quality of a life force that energizes both speech and action. It can be conceived of as a core of motivating emotions and desires, and it is very close to the drives that humans share with animals, such as hunger and sexuality. Indeed, the *nefs*, as an essence of passion, is what humans have in common with animals. In the case of humans, but not of animals, the *nefs* can be a driving impulse for behavior that is either noble or base. Neither of these distinctions applies to animal behavior because beasts are no more capable of doing "good" than they are capable of doing "bad."

To understand this difference, we have to consider a capacity that differentiates humans from animals. This is the faculty of the "intellect," as designated by the Turkish word *akıl*. By means of the *akıl*, the individual is able to know and accept a system of limits, prohibitions, or restrictions, such that the *nefs* is properly controlled and channeled. This is accomplished during the course of maturation as one passes from childhood to manhood or womanhood, a process that is synonymous with learning how to present oneself to others.[4] The result is a state of being (*hal*) whereby the individual is able to participate in social relations with other individuals. It is acknowledged as a condition of legitimate personhood (*namuslu bir adam, namuslu bir kadın*). The acknowledgment of legitimate personhood can come only from social others. It can never be claimed for oneself by oneself.

By the *akıl-nefs* theory, the individual's experience of social relations has an erotic quality. We can see this in two ways. First, the system of limits, prohibitions, or restrictions is not abstract or formal in character, but closely identified with intimate social relations. Accordingly, its regulations refer to body, dress, disposition, manner, and speech in a face-to-face, person-to-person setting. The individual is not merely demonstrating a learned skill but is also coming to know who he is and how he feels. Second, the constitution of legitimate personhood is accomplished not by suppressing but rather by shaping an interior of desires and emotions. Face-to-face and person-to-person relationships are a site of proper pleasures. They are occasions on which one contemplates happiness gained or lost. The personal experience of sociability potentially reaches toward a sublime of personhood achieved through association with others.

The language of familiarity and intimacy exhibits a metaphysics of personhood and sociability. A specific form of consciousness is associated with face-to-face, person-to-person relationships. Henceforth I refer to this consciousness as *popular intersubjectivity.*

Folk Traditions and Imperial Institutions

The portrayal of personhood and sociability in folktales can be shown to conform to the *akıl-nefs* theory. This means that folktales, insofar as they imagine interpersonal exchanges, stand as artifacts of popular intersubjectivity. In what follows, I examine two types of folktales as evidence of "popular" reflections on the official codes of the old regime. We shall see that the law of the sultan (*kanun*) and the law of Islam (*şeriat*) were perceived as high "orthodox" versions of a language of familiarity and intimacy. At the same time, everyday life was the locus of desires and devices that violated the proper bounds of relationships in the palace and mosque. The folktales point to a low "heterodox" version of a language of familiarity and intimacy in which subversive thoughts and practices implicitly contradict the legitimacy of imperial institutions.

Sultan and Vizier Stories

Folktales about the sultan's traveling in disguise with his vizier were commonly told in the old regime.[5] Such stories can be considered popular contemplations of imperial authority. Two mighty and august figures are imaginatively transposed from their official location in the imperial palace to the roadways, markets, and coffeehouses of everyday life. By means of the fabulous imagination—"once there was, once there wasn't (*bir varmış, bir yokmuş*)"—the "high" is conjoined with the "low" to produce a shock that provokes laughter.

The following sultan and vizier story can be considered in these terms. In this instance, the story does not relate the adventures of the sultan and vizier traveling abroad but rather an incident by which ordinary folk are brought into the confines of the palace to stand before the two. I provide only a summary of the plot rather than the full translated text:

> The sultan calls on his vizier saying he wishes to be provided amusement. The vizier finds three peasant brothers, each with an itch in a different place on his body—a dripping nose, an infected back, and a mangy scalp. Assembling them before the sultan, he tells them they will be rewarded with a gold piece if they can resist their irri-

tations for an hour. As the hour passes, the three peasants begin to reach the limits of their endurance. Unable to resist their nagging afflictions a moment longer, but unwilling to lose the proffered gold piece, they devise an ingenious response. The first brother points to the Bosphorus, saying, "Look at that fine boat that is passing," as he runs his sleeve past his sniffly nose. The second immediately responds, "Yes, and they are beating a drum on board," as he beats his head with his fists. And the third concludes, "And look how fast they are rowing," as he soothes his back by repeatedly hunching himself to ape the action of the rowers. The sultan laughs and the three brothers receive their reward from the vizier.[6]

On the elevated terraces of the palace, a little drama comically illustrates the constitution of personhood at a primary level of human experience. The urge to relieve an itch (*nefs*) is blocked by a prohibition against scratching. If desire can be controlled by accepting an imperial constraint, a handsome reward will be forthcoming. The three brothers fail the test because they scratch their itches before the allotted time has past. Even so, the sultan is pleased and the vizier gives the reward. Why is this the case?

As the three peasants call out to one another and perform their gesticulations, they refer as a group to the drummers and rowers in the passing boat. At the same time, their words and acts that describe this scene in the world at large signify their separate personal desires. That is, each response is part of a collective communication even as it is also an expression of individual desire. Hence, personal desires are controlled and channeled in accordance with the imposed constraints of interpersonal communication. If the peasants have violated the artificially conceived imperial prohibition, they have demonstrated the common law of sociability and personhood. Therefore they win the reward even though they fail the test.

This is almost right, but not entirely so. The peasants violate the common law of sociability and personhood even as they demonstrate it. Collective representations as expressions of individual desire should be *effectively,* not *artificially,* compatible with practical circumstances. From a legalistic point of view, the impracticality of collective representations as expressions of individual desire results in dissension and corruption. But from an everyday point of view, it is common knowledge that norms have to be compromised if sociability is to be sustained. To satisfy the *nefs,* which appears more as a low animal drive than as a high human ambition, the peasants have subverted the normative *akıl* (intellect) by resorting to a representational *akıl* (cleverness).

The story has staged a confrontation between the high imperial and the low plebeian. The palace formulates and enforces regulations that are intended to control and channel common desires. The peasants, who are the targets of these regulations, know that one can get what one wants only by conforming in form but not in fact. The performance of the three brothers is a reminder that imperial ideals are always defeated by everyday realities. The sultan erupts in laughter and the vizier proffers the gold piece.

The story is an artifact of a language of interpersonal relationship whose propositions are taken for granted. At the same time it suggests that this language is formally articulated in an imperial milieu but subversively manipulated in a plebeian milieu. This aspect of the tale may once have been far more obvious than it is now to citizens of the Turkish republic. The occasion that the vizier devises for the sultan's amusement bears a close resemblance to one of the most grandiose of all the imperial ceremonies staged within the palace grounds.

Palace Protocol and the Council of Victory

The ruling institution of the old regime took the form of a household organization. The sultan was a head of state who had the status of a family head. The center of his government took the form of family residence. High military and administrative officials were often raised in his residence from an early age and were considered his personal servants. The architecture of the palace grounds and ceremonies that were conducted therein were specifically designed to represent an "intimate and familiar" relationship between the head of state and his military and administrative officials. At the same time, these relationships were also rationalized and formalized in accordance with the requirements of a state organization.

On the occasion of the so-called Council of Victory celebrations in the Topkapı Palace, thousands of the highest military and administrative officials assembled in its middle court to manifest their personhood before the eyes and ears of the sultan, who was, in symbolism at least, personally present.[7] Positioned and dressed in accordance with the rules of palace protocol (*kanun*), officials stood silent and still, "as though hewn out of marble" for hours at a time.[8] Staged in part for the benefit of foreign dignitaries, these ceremonies were intended to demonstrate the power and glory of the Ottoman dynasty through the behavior of the officials so assembled. A member of the French embassy described one of these occasions held in 1573:

> The Ambassador saluted [the highest grandees of the court] with his head and they got up from their seats and bowed to him. And at a given moment all the Janissaries and other soldiers who had been standing upright and without weapons along the wall of that court did the same, in such a way that seeing so many turbans incline together was like observing a vast field of ripe corn moving gently under the light puff of Zephyr. . . . We looked with great pleasure and even greater admiration at this frightful number of Janissaries and other soldiers standing all along the walls of this court, with hands joined in front in the manner of monks, in such silence that it seemed we were not looking at men but statues. And they remained immobile in that way more than seven hours, without talking or moving. Certainly it is almost impossible to comprehend this discipline and this obedience when one has not seen it. . . . After leaving this court we mounted our horses where we had dismounted upon arrival. . . . Standing near the wall beyond the path we saw pass all these thousands of Janissaries and other soldiers who in the court had resembled a palisade of statues, now transformed not into men but famished wild beasts or unchained dogs.[9]

The mass of officials, standing silent and still before the symbolic presence of the sultan, were intended to illustrate the constitution of personhood as defined by imperial regulations (*kanun*). Similarly, the unruly and boisterous behavior of the soldiers upon leaving the palace illustrates, by way of contrast, the human energy controlled and channeled in the constitution of personhood.

The story of the three peasants required to stand before the sultan and the vizier without scratching their itches is an obvious parody of the Council of Victory ceremonies. Originally conceived to draw an invidious comparison between a pretentious imperial ceremony and the subversive practices of everyday life, its point was eventually forgotten in the course of its transmission from the Ottoman past to the republican present. For our purposes, the invidious comparison implies that the palatial and extrapalatial worlds are based on the same language of interpersonal relationship. The difference between the two is also suggested by the simple tale. The palatial world has the properties of a formalized and rational-ized construction. The extrapalatial world has the properties of a system of communication and behavior that is honored by its violation.

Nasrettin Hodja Stories

Sultan and vizier stories describe scenes in which the high and mighty come into contact with the low and plebeian. The results often involve ridicule, but the target of the tale is never predictable. Sometimes impe-rial pomposity and pretension are exposed by an encounter with the re-alities of everyday life. Sometimes popular hypocrisy and dissimulation are exposed by an encounter with the wisdom of the just ruler. In con-trast, Nasrettin Hodja stories more consistently tell of simple people doing ordinary things.[10] By the very logic of this difference, the humor of this kind of story is often at the expense of what is supposed to be right think-ing and practice.

Nasrettin Hodja stories tell of an individual who, by his very title (*hoca*), is understood to be an expert in the sacred Law of Islam, the code of proper personhood and sociability. More than a few Nasrettin Hodja stories are staged in, or very near, the mosque where adult men assemble for Friday prayers.[11] These features of the tales are intended to serve entirely mis-chievous purposes. The wily hodja teaches us that improper, illogical, and stupefying experiences disrupt and confuse what should be proper, log-ical, and sensible social behavior.

One of the best known, and one of the shortest, examples of this type of tale follows:

> The Hodja's neighbor wishes to borrow his donkey. The Hodja de-clines the request saying that he has no donkey to loan out. At that very moment, the neighbor hears the bray of the Hodja's donkey coming from the stable and rebukes the Hodja for telling a lie, say-ing, "Do you not hear the sound/voice (*ses*) of the donkey?" The Hodja replies, "You do not believe my word (*söz*), but you accept the word (*söz*) of a donkey?"[12]

In this story, the hodja selfishly does not want to lend his donkey and wishes to evade the obligation of neighborly reciprocity. Since he cannot legitimately refuse the request, he denies that he even has a donkey. When caught in this deception, the hodja accuses his neighbor of believing the donkey's sound (*ses*) in order to fault the word (*söz*) of the hodja. In effect, the neighbor improperly attends to the donkey, a brute beast wholly lacking in moral qualities. The joke of the story involves the hodja's attempt to invoke the norms of personhood and sociability at the very moment he is caught violating them.

As in the sultan and vizier story, the *akıl/nefs* theory is an implicit, not an explicit, feature of the Nasrettin Hodja story because its propositions are taken for granted. The contrast between the donkey's bray and the hodja's speech is a contrast between the utterances of living creatures with and without *akıl*. The hodja's words should reflect his recognition of the rules of personhood and sociability, a recognition whereby instinctive selfishness would be replaced with affectionate generosity. Once again, we see how the normative *akıl* (intellect), by which one registers social constraints, becomes instead a representational *akıl* (cleverness), by which one conceals motives, evades the law, and misleads others. Thus, the behavior of Nasrettin Hodja reveals the *nefs* as an anarchical and disorderly energy that subverts the proper form of interpersonal communication and relationship.

The Sacred Law and the Friday Prayers

Nasrettin Hodja, the hero of stories in which proper communication and relationship are subverted, is simultaneously a pillar of respectability, an expert in the sacred law of Islam, and a leader of Friday prayers in the mosque. He is betwixt and between the everyday utterances (*parole*) and the orthodox grammar (*langue*) of a language of interpersonal relationship. As a master of the former, he is a punster and trickster. As the master of the latter, he knows the law, delivers the Friday sermon, and leads the prayers. So the language of interpersonal relationship, which is "at risk" and "in play" in the Nasrettin Hodja stories, is assumed within the narrative tradition itself to have a connection with the beliefs and rites of Islam.

The connection is clearly spelled out in a contemporary "science of being" manual (*ilmihal*) published to provide instructions for the proper observance of religious obligations.[13] In the section on "Worship," for example, the author explains the obligation to perform the five daily prayers in terms that recall the language of interpersonal relationship we have been considering. He begins with the sentence, "Worship is a way of honoring and revering God."[14] Its terms "honoring and revering" (*saygı ve ta'zim göstermek*) could also be applied to the kind of behavior that is enjoined before the father, elder, patron, lord, or sultan.

In his next sentence, the author describes the relationship of worshiper and divinity as though it were a relationship of client and patron. The believer has the duties of a servant (*kulluk görevi*) who has received generous gifts from his august and mighty (*yüce*) creator. The believer is obliged to return his thanks to God just as he would be obliged to someone "who offers his place on a bus or a glass of water." The author then characterizes worship as a form of spiritual nourishment (*ruhun gıdası*) that is equivalent to bodily nourishment (*yemek ve içmek*). The theme of the quenching of hunger and thirst leads to a description of prayer as the means for controlling and channeling the *nefs*:

> In worship, we always fight with the bad feelings of the *nefs* and we draw them out of the spirit. We cleanse bad thoughts from our spirit. In this way, we become a completely clean human being both inwardly and outwardly. In the truest sense, someone who performs prayer has become the master of the desires of the *nefs*. He has become bridled (*gem vurmuş*). He does everything in its proper place and by its proper measure. The greatest battle is the war with the *nefs*. The greatest form of bravery is to become the master of the *nefs*.[15]

The author concludes by portraying the five prayers as the means for constituting personhood before the presence of divinity. The result is a sublime of personhood achieved through association with God, rather than through association with others:

> With the five prayers one is able to be nourished by God's great riches, to be purified by contact with his mercy, to present oneself and to humble oneself before the God of man and to come into a relationship with His meaning, and to establish in the body the material and spiritual order in the cosmos.[16]

The same metaphysics of personhood and sociability that is part of everyday life reappears on the level of state and religion. From the perspective of the language of interpersonal relationship, the Friday prayers and the Council of Victory are paradigmatically equivalent. Believers perform their ablutions and then assemble with their neighbors in the mosque. Standing in ranked formation before the niche (*mihrap*) oriented toward Mecca (*kıble*), they enact in unison words and deeds that are addressed to God and scripted by the sacred law (*şeriat*). Substitute sultan for God, *kanun* for *şeriat*, officials for believers, palace for mosque, and sovereign power for religious truth and the result is the Council of Victory. This means that the imperial palace and the imperial mosque each stake a separate claim on popular intersubjectivity. Rationalized and formalized as *kanun*, it is the basis of a ruling institution. Rationalized and formalized as *şeriat*, it is the basis of divine creation.

With this understanding of the cultural weight and structural position of a language of interpersonal relationship, we can now examine the sites of the memorial tomb and Kocatepe Mosque. As in the old regime, representations of state and religion in the new regime stake a claim on popular intersubjectivity. The entirely new environment of a mass society of anonymous others drives these representations in new directions.

The Memorial Tomb

In the fall of 1922, the Grand National Assembly, at the urging of Mustafa Kemal, resolved that a government consisting of the "sovereignty of an individual had ceased to exist . . . and passed forever into history," thereby bringing to an end the Ottoman sultanate.[17] In the spring of 1924, having already proclaimed the republic with its capital at Ankara, the Grand National Assembly, again persuaded by Mustafa Kemal, abolished the caliphate and the sacred Law of Islam.[18] These events recall how the new nation-state was contingent on the suppression of two key institutions, Ottomanism and Islamism—one the sovereignty of an individual, and the other a system of a divinely revealed law. The citizens of the republic would represent their existence in terms of a new past, present, and future. A new way of being would displace the old. Ottomanism would be inoperable because it would have no register in thought or feeling. Islam would remain a matter of private practice and sentiment, rigorously excluded from public life.

Soon after Atatürk's death on November, 10, 1938, the decision was taken to erect a monument in his memory (figs. 10.1, 10.2). From the outset, the Atatürk Memorial Tomb (*Anıtkabir*) was conceived of as a great ceremonial center for the Turkish nation. In this respect, it was part of the effort of Turkish nationalists to define, and thereby control, the symbolism of public life.[19] It would be sited on a prominent hill overlooking Ankara and surveying the plains of central Anatolia. Its spaces and buildings would be of exceptional magnificence and grandeur, making it one of the most ambitious architectural projects of the republican period. Its

10.1. Anıtkabir, the Atatürk Memorial Tomb, from the central square looking toward the Hall of Honor. (Photograph by the author.)

10.2. Anıtkabir, from the Hall of Honor looking toward the central square. (Photograph by the author.)

material composition, consisting of marble and stone quarried in dispersed sections of the new national domain, would reflect the territorial integrity of the nation. After a design competition was held in 1941–42, a jury of international membership selected the project of a Turkish team, Onat and Arda, for the realization of the monument.[20] Ground was broken on September 9, 1944, and construction proceeded for almost a decade, during which time the original design continued to be reworked.[21]

On November 10, 1953, the fifteenth anniversary of Atatürk's death, his body was transferred by official state procession from the Ethnographic Museum and laid to rest in a crypt in the Hall of Honor.[22] Since that time, the memorial tomb has served as a site for rites commemorating the founder of the Turkish republic. Official ceremonies are conducted there on the anniversary of Atatürk's death, during visits to Turkey by foreign heads of state, and on other official occasions of state. Members of private and public associations—including schoolteachers, schoolchildren, military officers, business executives, municipal officials, and club members —may assemble at the tomb to pay their respects to Atatürk. Groups of ordinary citizens also visit the site to browse through its museum displays, admire the views of the countryside from its walkways and courts, and pause for a moment before the founder's resting place.[23]

Though completed some thirty years after the founding of the republic, the memorial tomb commemorates the ambitious projects of nationhood so vigorously pursued during its first decades. In this respect, various theses of nationalist ideology, firmly in place by the 1930s, are referenced by the features of its buildings' decors and facades. Thesis: the arts of civilization will flourish in the new Turkish republic. Reference: bas-reliefs and sculptures represent the people of the new nation. Thesis: the Turks have been a nation of Anatolia since ancient times, their earliest representatives being Sumerians and Hittites. References: the pathway from the outer wall to the central court is lined with Hittite lions, and the Hall of Honor was intended to resemble a Sumerian ziggurat.[24] Thesis: the Turkish republic is a representative of the Turkish folk of Anatolia. Reference: walls and ceilings feature abstracted motifs of Turkish flatweaves in paint and mosaic.

Though such references are encountered, the memorial tomb was designed as a place for solemn visitations and observances rather than for the display of nationalist ideology. During informal and formal visits, citizens of the Turkish republic would recall its founder and pay him their respects. In this regard, the tomb is a site for interpersonal exchange between citizen and founder. Symbolically at least, the citizen can be heard and seen by the founder, just as the founder can be heard and seen by the citizen.

Informal Occasions: The Personhood of Atatürk

On informal occasions, visitors view the sculptures, inscriptions, and artifacts of the memorial tomb as they stroll about its walkways, courts, and museums. Hard-edged bas-reliefs depict Atatürk leading the Turkish people during the War of Independence. Excerpts from his speeches, inscribed in the new romanized script, appear in the form of gigantic tableaux. At one corner of the site, visitors see the cannon carriage that was used to transport Atatürk's body to the tomb. At another corner, they see his official and ceremonial cars, in which he toured the nation. At another location, designated the Atatürk Museum, they can view his personal possessions: shoes, suits and hats, shirts, collars, handkerchiefs, cuff links, walking sticks, a stickpin, ties, toiletry articles, his hand mirror, eyeglasses, cigarette holders, military medals, a uniform, a pistol, a desk set, samples of his handwriting, a library, and twinned photographs of himself and his mother. They also find a display of personal gifts from the heads of the newly organized institutions of the republic, such as the Industrial Bank, the Post, Telephone, and Telegraph, and the Grand National Assembly.

Going on to the rooms designated the Art Gallery, they see money and stamps with representations of the face and figure of Atatürk. Eventually, they enter the Hall of Honor itself and approach the symbolic tomb of Atatürk, located above the actual tomb. Here they contemplate a national leader and founder of the republic against the backdrop of the Anatolian countryside.

The informal visitor to the memorial tomb is able to know the personhood of Atatürk through the lens of national destiny, most coherently by his leadership during the War of Independence, but also, more vividly and intimately, by personal possessions from the period in which he was president of the Republic of Turkey. In this respect, the memorial tomb does not tell the story of national history, refer to attributes of a national tradition, teach the principles of national citizenship, or explain the national constitution. At the most important site of the republic, the nation is not conceived of through its history, ideology, laws, or constitution. Rather, the argument of a language of familiarity and intimacy has been reformulated in the terms of citizen and nation.

Formal Occasions: Assemblies in the Central Court

The coordination of architecture and ceremony during formal visits to the Atatürk Memorial Tomb demonstrates this reformulation openly and explicitly. On state occasions, smaller or larger assemblies pay their respects to the founder of the Turkish republic. Individuals stand in ranked formation in the central court, before the Hall of Honor. They are in the personal presence of the national leader and founder. He observes and listens as they stand silent and still.[25]

Before their eyes, they can see a plinth on the steps leading to the Hall of Honor. On it they can read a message from the founder, inscribed in romanized letters: "Without condition or restriction, sovereignty belongs to the nation" (*Hakimiyet kayıtsız şartsız milletindir*). The message announces not the democratic principle of popular representation but the condition of external constraints that impinges on each individual, not the least of whom would be the founder himself. Personhood is constituted within the space and time of nationhood.

Looking to the left, participants can make out the "Address to Youth" behind the frontal colonnade of the Hall of Honor. This address calls for defense of the homeland in the worst of times. Its message concludes with a call for individual sacrifice: "O Turkish children of the future! . . . save the republic! The power exists in the noble blood that runs in your veins!" Looking to the right, viewers can make out the address to the Turkish nation on the occasion of the "Speech of the Tenth Year," again behind the frontal colonnade of the Hall of Honor. This message concludes with a sublime of personhood achieved through *national* association: "How fortunate is he who can say, 'I am a Turk.'"

The citizen stands before the Hall of Honor in the presence of the leader and founder in order to pay his respects. The three written communications announce the framework within which this interpersonal exchange takes place. Citizen and founder interact within a framework of constraints imposed by nationhood. In exchange for individual sacrifice there is the promise of the sublime.

At the site of the memorial tomb, architecture and ceremony are coordinated in accordance with a paradigm that recalls the Council of Victory at the imperial palace. Tomb substitutes for palace, the symbolic presence of national founder for that of dynastic ruler, a central court (*iç meydan*) for a middle court (*orta yer*), high officials of the republic (*cümhürreisi, b.m.m reisi, generaller*) for high officials of the palace, representatives

**Kabir iç meydanındaki
merasim planı**

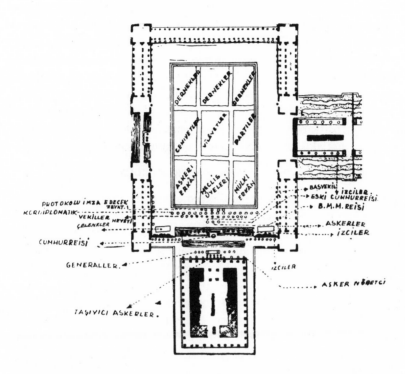

10.3. Anıtkabir, plan for ceremonies in the central square. (Reproduced from the memorial tomb brochure, *Devrim Gençliği İlavesi,* ca. 1953.)

of a national polity (*meclis üyeleri, mülki erkân, askeri erkân, vilayetler, cemiyetler, dernekler, ve partiler*) for household staff (*kullar*), diplomatic officials in residence (*kordiplomatik*) for visiting foreign embassies, and modern dress (*şapka, kravat, and kostüm*) for imperial sumptuary (fig. 10.3).[26] A narrow loyalty between a dynastic ruler and his household staff has been converted into a broad loyalty between a national founder and a national elite representing a national citizenry.

In the Atatürk Memorial Tomb, we have a ceremonial center of the nation-state, first chosen as a design in 1942 and finally completed in 1953, that parallels a ceremonial center of the old regime, already defunct in 1853.[27] But insofar as this is the case, the imperial legacy in Turkish nationalism does not pass directly from palace to tomb. It detours from palace downward to a form of popular intersubjectivity (engendered by imperial institutions) and then upward to tomb.[28] The paradigmatic similarities between the architecture and ceremony of nation and empire are not intentional; the early Kemalists would have had no interest in imitating the late Ottomans.[29] The similarities result incidentally from the Kemalist effort to stake a claim on the experience of personhood and sociability that was left intact by the nationalist program of reforms. Nationalism was to be presented to the people of the Turkish republic as an official and codified version of a language of interpersonal relationship. The experience of participants in the formal ceremonies held in the central square of the memorial tomb can be easily read from this point of view.

Symmetry, Rectilinearity, Proportion

The scripting of architecture and ceremony at the memorial tomb emphasizes an interpersonal exchange, rather than the various strands of nationalist history, ideology, or constitutionalism. Nevertheless, the site leaves visitors with a strong impression about the character of public life in Turkey. It does so by means of geometric forms and voids, rather than through myth and symbol.

By principles of symmetry, rectilinearity, and proportion, the memorial tomb constructs "a unitary space of geometric structure."[30] The result is an arrangement of pathways, courts, and buildings that affirms the possibility of a rational analysis of space. The monument represents a consistent and pervasive intention. The form of the parts always points to the presence of the whole. The overall lack of emphasis on decor and facade at the monument does not allow visitors to miss this point. The relative absence of historical references and aesthetic intentions, given the elaborate ideologies of the nationalist movement, forces visitors to recognize the abstract logic of its geometric rationality. In the Turkish republic, the combined projects of modernity and nationhood involved the planning and construction of a public space and time for a mass society of anonymous others. The principles of reason and science set the new modernist and nationalist regime apart from the old personalist and imperialist regime.

The striking feature of the design principles at the memorial tomb is the omnipresence of geometrical frames. Walkways and courts, quotations and bas-reliefs, colonnades and arches, borders and pavements all take the form of rectilinear frames. One is always obliged to walk, to read, and to look through frames set within frames. When the eye shifts toward the capital city and the Anatolia countryside (and they are constantly visible as one moves about the site), they are always seen through frames set within frames. Frames within frames impose themselves on the movements and perceptions of the ordinary citizen during his or her informal visits to the site. Frames within frames organize the officials who stand in ranked assemblies during the formal occasions of state. In this fashion, architecture and ceremony at the tomb define a space that obeys a consistent and coherent rationale, signifying a consciousness of citizenship defined by limits and boundaries.

If this is a modernist-nationalist public space and time, however, it is of a special kind. The memorial tomb does not invite the individual to comprehend his or her status as citizen of a nation so much as it defines subjectivity by limits and boundaries. This is not so much a space of Enlightenment reason and history as a space of *akıl,* a space experienced as a constrained interpersonal relationship. The memorial tomb is not a Hobbesian, Kantian, Hegelian, or Durkheimian site. Its philosophical underpinnings are elsewhere.

Designed in accordance with the new techno-scientific norms of rationalized public space and time in the Turkish republic, the memorial tomb takes on a very different meaning in its address of popular intersubjectivity. Brochures about the tomb, featuring a bust of Atatürk on their covers, represent the site itself as empty of a human presence.[31] Schematics of the site that illustrate the layout of its buildings and museums feature recticulated grids.[32] Pictures of the site usually show its walkways and courts as voids. When one visits the memorial tomb, one should not hold hands. One should not sit. One should not laugh. A unitary space of geometric structure oscillates between national identity and individual sacrifice and death. As a pure representation of the limits and boundaries of consciousness, there is nothing left for interior desire save its extinction in the name of the nation.

The Kocatepe Mosque

The Atatürk Memorial Tomb is arguably the most important site of state ceremony in the Turkish republic. Designed and built at a time when modernist influences on the nationalist movement were on the rise, it stands as a monument to the project of replacing an old order with a new order. And yet we have found that the Kemalist encoding of the nationalist imagination cannot be understood apart from its attempt to claim and exhaust the sphere of popular intersubjectivity. Turning now to the Kocatepe Mosque, we find that the tables are turned. This "great place of worship" (*ulu mabet*), newly completed in 1987, was designed and built during a period of Islamic resurgence and was intended to stand as a monument to the place of religion in Turkish society. If, however, we consider the coordination of architecture and ceremony at the mosque in terms of both the intentions of its architects and the perceptions of its caretakers, we discover that it is locked in an argument with the memorial tomb.

The idea of building a mosque in the new capital of the Turkish republic may have been proposed as early as 1934.[33] In any case, such a project was being discussed shortly after the decision was taken to build the memorial tomb. With the encouragement of officials in the Ministry of Religious Affairs, a building committee was formed in 1944, and a design competition was held in 1947. None of the entries was awarded first place, but the project submitted by Alnar and Ülgen, which proposed a structure in the simple and modest style of the earliest Ottoman mosques, received considerable support.[34] The initiative then faltered until 1956, when a personal intervention by the prime minister revived it.

Now the decision was taken to build a great place of worship in an architectural style that would "reflect the republican period" (*Cumhuriyet dönemini temsil edecek*).[35] The site of Kocatepe was chosen so that the structure would be within the urban precincts on a hill "dominating Ankara" (*Ankara'ya hakim*).[36] After another design competition in 1957, the jury awarded a first prize to the project submitted by two Turkish architects, Dalokay and Tekelioğlu, but it was not recommended for construction until certain revisions had been undertaken. The winning project proposed a mosque in the form of a sectioned "rind" or "skin" with minarets stationed at each of its four corners. This modernistic structure was to be set among, or coordinated with, other buildings, a practice that otherwise recalled the classical Ottoman "mosque complex" (*külliye*). These buildings were to house a library, a conference room, a museum, a two-hundred-vehicle autopark, a tourist market, a kitchen, a polyclinic, the offices of the Ministry of Religious Affairs, and the campus of an Advanced Islam Institute.

Although some of the buildings, such as the offices of the Ministry of Religious Affairs, were eventually completed, the design for the mosque remained controversial. Objections to the structural soundness of the "rind" or "skin" design, which some defenders of the mosque considered entirely specious, eventually prevailed. Yet a third design competition was

10.4. Kocatepe Mosque, from the stairways leading to the plaza. (Photograph by the author.)

opened in 1967. The winning project, submitted by Tayla and Uluengin, proposed a gigantic structure that closely resembled an Ottoman mosque of the classical period. Construction began on October 30, 1967, and continued off and on for twenty years, owing to periodic shortages of funds. Eventually, in 1981, the Religious Endowments of Turkey took over the financing, and construction proceeded apace. First proposed in the 1930s, debated as a project for thirty years, and fitfully under construction for twenty, Kocatepe Mosque was officially opened on August 28, 1987, as a "national place of worship" (fig. 10.4).

The reference point for the design of the new mosque had shifted back and forth in historical time. In 1947, the mosque proposed for the capital had been one of modest dimensions that drew upon the single-unit mosque of the early, pre-imperial Ottoman period. In 1957, the concept of a national place of worship was explicitly formulated, the projected size of the mosque expanded accordingly, and a postimperial, modernist design was favored. By 1967, the national place of worship was contemplated in conjunction with a capital city whose population now exceeded one million souls, and the projected size of the mosque complex surpassed the scope of the 1947 and 1957 designs by far.[37] The new mosque was to be modeled on the classical Ottoman mosque, the glorious architectural achievement of the high imperial period. Its prototype is said to be the Sultanahmet Mosque, a late Ottoman mosque of the early seventeenth century, save that the scale of the new national mosque is intended to exceed that of the imperial structure it emulates.[38]

My Visit to the Kocatepe Mosque

In the fall of 1987, I was graciously welcomed at the Kocatepe Mosque by two officials of the Religious Endowment of Turkey. They were enthusiastic about the new mosque, which had been inaugurated little more than a month earlier, an occasion that was attended by many thousands of citizens. During a tour of the site, one of my hosts explained the history of the mosque's construction, its purpose and symbolism, its relationship with the surrounding buildings and landscape, and the significance of what could be seen from its various prospects.

Taking me first to the central mosque building, my host claimed that the interior (*harem*) was considerably larger than that of the classical Ottoman mosque. Whether this is true or not, my host's emphasis on its immensity is impressionistically exact. The space beneath the dome of the mosque seems very, very large in comparison with its classical predecessors. The effect had been achieved, my host explained, by the use of advanced techniques of construction, that is to say, reinforced concrete. Contemporary architects and builders could mimic the form of the classical mosque but free themselves from the limits of a dome system fashioned from stone and mortar. The four inner columns that support the dome in the classical mosque are necessarily huge for structural reasons, but the four inner columns of the Kocatepe Mosque could be reduced in width and yet raise the central dome (*ana kubbe*) to a greater height. Accordingly, the dimensions of the furnishings and accouterments of the mosque also had to be expanded. The niche indicating the direction of prayer (*mihrap*) and the staired pulpit (*minber*) are towering. The galleries (*mahfel*) are doubled to fill the space between the floor and the elevated dome.

Kocatepe Mosque does not just imitate, it also exaggerates its imperial exemplar—but by what logic? As we shall see, the mosque would symbolize the public sphere of the nation, but in a peculiar way. As one might have guessed, the use of advanced construction techniques is supposed to symbolize the modernity of Islam during the republican period. To some degree, this must have been the architects' intention, and it was certainly on the minds of my hosts. They mentioned various features of the mosque building which demonstrated that Islam during the republican period was modernist (*çağdaş*) in the sense of being technically advanced and sophisticated. Each of the four minarets is equipped with an automatic elevator. A centralized heating system warms the floor. A conference room features an intercom system connecting each seat with the podium. Lighting is provided by electrified chandeliers taking the form of large illuminated globes.

But my hosts did not consistently argue that the mosque demonstrated the technical prowess of its designers and builders. On the contrary, they justified the abandonment of the "rind" design of 1957 by claiming that it exceeded the capacities of Turkish construction firms.[39] Rather, the logic of the Kocatepe Mosque, which differentiates it from the Sultanahmet Mosque, has to do with its referencing of the nationalist imagination, the experience of a mass society of anonymous others. This is what lay behind my guide's repeated emphasis on numerical quantities and measurements. The Kocatepe Mosque projects an image of a vast throng of believers coming from all over the nation and assembling as a great indivisible unity. Viewing a series of spatial voids and hearing a litany of magnitudes conjured up the presence of an immense crowd of interacting believers.

Leaving the interior of the mosque building, my host took me to the adjoining auditorium, where conferences could be held. The seating capacity (six hundred persons) was duly noted, and the intended purpose of the intercom system was demonstrated. We then explored three further floors under the mosque itself, consisting of 15,000 square meters of space. Still under construction at the time, these floors had been provisionally set aside for a vast supermarket with luxury goods. But some were arguing that the space would be better used for cultural and educational purposes, such as book fairs or museum displays.[40] Leaving the buildings, we walked about the monumental forecourt, which is bordered by domes the dimensions of which are not very different from those of the largest Ottoman mosques.

Then, as we exited the forecourt, my guide's narrative became more animated and acquired a new intensity. A vast, paved space with no exact precedent in the older mosque complexes surrounds the new mosque building. My host claimed that 24,000 people could assemble to perform the prayers within the mosque and 100,000 could be accommodated in the combined space of the interior, forecourt, and surrounding plaza. As the tour continued, he pointed out the various features of the mosque that were designed to accommodate, but also to symbolize, the assemblage of large masses. There are three large, marble-paneled rooms for performing ablutions (*gasilhane*), two for men, one for women. There are eight marble slabs (*musalla taşları*), set out in a single line, for laying out the corpse on the occasion of funeral ceremonies.[41]

My host led me through covered passageways lined chock-a-block with hundreds, perhaps thousands, of little compartments for the depositing of shoes. He took me to view the wide stairways rising to the site where he spoke of thousands and thousands of believers coming and going. He then explained how a main thoroughfare of Ankara (between Küçükesat and Mithatpaşa) passed directly under the mosque building. This meant that the Kocatepe Mosque was connected with the mass transportation system of the capital city. Descending into the two-story, underground garage, he described how it would enable the efficient massing of believers.[42] Large numbers of citizens might arrive by bus or automobile (vehicle capacity 1,200), move quickly by foot to the interior of the mosque, perform their ablutions and prayers, and return to their vehicles to make their way back to their homes or workplaces.

The classical Ottoman mosque took the form of an intricate structural system of domes, half domes, and small domes. This peculiar structure, achieved only after decades of variation and experimentation, was determined by the objective of raising as large a dome as possible over as large an open space as possible.[43] The result was a magnificent interior where thousands of believers might assemble on the occasion of the Friday prayers. Such a mosque monumentalized Ottoman support for Islamic society, but it had nothing to do with masses and anonymity.[44] In the late twentieth century, during the age of the nation-state, a replica of the imperial mosque has taken on a new meaning altogether: it is a place of worship in a mass society of anonymous others. As my host took me from one spatial void to another, he always saw them filled with people coming from all parts of the capital and all parts of the nation.[45] The brochure he provided, here translated and quoted verbatim without omissions, makes the same point:

> "The mosque" . . . as its name implies, gathers together . . . At the delayed opening of Kocatepe during Ramazan of 1986, this mean-

ing was actually experienced . . . Kocatepe was filled to overflow-
ing with the faithful who hurried to come from surrounding
provinces (*il*), districts (*ilçe*), and regions. . . . [T]his streaming to
Kocatepe, the greatest place of worship of the Republican period
. . . was explaining the yearning of the Turkish nation for growing
and uniting.[46]

Here again is a sublime of personhood achieved through national association, but it has been strangely transformed into a scene of an anonymous nation-state solidarity (complete with references to bureaucratic districts) that nonetheless satisfies a personally experienced yearning (*hasret*)
for coming together.

As we have seen, "science of being" manuals (*ilmihal*) commonly explain canonical beliefs and practices as the means for controlling the passions of the self (*nefs*). According to such a logic, the Friday assembly is
that occasion when individuals come together as a community, stand before the niches in the mosque, orient themselves toward Mecca, and manifest their personhood before the presence of divinity. I have taken pains
to repeat these matters because neither my guide nor the brochure contemplated the mosque according to such an Islamic canon, but associated it with an image of a desire for assembly among thousands and thousands of believers coming from here and there all over the Turkish
nation-state.

Guide and brochure reveal that the Kocatepe Islamists are contemplating
the new mosque as a means of composing the two horizons of experience: circuits of interpersonal exchange and a mass society of anonymous
others. Having reached this conclusion, I can see in my mind's eye the
crisscrossing and intersecting lines that inscribe the broad plaza of the
mosque, the curvilinear arabesques of the painted walls and ceilings, and
the geometrical interlacing of windows, doors, and their framing. But at
the same moment, I also recall the main thoroughfare by which buses
and cars reach its underground parking garage, the conference room where
each seat is fitted with devices for electronic communication, and the
vast space beneath the forecourt that was to be a supermarket, department store, or book fair. Architectural motifs of the classical mosque and
techno-scientific artifacts of mass society are jarringly fused together out
of a yearning for association.

The Kocatepe Mosque offers the promise of a faceless national massing that would nonetheless fulfill a personal longing for interpersonal as-

10.5. Kocatepe Mosque, from the minaret looking down to the plaza. (Photograph by the author.)

sociation. Kocatepe Mosque may look like a classical Ottoman mosque of the high imperial period, but it is intended to stake an Islamic claim on popular intersubjectivity in a mass society of anonymous others. The Kocatepe Mosque, like the Atatürk Memorial Tomb, also grapples with two horizons of experience, but in a different way.

Clearing a Space in the City

The mosque, like the tomb, moreover, is designed to impose itself on the city. Before beginning my tour, my two hosts explained why Kocatepe had been chosen as the site for constructing a "national place of worship." First, it was a hill that was clearly visible from many points in the city of Ankara. And second, the existing structures on this hill could be demolished to provide a sweeping view of the city.[47] The mosque complex was to appear as a distinct silhouette visible from many other parts of the city, just as most of the city would be visible from the grounds of the mosque complex. The site was chosen, therefore, to establish a relationship between the mosque and the capital. The space and time of the former would be coordinated with the space and time of the latter. This objective had a direct influence on the design of the minarets and the plaza. The four triple-tiered minarets are higher than any others in Turkey.[48] The plaza achieves more than providing a large space for the overflow of believers who might assemble at the mosque. Described as a "plateau" (*plato*) in the brochure, it is constructed as an elevated viewing platform that provides sweeping vistas of the surrounding city (fig. 10.5).

During our walk together outside the mosque building, my host took me out to the plaza's edge. Making a gesture, he said, "Look there in the distance, what do you see?" Following the motion of his hand, I saw the outline of the Hall of Honor of the memorial tomb in the distance, seemingly more or less at the same level as the plateau on which we stood. The new national place of worship, no less than the memorial tomb, occupied a prominent place in the landscape (the minarets of the mosque are clearly visible from the central square of the tomb). This had been, he told me, the explicit objective of the designers and builders of the Kocatepe Mosque. As its architects planned their mosque, as its caretakers provide tours of the mosque, and as ordinary citizens visit the mosque, they have had the principal monument of the Turkish republic in the back of their minds.

Later, my host insisted that we take an elevator and ascend to the top of a minaret. From atop it, he described once again how the mosque dominated the capital as we enjoyed the splendid view of the city of Ankara. And once again, he pointed out the memorial tomb, which was not in the center but on the edge of the city and which was now not merely on a level with but actually well below our station. The Kocatepe Mosque, no less than the memorial tomb, had been conceived within the framework of the nationalist imagination. Indeed, the tomb is the precondition for the mosque, which does not stand singly and alone in the imagination of its designers or caretakers but stands as a response to the challenge of its predecessor in the distance. The Kocatepe Mosque is intended to compete with the Atatürk Memorial Tomb for the definition of the space and time of capital and nation.

This leaves us with the following questions: In what way do the two monuments compete with one another? How do they differently define the experience of space and time in the city and the nation? To find answers to these questions, we have to understand how the two monuments draw different relationships between the two horizons of experience: circuits of interpersonal exchanges and a mass society of anonymous others.

Here and There, Presence and Absence

After the tour, I again sat with my two hosts in their offices. Without my raising the issue, they explained how the Kocatepe Mosque represented a side of the Turkish nation (*millet*) that had been heretofore unrepresented at the memorial tomb. For them, what was "present" at the mosque had as its precondition what was "absent" from the tomb. What was this thing? One could easily answer by stating that the Kocatepe Mosque represented the place of Islam in the life of the nation. But what does such an answer tell us, after all? What would this proper name, "Islam," have meant for my two hosts? To what aspect of their individual experience would such a term, "Islam," refer? My hosts did not speak of so vague a generality as "the place of Islam in the life of the nation." They explained what was present at the mosque and absent at the tomb by pointing to our experience together in the privacy of their offices.

During our meeting, we had exchanged greetings, we had sat together, we had sipped tea together, and we had conversed together. As is usually the case on these occasions, I had been asked my name, my profession, and my place of residence. They inquired about my father and mother and about my own family. Now, as we contemplated the difference between the mosque and the tomb, one of my hosts posed the question, "Don't you notice something different about your visit here and your visits to other government offices?" I did not understand what he meant. "Here," he said, "our relationships are softer and our conversation is more pleasant." His colleague nodded in agreement. I understood then that they were pointing to the experience of interpersonal relationships, and in doing so, claiming this experience to be exclusively associated with the relationships of believers.

This is the same sentiment that had been articulated in the mosque brochure, in which a mass desire for a sublime of personhood achieved through national association is described as "the yearning of the Turkish nation for growing and uniting." For my two hosts, Kocatepe Mosque draws a new kind of relationship between popular intersubjectivity and a mass society of anonymous others. The experience of a mass society of anonymous others opens up a void in the psyche of Turkish citizens. Moreover, the memorial tomb, where the relationship between personhood and nationhood demands sacrifice and death, symbolizes that very void. In response, a gigantic Islamic monument is a countersymbol that represents the possibility of filling this void. Kocatepe Mosque figures a national solidarity as an Islamic experience of personhood through sociability.

Thinking about this conversation sometime after my visit, I recalled an incongruous element of the gigantesque mosque complex. At the center of the complex, tucked away among its colossal buildings, an open-air grape bower is maintained for the pleasure of its higher officials. Sometime around 1970, I was served tea there by acquaintances in the Ministry of Religious Affairs, which had recently been completed as the first phase of the Kocatepe complex. Throughout all the razing and demolition that took place during the twenty-year construction of the site, it was somehow preserved intact. The survival of the grape bower, an exemplar of hundreds of thousands in the towns and villages of Anatolia, is perhaps not an accident. It stands as a naked representation of intimate and familiar association, which the Kocatepe Mosque, now looming before it, monumentalizes as a dimension of nationalist space and time.

Conclusion

When the Atatürk Memorial Tomb was completed was 1953, the single-party system had given way to the multiparty system. The tutorial democracy of the Turkish republic had become a practicing democracy. Nonetheless, the architecture and ceremony of the new site did not represent concepts of citizenship, assembly, and constitution so much as they refigured an older grammar and vocabulary. For the Kemalists, the constitution of personhood had to be removed from circuits of interpersonal exchange and transposed to a mass society of anonymous others. This was accomplished by staking an *absolute* claim on a language of familiarity and intimacy, such that nothing was left over for the interpersonal loyalties of everyday experience. The colonnades, buildings, pavements, and facades of the memorial tomb feature rectilinear frameworks signifying the extinction of individual desire. The exchange between citizen and founder represents personhood though sacrifice and death in the name of nationhood. The architecture and ceremony of the memorial tomb therefore articulate a contradiction. They stake a claim on a language of familiarity and intimacy, even as they refuse to recognize its place in everyday life.

Thirty-four years after its completion, the Kocatepe Mosque responds to the challenge of the memorial tomb by addressing precisely this contradiction, but only to invert its terms rather than resolve it. The mosque is understood to represent a yearning for growing and uniting that is coursing through the entire nation. This interpretation on the part of both my hosts and their brochure depends on two thoughts, neither of which was entirely in place before the founding of the Turkish republic.

First, the Kocatepe Islamists identify the performance of Islamic beliefs and rituals with a desire for interpersonal association rather than primarily with believer, divinity, and cosmos. That is to say, religion now refers, as it never did before, to the experience of personhood through sociability. In effect, the Kocatepe Mosque stakes an Islamic claim on popular inter-subjectivity in everyday life.

Second, the Kocatepe Islamists also impute to the nation a desire for intimate association. That is, they conceive of a mass society of anonymous others in terms of the experience of personhood through sociability. In doing so, they recognize the existence of a mass society, but they understand it in terms of circuits of interpersonal exchange rather than recognize it for what it is.

The two monuments are locked in an argument for sovereignty over a psychic terrain. The one poses the problem that a mass society of anonymous others represents for a language of familiarity and intimacy; the other reacts to the absence implicit in this formulation with an impossible figure of nationhood as desire for association.

Notes

1. In the spring of 1994, large crowds gathered at the Atatürk Memorial Tomb to protest the defamation of Mustafa Kemal's reputation by a member of the Welfare Party (Refah Partisi). Other officials of the party disowned these remarks and reaffirmed their respect for the founder of the Turkish republic.

2. See Jürgen Habermas, "Modernity: An Incomplete Project," in Hal Foster, ed., *The Anti-Aesthetic: Essays on Postmodern Culture,* Port Townsend, Washington: Bay Press, 1983, 13. In reference to the nation-states of western Europe, Habermas differentiates "the project of modernity" from "the vital heritages of everyday life." See also Alexis de Tocqueville, *Democracy in America,* vols. 1 and 2, New York: Vintage Books, 1945. His account of the United States is divided into a study of institutions, laws, and government (vol. 1) and a study of intellectual movements, personal sentiments, social mores, and political society (vol. 2). See also Şerif Mardin, *Religion and Social Change in Turkey: The Case of Bediüzzaman Said Nursi,* Albany: State University of New York Press, 1989, 163–64. He differentiates two levels of

late Ottoman thinking: concepts of state institutions and social orders and concepts that consisted of a "personalistic view of society." I have also relied on the discussion of the nationalist imagination in Benedict Anderson, *Imagined Communities: Reflections on the Origin and Spread of Nationalism,* London: Verso, 1983, and the discussion of circuits of interpersonal exchange in James Siegel, *Solo in the New Order: Language and Hierarchy in an Indonesian City,* Princeton, New Jersey: Princeton University Press, 1986.

3. For a brief foray into this problem, see my "Oral Culture, Media Culture, and the Islamic Resurgence," in Eduardo Archetti, ed., *The Anthropology of Written Identities,* Oslo: Scandinavian University Press, 1994.

4. By this explication, the *akıl* is not really equivalent to the faculty of reason, calculation, imagination, or fantasy (although the same Turkish word can be used in most, if not all, of these senses). In contrast to these more active concepts of mental function, the *akıl* (in the specific sense of the word that I am using here) is a passive, if not entirely perceptive, faculty that points toward the existence of externally imposed constraints.

5. Sultan and vizier stories are still told in the Turkish republic. I have heard many of them in the province of Trabzon since my first visit in 1965. Warren S. Walker and Ahmet E. Uysal recorded a number of such stories, including the one cited here; see their *Tales Alive in Turkey,* Cambridge, Massachusetts: Harvard University Press, 1966. Many sultan and vizier stories have probably not changed significantly since the collapse of the old regime, but they have more or less lost whatever political bite they may once have had.

6. Walker and Uysal provide two variants of this kind of tale. The first was collected in the *kaza* of Ceyhan (Adana) during 1962, and the second, in İskenderun (Hatay) during 1962. See their *Tales Alive in Turkey,* 142–43.

7. Gülru Necipoğlu, "The Formation of an Ottoman Imperial Tradition: The Topkapı Palace in the Fifteenth and Sixteenth Centuries," Ph.D. dissertation, Harvard University, 1986; Gülru Necipoğlu, *Architecture, Ceremonial, and Power: The Topkapı Palace in the Fifteenth and Sixteenth Centuries,* Boston, Massachusetts: MIT Press, 1991.

8. Necipoğlu, *Architecture, Ceremonial, and Power,* 66.

9. Necipoğlu, *Architecture, Ceremonial, and Power,* 65–66.

10. Stories that tell of Nasrettin Hodja's encounters with Tamerlane, the great conqueror of the Turko-Mongol world, are exceptions to this rule.

11. See the many examples of this association in the stories presented by K. R. F. Burrill, "The Nasrettin Hoca Stories: An Early Ottoman Manuscript at the University of Groningen," *Archivum Ottomanicum,* vol. 2, 1970, 7–114.

12. The text is an English translation of the Turkish given by P. Wittek, *Turkish Reader,* London: Percy Lund, Humphries & Co., 1945, 21.

13. Süleyman Ateş, *Muhtasar İslam İlmihal,* Ankara: Kılıç Kitabevi, 1972.

14. Ateş, *Muhtasar İslam İlmihal,* 50.

15. Ateş, *Muhtasar İslam İlmihal,* 53.

16. Ateş, *Muhtasar İslam İlmihal,* 54.

17. Bernard Lewis, *The Emergence of Modern Turkey,* New York: Oxford University Press, 1961, 253–54.

18. Lewis, *The Emergence of Modern Turkey,* 256, 260.

19. Lauro Martines, *Power and Imagination: City-States in Renaissance Italy*, New York: Knopf, 1979, 275. Compare his assessment of the shift from late medievalism to early modernism in Renaissance Italy of the fifteenth century: "The quest for the control of space in architecture, painting, and bas-relief sculpture was not [merely] analogous to a policy for more hegemony over the entire society; it belonged, rather, to the same movement of consciousness."

20. The competition for the design of the memorial tomb was opened on March 1, 1941, and closed on March 3, 1942. The forty-nine entries included teams from Turkey (20), Germany (11), Italy (7), Austria (7), Sweden, France, and Czechoslovakia. The international jury awarded three first prizes, to entries submitted by a German (Kruger), an Italian (Foshini), and two Turks (Onat and Arda). See Necdet Evliyagil, *Atatürk ve Anıtkabir*, Ankara: Gazetecilik ve Matbaacılık Sanayii, 1988, 50.

21. Üstün Alsaç, "The Second Period of National Architecture," in Renata Holod and Ahmet Evin, eds., *Modern Turkish Architecture*, Philadelphia: University of Pennsylvania Press, 1984, 99–100. Alsaç (94–96, 100–1) observes that the memorial tomb, as it evolved during its construction, came to feature both "national" and "modern" elements. The tomb was first designed during a resurgence of nationalism as economic crisis forced Turkish architects to turn to regional building materials and methods of construction. But it was completed over a decade later, after a series of redesigns, when Turkish architects were beginning to favor internationalism once again. The categories of "national" and "modern" are puzzlingly opposed in Turkey. By "national" (a category that was itself thoroughly modernist in character), Alsaç is referring to those traditional materials, designs, or structures that had come to signify a Turkish "folk" or "people" for the Turkish nationalists. By "modern" (a category that is otherwise closely associated with nationalism), he is referring to materials, designs, or structures that were recognized in Turkey as international and therefore not specifically Turkish in character.

22. See Evliyagil, *Atatürk ve Anıtkabir*, 37–49.

23. Over the years, the memorial tomb came under the control of military authorities. After its construction by the Ministry of Transportation, it was administered by the Ministry of Education (from 1956) and then by the Ministry of Culture (from 1970). After the military coup of 1980, it was taken over by the Ministry of the General Staff (from 1981) to be administered in the name of the Memorial Tomb Command (from 1982). See Evliyagil, *Atatürk ve Anıtkabir*, 67. All the presidents of military background have been buried at the memorial tomb, but not the two presidents of civil background, Bayar and Özal. Two days after his death on December 12, 1973, İsmet İnönü, "comrade in arms," "the second president," and "founder of democracy," was buried at the memorial tomb just across from the great square, facing in a direct line bisecting the Hall of Honor. See Evliyagil, *Atatürk ve Anıtkabir*, 65.

24. Since the Hall of Honor was not completed as originally planned, the resemblance is not plainly apparent.

25. For example, Evliyagil, *Atatürk ve Anıtkabir*, 85, includes a picture of the Monument to the Martyrs at Çalköy in which Atatürk's eyes appear clearly between the clouds above the site. Moreover, there is a moment during occasions of state when officials inscribe personal messages to Atatürk in a ledger.

26. Figure 10.3 is adapted from the brochure *Anıtkabir: Devrim Gençliği İlavesi*, Başvekâlat Devlet Matbaası, n.a., n.d. This is a free handout that includes maps of the procession and burial ceremony held in 1953. The original figure illustrates how the officials and delegations that I have listed are assigned specific stations during the funeral ceremonies. The brochure, which must have been first published in the 1950s, was still available at the memorial tomb in 1987.

27. In 1853, the Topkapı Palace was abandoned as a residence, and the government was moved to Dolmabahçe Palace. Necipoğlu, *Architecture, Ceremonial, and Power,* 258.

28. The criteria laid down at the time of the design competition in 1941 are more or less sufficient to account for the similarity between the memorial tomb and the Topkapı Palace: (1) The tomb will be a place of visitation. Visitors will enter a large hall of honor in the presence of the Father (*Ata*); they will stand before Atatürk and offer him their respects. (2) The tomb will represent Atatürk's practical and creative qualities as a soldier, head of state, politician, and scientist. (3) The design of the memorial tomb should be such that its appearance is striking both close up and at a distance. Architectural motifs will be realized in the form of works that will express its power. (4) So that the Turkish state under Atatürk's name and personality are symbolized, those who want to demonstrate their respect for the Turkish nation will manifest these feelings by bowing before the tomb of Atatürk. (5) A large Hall of Honor will be located on the site of the memorial tomb and visitations will be made at this hall. See Evliyagil, *Atatürk ve Anıtkabir,* 50.

29. During the 1940s, the dynastic tradition of the Ottoman Empire was still anathema to Kemalists. Unlike Turko-Islamists of more recent date, they had little nostalgia for the old regime. Even had the architects of the memorial tomb wished to refer systematically to the Topkapı Palace, they would have lacked the detailed information necessary for doing so. Uzunçarşılı did not publish his study of the organization of the Topkapı Palace until 1945. Necipoğlu did not publish her analysis of architecture and ceremony until 1991.

30. Giulio Carlo Argan uses the quoted phrase to describe the squares in fifteenth-century Renaissance cities. See his *The Renaissance City,* New York: Braziller, 1969, 21.

31. *Anıtkabir: Devrim Gençliği İlavesi* (see note 26). See also Nurettin Can Gülekli, *Anıtkabir Guide,* n.d. This brochure was published by the Memorial Tomb Association for the fiftieth anniversary of the Turkish republic and was still on sale at the site in 1987.

32. *Anıtkabir: Devrim Gençliği İlavesi.*

33. During my visit to the Kocatepe Mosque, I was told that Rifat Börekçi, one of the Ottoman learned doctors (*ulema*), had first proposed such a mosque. This man would have standing in the eyes of even the most secular nationalists. On May 5, 1920, he had issued a *fetva* on behalf of the nationalist movement that invalidated an antinationalist *fetva* issued by the Şeyhülislâm; see Lewis, *The Emergence of Modern Turkey,* 247.

34. A very small reproduction of the design of the mosque is included in the brochure by Hamdi Mert, Halil Kaya, and Abdullah Manaz, *Ankara Kocatepe Camii: 1967 – 1987,* Ankara: Türkiye Diyanet Vakfı, n.d. It shows a mosque somewhat

like that of Orhan Gazi in Gebze, but with two minarets and a monumental court, as in the instance of the Sultan Beyazid Mosque in Edirne; see Aptullah Kuran, *The Mosque in Early Ottoman Architecture*, Chicago: University of Chicago Press, 1968, 37, 57–59. Kuran (p. 48) classes such a mosque as a "single-unit mosque with complex massing."

35. Mert, Kaya, and Manaz, *Ankara Kocatepe Camii*, 2.

36. Mert, Kaya, and Manaz, *Ankara Kocatepe Camii*.

37. Mert, Kaya, and Manaz, *Ankara Kocatepe Camii*.

38. Mert, Kaya, and Manaz, *Ankara Kocatepe Camii*, 8. The Kocatepe Mosque would not have six minarets, like the Sultanahmet Mosque, but only four.

39. They claimed that the collapse of another structure of the "rind" type had contributed to the abandonment of the modernistic design. Turkish construction firms have undertaken a variety of projects requiring advanced technical procedures since the 1960s. There is reason to doubt whether the "rind" type of mosque was beyond their capabilities by the time ground was broken for the Kocatepe Mosque in 1967.

40. At the time of my visit, a final decision had not yet been taken, because this section had not yet been completed. Now a department store and supermarket are located below the mosque. See Aydan Balamir, "Architecture and the Question of Identity: Buildings for Dwelling and Prayer in (Post) Modern Turkey," paper presented at the conference "Rethinking the Project of Modernity in Turkey," March 10–13, 1994, MIT, Boston, Massachusetts. The name of the firm, Beğendik ("we were pleased") is further evidence of the attempt in certain quarters to meld consumerist and Islamist desire, but this is another topic beyond the scope of this chapter.

41. I believe the Eyüp Mosque in Istanbul has as many as six such slabs.

42. The autopark was being used as a garage for ambulances at the time of my visit.

43. Kuran, *The Mosque in Early Ottoman Architecture*, 198.

44. I am told that most Turkish families in Ankara and Istanbul prefer to hold funeral, circumcision, and memorial (*mevlit*) ceremonies at the smaller mosques in these cities, precisely because the large imperial mosques are too impersonal.

45. The brochure features a similar preoccupation. It includes a full-page photograph of the interior (*harem*) filled with believers performing the prayers, and it describes the doubled galleries (*mahfeller*) as places from which one can have a special view of the interior section (*harem kısmına özel bir görünüm*). See Mert, Kaya, and Manaz, *Ankara Kocatepe Camii*, 9, 11.

46. The quote as it appears in the brochure reads as follows: "'Cami' . . . adı üstünde, toplayan . . . 'Kocatepe'nin 1986 Ramazanındaki geçici açılışında bu mana fiilen yaşandı . . . Kocatepe, civar il, ilçe ve bölgelerden koşup gelen mü'minlerle dolup-taştı . . . Cumhuriyet döneminin en büyük mabedi 'Kocatepe'ye bu koşuş, Türk milletinin büyümeye ve bütünleşmeye olan hasretini ifade ediyordu." See Mert, Kaya, and Manaz, *Ankara Kocatepe Camii*, 7. The opening of the mosque for the performance of prayers in 1986 preceded the official opening during the summer of the following year.

47. To accomplish this objective, numerous apartment buildings had to be razed

to open up the space around the structure. At the time of my visit, seventeen more were scheduled to be pulled down as soon as funds were available.

48. Mert, Kaya, and Manaz, *Ankara Kocatepe Camii.* The minarets seem disproportionately high and thin by classical standards. The increased height of the minarets, it appears, exceeds what was necessary to accommodate the increased height of the dome.

11/ Silent Interruptions

Urban Encounters with Rural Turkey

GÜLSÜM BAYDAR NALBANTOĞLU

The architecture of rural Turkey has been a recurrent theme in the grand narrative of modern Turkish architecture. It was captured by a wave of nationalist and regionalist interests in the 1930s and early 1940s, valued by disappointed modernists in the 1960s, and rediscovered for its consumptive value in the 1980s. In the earlier phases, the proponents of regionalism had to draw careful distinctions between an ideal, sanitized, and immaculate rural imaginary and the unenviable state of real Turkish villages. Paradoxically perhaps, the rural imaginary privileged the model of an ideal, clean, orderly city and used it as a cultural and physical exemplar.[1] The impossibility of realizing this impeccable model became apparent after the unprecedented urban migrations of the 1950s onward—articulated with other social, political, and economic forces beyond the scope of this essay—which threatened the sanitized, controllable, and homogeneous urban vision of the republic's early leaders. The material effects of this process remain at the core of contemporary cultural studies in Turkey. Opinions are divided. While some lament the phenomenon, interpreting it as the evaporation of the last hopes of the Kemalist vision of cultural modernity, others celebrate it as a much desired plurality that strikes the final blow to homogenizing, elitist, and sterile attempts to create culture from above.[2]

This essay is written from a position calling for the opening up of a third space that neither authorizes "one" nor privileges "many." It attempts to uncover a cultural-architectural space of difference that disrupts preconstructed identities and essences, contesting plurality as a multiplication of sociological totalities; a space in which both essentialist constructions and relativist celebrations are avoided; a space of translation across the urban-rural boundaries set up by the nation's founding fathers.

Translation, as Walter Benjamin put it, "instead of making itself similar to the meaning of the original, must lovingly and in detail form itself according to the manner of meaning of the original, to make them *both* recognisable as the broken fragments of the greater language."[3] Although Benjamin's description concerns languages, which is somewhat different from my interest here, I find it useful for the framework of my analysis because it recognizes both fluidity and difference. I believe that the cultural border between the city and the village, which architectural discourse has sharply delineated, is a fluid one. Both acknowledgment and repression of difference is made possible by this fluidity. My position calls for the recognition of negotiations without surmounting the space of incommensurable meanings and judgments.

Such spaces of negotiation have hitherto been excluded from or silenced by dominant modes of architectural discourse and practice. Architectural (re)constructions of rural Turkey have long been dominated by worn-out discussions of regionalism and contextualism that take place on a highly prescriptive plane and help perpetuate the status quo. Through sophisticated processes of aestheticization and legitimation, architectural discourse in Turkey has repressed and domesticated its "rural" component by reducing it to building forms. I argue that this repression can be overcome by recognizing the irreducibility of space to form and acknowledging connections between architectural and cultural production.

My aim, however, is neither to undertake a detailed historiographical critique of modern Turkish architecture nor to extend its historical breadth by introducing new and unexplored topics. I am interested, instead, in highlighting particular cultural, historiographical, architectural, and urban moments to generate possible critical openings for present practices of writing and building. In what follows, I analyze three such instances in the spatial history of Ankara in order to explore a possible dialogue at the intersections between urban and rural cultures. My argument flows between textual, architectural, and urban spaces and attempts to engage these with cultural production. All three instances are particular readings of urban scenes that reveal possibilities for erasing ideological constructions of harmonious cultural totalities; they disrupt, betray, and subvert homogenizing tendencies.

Beyond the Monumental Narrative of Urban Space

In urbanistic terms, the planning of the capital city of Ankara is an unsurpassed example of the monumental narrative of modern Turkey. It is also one of the exemplary sites of the relative success and unforeseen failure of the Turkish modernists' attempts to transcend the inherent con-

11.1. İstasyon Avenue, view toward the railway station, 1936. (Reproduced from *Ankara*, Turkish Ministry of Culture, 1991.)

traditions between urban and rural cultural landscapes. The creation of the modern capital from a small central Anatolian town is well known.[4] What is often overlooked is that from the early days of the capital's foundation, encounters between old (traditional, rural) and new (modern, urban) Ankara engendered significant tensions that disrupted the proper image of the city. I believe these encounters help reveal not one but multiple layers of architectural and urban space, and they enable us to imagine other spatial stories beyond pedagogical narratives.[5]

Herman Jansen, the German urban planner of Ankara, mapped the modern capital along two major axes, Gazi Boulevard and İstasyon Avenue, which intersected at a T-junction adorned by a monumental statue of Mustafa Kemal Atatürk, the founder of the Turkish republic. These Haussmanian arteries were symbolic connections, the meanings of which far surpassed their function as traffic regulators. Gazi Boulevard, on the north-south axis, marked the direction along which the new city developed. İstasyon Avenue connected the railway station to the boulevard and, in a somewhat less definitive manner, continued east to reach the outskirts of the citadel. The station building was a historical landmark that hosted Mustafa Kemal during the War of Independence. It was the "gateway" to the city.

By 1928, İstasyon avenue was lined on both sides by such key buildings as the National Assembly, the Ankara Palas Hotel, and housing for
bureaucrats; it was paved and widened to incorporate two lanes separated
by a green strip and delineated by regular rows of trees. From the gates
of the railway station it was a powerful physical connection to Gazi Boulevard that led the newcomer into modern Ankara. The pride taken in İsta-
syon Avenue is best reflected in the numerous period photographs that
offer a variety of impressive perspectives from all angles (fig. 11.1). The
ornamental facades facing İstasyon Avenue that led to the monumental
statue of Atatürk were set against the picturesque backdrop of the castel-
lated walls of the citadel. "The extraordinary view of the citadel and its
timber framed houses," as Jansen described it, was carefully preserved for
the visual consumption of the modern city.[6] "In new town planning practices," stated Jansen, "the new sections of the town should be clearly separated from the old. *Theoretically, the old town should be covered by a bell
jar* [emphasis mine]."[7] The astounding metaphor of the bell jar summarized the monumental narrative of modern Ankara that silenced "other"
narratives in its own interest.

Most importantly for my argument, the monumental narrative often
overlooks the fact that the very boulevards that distanced the old city
from the new were also connections enabling the flow between them.
Some significant instances reveal the ways in which inhabitants of old
and new Ankara enacted these urban spaces and made local sense out of
the city that was shaped for them. In a much-quoted episode narrated by
a leading Turkish intellectual, Yakup Kadri Karaosmanoğlu, in his re-
knowned novel *Ankara,* inhabitants of old Ankara have gathered on New
Year's Eve outside the monumental entrance of the Ankara Palas hotel
on İstasyon Avenue to watch the elite arrive at the ballroom. They engage in the following conversation:

> "So you think you have seen it all from here, hah, hah," one says
> to another, who replies with a grin, "I know what they do inside,
> but I won't say it." "I will," interferes a third, "there is tango in-
> side." "Who is tango?" asks another.

And the conversation continues along these lines as modern Ankara flows
into the ballroom and police try to control the entrance.[8]

I am intrigued by the striking similarity of Yakup Kadri's story to Baudelaire's "The Eyes of the Poor," which depicts an encounter between two

11.2. Facade of the Ankara Palas. Architects Vedat Tek and Kemalettin Bey, 1924–27. (Photograph by the author.)

lovers and a poor family in front of a cafe on a new boulevard in 1850s Paris.[9] İstasyon Avenue functioned, on a much smaller scale, like the boulevards designed by Haussmann for Paris in creating a new basis for drawing the different strata of the urban population together. The boulevards, as Marshall Berman articulated it, surfaced the contradictory effects of modern culture. On one hand, they had an unprecedented liberating effect in enabling new forms of privacy within the anonymity of the public—intense forms of self-discovery, dreamy and magical experiences. On the other hand, they highlighted disturbing social and cultural differences and revealed insurmountable communication gaps. In Berman's words, Baudelaire's story "shows us how the contradictions that animate the modern city street resonate in the inner life of the man on the street."[10]

In the doubly complicated Turkish scene, where the liberation of the self is bracketed by the liberation of the nation, and where modern culture is imposed from above, Yakup Kadri seeks a nationalist synthesis to surmount difference. Yet the episode he narrates enables us to see multiple layers of meaning in both İstasyon Avenue and the Ankara Palas, beyond the conventional accounts of architectural or urban history. The Ankara Palas, for example, can no longer be sufficiently described as an

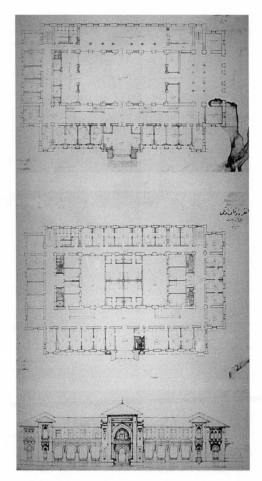

11.3. Original ground-floor plan of the Ankara Palas. (Reproduced from Renata Holod and Ahmet Evin, eds., *Modern Turkish Architecture*, Philadelphia: University of Pennsylvania Press, 1984, 55.)

excellent example of the First National Movement (fig. 11.2). Any history of the building would be incomplete without mentioning the "production" of the interior space by mechanisms of control, the gaze of those who are denied entry, and the power of these outsiders' imaginations.

The narrative multiplies when we cross the physical boundary and realize that the people who populated the ballroom enacted a cultural space that rendered them as ambivalent as their voyeurs outside. For the priv-

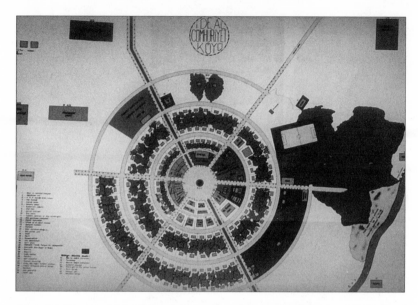

11.4. "An Ideal Turkish Village." (Reproduced from Afet İnan, *Devletçilik İlkesi ve Birinci Sanayi Planı* [The principle of etatism and the first industrial plan of the Turkish republic], Ankara: Türk Tarih Kurumu, 1933, appendix.)

ileged inhabitants of Ankara, dressed elegantly in accordance with the fashion pages of local newspapers that brought the latest news from Paris, and having adopted appropriate codes of behavior based on how-to books on "modern manners," ballroom dancing was part of a performance that they rehearsed only ambivalently. At a gathering to celebrate the anniversary of the republic, Mustafa Kemal is said to have called the reluctant women to the dance floor this way: "I cannot imagine a woman who can possibly reject the dance proposal of a Turkish man in his military uniform. Now I command: To the dance floor! Forward! March! Dance!"[11] The astounding military, nationalist, and sexist tone of the command reflected the contradictions in the construction of a monolithic modern culture imagined by the founders of the republic. One wonders whether it was the citadel or the Ankara Palas hotel that was covered by a bell jar.

A standard source on modern Turkish architecture describes the Ankara Palas as "a two storey, rectangular building with a great ballroom at the center, reminiscent of the historical Ottoman inns with central courtyards surrounded by guest rooms on two floors" (fig. 11.3).[12] If the architect was indeed inspired by the Ottoman inns, the irony of the inversion of the function of the central courtyard from that of a functionally inclusive space (all travelers are welcome) to that of a culturally exclusive space cannot be overlooked. Noting the fluidity of the way the central hall opens to the surrounding spaces, I believe that further research may reveal other forms of control and boundary (such as gender-based ones) no less significant and complex than those symbolically embedded in the monumental entry. The architectural literature on Ankara Palas that comfortably locates it in the First National Movement and describes solely its formal composition and spatial inspiration powerfully forecloses alternative ways of understanding the complexities of the architectural and urban space it has generated.

To summarize, the sanitized monumental architectural and urban spaces of modern Ankara attempted to guard the proper image of the new city. The practice of everyday life, however, insidiously disrupted the grand narrative by bringing to the surface meanings and values that were generated in between the cultural and spatial boundaries the city fathers delineated with utmost care.

Same Words, Different Languages

The relationship between the modern Turkish city and its "other"—that is, rural Turkey—took different forms in architectural discourse and practice. Much has already been written about the architectural appropriation of rural vernacular forms and the civilizing mission of Turkish architects in rural areas. I will briefly summarize some relevant points before continuing my discussion of spatial and architectural interruptions.

Typological studies of the Turkish house and the enthusiastic assimilation of rural forms in urban buildings have been recurrent obsessions in architectural circles since the 1930s. At that time, extensive academic work was based on rigorous research on the house types of various geographical regions. Many urban residences boasted such features as projected roofs or centralized plans based on vernacular examples. Much of the research was carried out in conjunction with intense debates over the appropriate choice between regionalism and modernism. This discourse was evidently located within a larger cultural discourse that sought to synthesize culture and civilization to project a modern Turkish identity. As a survey of architectural journals from this period shows, debates among Turkish architects often came to a standstill when belief in the inevitable Turkishness of modern architecture converged with a conviction about the essential modernity of the Turkish vernacular.[13]

Along with the assimilation of rural forms by leading Turkish architects, the 1930s and early 1940s saw unprecedented efforts to accumu-
late and systematize rural data and to realize the republic's civilizing mission in rural settlements. In architecture, these attempts yielded a series
of ideal types, both built and unbuilt, ranging from model villages to individual houses. These were inspired by a host of Western examples, including German *Siedlungen* and *existenzminimum* housing principles.[14]
Model villages consisted of neatly arranged rows of identical houses reminiscent of the disciplinary environments of nineteenth-century factory
towns. Typical rural houses were miniaturized versions of urban apartments. I was astounded to find the plan of "An Ideal Turkish Village" ap-
pended to a 1933 publication of the Turkish Historical Society (fig. 11.4).[15]
Unmistakably inspired by Ebenezer Howard's Garden City, the centralized plan for the ideal village consisted of clearly demarcated zones for
sports, health and educational facilities, commerce, and even industry.

I believe these two positions—assimilation of rural elements in urban
environments and the use of urban models in rural settings—are in fact
one. Both search for a center, ultimately a nationalist core, in which to
dissolve all forms of difference. This marks the desire for a moment of
transcendence when the nostalgia for lost origins and the demand to civ-
ilize reveal themselves as two sides of the same coin. By reducing complex differences to conveniently formulated binary opposites of urban
versus rural, traditional versus modern, and regional versus international, these positions refuse to see the complexity that emerges from the
gap between fluctuating feelings of fascination and contempt for the rural
Turkey they relentlessly homogenized. It seems important, then, to question what they did not say or what they refused to say by working with
and through their work and by asking questions from the margins of their
powerful claims.

Amidst the mostly unified voices of the humanistic project of the civilizing missioners who visited numerous villages during the 1930s, there
were a few that disturbed the tone of the dominant discourse to a significant extent.[16] I refer to two articles by Nusret Köymen, a prolific writer,
that appeared in *Ülkü,* the official journal of *Halkevleri* (People's Houses).[17]
These articles were important not only for their uniqueness in voicing
an alternative opinion in a largely univocal journal but also for reflecting on some critical issues in a sophisticated manner. Köymen pointed
out two fundamental difficulties in carrying out the civilizing mission in
rural Turkey. First, on a pragmatic level, he believed that given the ex-

tremely limited resources of many of these efforts, even the most agreeable ones, those involving issues like health education and technical support, were bound to remain partial and short-lived. Second, and more significant for my argument, he pointed out a fundamental incommensurability between urban and rural cultural practices. An insightful paragraph offers the following observation:

> The languages of the urban dweller and the peasant are different *even if they use the same words;* [they are different] to such an extent that a peasant from a village who has had no contact with any city and an urban dweller who has had no previous rural exposure cannot possibly understand each other. . . . There is no way to cancel this difference. . . . The thing for the village reformer [*köycü*] to do is . . . to make use of those instances *when the peasant's personality is temporarily split* to make room for penetration to influence him. Those are the times when the peasant is in the city. [Emphases mine.]18

In the village, the author continues, because there is no possibility of communication, peasants do not speak to the reformers. They "merely nod" at whatever they hear.

In its recognition of the incommensurability of the two voices, the peasants' and the reformers', Köymen's position differs fundamentally from that of his contemporaries. He observes that the peasants, vis-à-vis the village reformers, have no voice. They are silenced. They merely nod. Recognizing the opaqueness of language, Köymen refuses to fill the silence with his own voice. Yet that refusal is only momentary. He is not prepared to resign. Once the peasant comes to the city, he notes, again with astonishing insight, his personality is split—that is, he is decentered through his exposure to a second symbolic order, which makes room for intervention. The reformer should use the opportunity to filter through the gap that is created in the process of decentering.

At this stage Köymen calls upon architecture for help. He notes that peasants come to the cities mostly on a temporary basis to settle bureaucratic or administrative matters. Believing in the necessity of gathering the temporary rural population in one center, he suggests building "peasants' inns." These, he continues, should be made with regional materials and "according to architectural principles that have been developed through thousands of years of experience." By mimicking the familiar, the exterior of the building would call upon the peasants' yearning for home. The interior, on the other hand, should be furnished with easy-to-make objects in a manner that would arouse the peasants' "civilizing need." Hence the standard process is reversed: instead of going to the village, the reformer remains in the city to carry out the civilizing mission. As one architect put it in a slightly different context, this meant to "introduce beds to those who are used to sleeping together on earthen floors, to teach those who sit on the floor how to use chairs, to provide tables for those who eat on the floors, *to revolutionize lifestyles.* [emphasis mine]."[19]

Köymen's idea of peasants' inns was never realized. It is difficult for me to agree with his agenda, and it seems to me that Köymen was too easily convinced that the peasant in the city would take myth for language.[20] Ironically, a few decades later, his kind of architectural myth (the sanitized facades of the vernacular) would be readily consumed by the urban bourgeoisie in the form of holiday villages in the countryside rather than peasants' inns in the city. Besides his pointed analysis of the peasant's subjectivity, what should not be overlooked in Köymen's call is the feeling of urgency to do something about the peasant in the city. Lurking behind his proposal is the realization that the peasant's split personality might engender the unknown. If the split was not sealed and surmounted by the pedagogy of the reformers, unknown and intolerable forms of expression might emerge. Indeed, Turkish cities faced this challenge after the late 1940s, when the peasants came to stay.

Limits of (In)tolerance

When the peasants came to stay in Ankara and other major Turkish cities in the late 1940s, there were no peasants' inns to welcome them. The early stages of migration saw the erection of a few shacks that sporadically spotted the city. Then they multiplied. Between 1937 and 1950 their numbers in Ankara increased from 20,000 to 100,000.[21] At that time the migrants' labor was only marginal in the economy. Ankara had neither organized industrial accumulation nor widespread small industries to employ them. Hence the migrants settled in areas that were close to the business center but were also topographical thresholds such as steep slopes and areas threatened by landslides and floods (see fig. 9.4).

The new urban phenomenon disturbed the city fathers. In the late 1930s, the Ministry of Interior Affairs assured the "citizens" that Ankara would be cleared of "these unsightly places with miserable roads."[22] The following decades saw the development of a series of economic and political agendas layered over the issue of rural migrants that lies beyond the scope of this essay. As John Berger says of migrant workers in *A Seventh Man,*

> his migration is like an event in a dream dreamt by another. As a figure in a dream dreamt by an unknown sleeper, he appears to act autonomously, at times unexpectedly; but everything he does—unless he revolts—is determined by the needs of the dreamer's mind. Abandon the metaphor. The migrant's intentionality is permeated by historical necessities of which neither he nor anybody he meets is aware. That is why it is as if his life were being dreamt by another."[23]

Although there is no point in denying the power of the dreamer, I believe the autonomous and unexpected acts of the migrant deserve more attention than they have received so far. They have displayed the potential to disrupt historical constructions of Turkish architecture, on one hand, and homogenizing accounts of rural forms, on the other. From an architectural viewpoint, unlike most other buildings, the squatter's house, known as a *gecekondu,* is not built on the premise of permanence; it is under continuous threat of demolition. Thus the survival of the early *gecekondu* dwellings was enabled by their inhabitants' tactical operations against the relentless strategies of the city fathers.

Strategies, Michel de Certeau proposes, are calculative, rationalized, and manipulative operations of control from positions of power.[24] Strategic rationalizations distinguish and demarcate their own space in an environment "in an effort to delimit one's own place in a world bewitched by the invisible powers of the Other." Tactics, on the other hand, are calculated actions "determined by the absence of a proper locus." Both required and produced by strategies, the de-privileged subjects of tactical operations have no place. They utilize a land that belongs to others. Tactics require a clever use of time. They are ingenious ways in which the weak turn events into opportunities and make use of the strong, and they "thus lend a political dimension to everyday practices." The architecture and landscape of the early *gecekondu* areas display ingenious tactics of determined survival.

Here I would like to propose a reading of these areas different from those which described them as "ugly" and "unsightly" and viewed them as "the city's garbage to be disposed of." As these descriptions recognized in a rather negative manner, the *gecekondu* neighborhoods rendered the city opaque. They threatened the transparency of the boulevards that had been proudly described as "the mirror of a beautiful and clean city." The snaking pathways of the *gecekondu* areas stood in shameful opposition to the straight axes of modern Ankara. A 1949 newspaper essay on Altındağ—one of the earliest hillside *gecekondu* settlements in Ankara—likened the street network to a maze. It was "like solving a child's puzzle," the author wrote, "where you have to find the exit by tracing the correct path within a jumble of lines."[25]

The mazelike pathways were indeed a challenge to the panoptical transparency of the boulevards. Yet they made possible a kind of countercontrol and surveillance on the part of the inhabitants. The opacity of the maze enabled an entire neighborhood network of communication that was vocal and gestural rather than visual. Once that network was activated, news of an intruder reached all the way to the summit within a matter of minutes. One *gecekondu* dweller, a woman, recounted:

> We received the news that the demolishers had arrived, with the police. We didn't know what to do. Our neighbors advised us. We locked our little kids inside, we remained out of sight. The police came to the house: "Vacate the house, we will demolish." The kids were all alone inside; they got scared, they started crying and screaming. The police are the police but they are not heartless. . . . They left when they heard the children's cries. Since that day, whenever the demolishers come we lock our kids inside and hide away. . . . This house that you see here has never been demolished.[26]

In the late 1940s, one widespread method of constructing *gecekondu* dwellings in Ankara was as follows: Eight wooden posts were joined in pairs by scrap wood pieces to form four wall panels on the ground, which were then plastered with mud. Rectangular openings were left in two of the panels for a door and a window, respectively. When night fell, these panels were anchored to the ground at four corners and the exterior was covered with scrap metal. When city authorities came to demolish this "house of cards," all they had to do was push one of the walls for the entire structure to collapse. Yet it was, of course, simple to reerect the panels very quickly. Some such "homes" were rebuilt as many as eleven times.[27] The uncanny repetition of this process is brilliantly captured in Latife Tekin's novel *Berci Kristin: Tales from the Garbage Hills,* in which, upon their umpteenth arrival at the same site, the demolishers see only a little girl playing house with a tiny shack she has made from the remains of demolished *gecekondu*s surrounding her. They leave the place, never to show up again.[28]

In developing their tactics, rural migrants responded less to such regionalist concerns as climate and topography than to the very conditions that simultaneously affirmed and denied their urban existence. In doing so, they did not necessarily discard ages of accumulated experience from the countryside. In one of the most striking examples in late 1940s Ankara, dwellings were carved into the sloping ground between two roads leading to a hilltop. The only markers of these houses above ground were upside-down earthen pots with holes in their bottoms that, as journalist Adviye Fenik put it, "function[ed] as windows as well as chimneys."[29]

Fenik wrote a series of articles in 1949 on the Altındağ *gecekondu* district in Ankara. Amid many statistical, economical, and administrative analyses of the early *gecekondu* settlements, hers is the only account I know of concerning everyday life. It is invaluable in providing insights into the tactical operations of *gecekondu* environments. Fenik's description of the earthen pots follows her story of how, upon stumbling on one of them, she was asked to step aside because she was "walking on the roof." Stepping back, she felt as if she had "stepped on a grave." "Grave" is a chilling metaphor for a house, something I would like to dwell on in relation to another architectural moment that took place less than two decades before Fenik's encounter with the carved *gecekondu*s.

In 1933, Abdullah Ziya, an architect with the Ministry of Education, made a regional classification of rural buildings in Anatolia.[30] The only category for which he had no word of praise was what he called "negative villages," where houses were carved into rocky mountains. "When you look at these villages from afar," he reported, "you see numerous bodies wiggling in the cavities of the slope." Apparently unimpressed, he decided that since the negative villages did "not have any formal or aesthetic value," he did "not find it necessary to write about them at length."

It appears that "negative" dwellings were denied existence in legitimate discourse whether they were located in the city or in the countryside. Their inhabitants were likened to dead bodies ("I felt as if I stepped on a grave") or to nonhumans ("bodies wiggling in the cavities of the slope"). Topographical and climatic necessities might have generated the negative villages in the first place. Abdullah Ziya's acknowledgment of built form for its visibility and construction, however, caused him to fail to comprehend carved settlements as architecture. In the city, the carved *gecekondu*s served rural immigrants in a number of vital ways. Besides defying the conventional meaning of urban lot, they were inexpensive to build, difficult to notice, and, most importantly, almost impossible to demolish.

The tactics of the rural migrants displayed the fluidity of architectural and other languages. They did not polarize cultural entities, nor did they attempt to fix meanings. Although it may have no direct bearing on architecture per se, I am tempted to relate one instance in which Quran cases on the walls of *gecekondu* dwellings contained carefully folded doctors' prescriptions. The sick were taken to the doctor, but there was no money to buy the prescribed medicine. A traditional healer was called in to cure the patients. The prescription, however, was treasured as "the passport to heaven" and kept inside the Quran case.[31] The intriguing inversion here seems particularly relevant now, when the medical profession itself takes traditional healing methods seriously.

In architectural terms, the *gecekondu* buildings and settlements interrupt the conventional meanings of such terms as boundaries and walls, inside and outside, and public and private. First, they defy mapping because their size keeps changing. A unit with one room and a detached toilet can turn into a seven- or eight-room house within a matter of months. The additive nature of building is more complex than the similar process in the village, however, because elements of urban apartments are gradually introduced in a selective manner. The study of changes in domestic politics depending on the inclusion or exclusion of corridor spaces (borrowed from urban apartments), for example, will disclose further layers of complexity in spatial relationships. In the *gecekondu* environments, the languages of the city and the village clash, and other languages emerge.[32]

In order to survive, rural immigrants had to discover spatial and architectural tactics of survival and resistance about which the discipline of architecture has so far remained silent. Rural immigrants assimilated, subverted, and mimicked. In doing so, they never denied, in a stubborn traditionalism, the language of the city. I think it is significant that as early as the 1950s *gecekondu* inhabitants organized to demand modern urban services.[33]

The city made use of the immigrants without tolerating their physical presence. Urban professionals recurrently made the rural immigrant their cultural object of analysis whose integration into the city had to be guaranteed. In 1966, a publication by the Social Services Division of the Ministry of Health and Social Welfare suggested that *gecekondu* communities should not be mistaken for settled, balanced, self-satisfied groups. "A long time is needed for these families to be fully settled and integrated into the urban community. To enable necessary measures, they must be seen as transitory communities settled in transitory areas."[34] For urban professionals, integration meant speaking the given language of the city. In the early phases of *gecekondu* building, rural immigrants spoke *through* rather than *in* the city they had come to inhabit.

Architectural discourse and practice, which had been obsessed with rural buildings and settings, remained silent about this entire phenomenon. *Modern Turkish Architecture,* the standard English source on the topic, devotes three sentences to *gecekondu* settlements in a chapter titled "International Style: Liberalism in Architecture." Summarizing the economic roots of the rural migration process, it states: "This migration had a profound effect on the urban texture. Big cities such as Istanbul, Ankara and Izmir, where employment opportunities were high, became surrounded by *gecekondu*s. These squatter areas, unsanitary and lacking infrastructure, came to house forty to fifty percent of the urban population." The next paragraph, on the development of "a lucrative estate market," is followed by an informative study of major public buildings of the 1950s.[35] I propose that the absence of any architectural elaboration of the *gecekondu* environments cannot be interpreted as the author's oversight. An architectural writing tradition based on the study of forms and styles, even when such analysis is backed by sociocultural data, is unable to allocate space for such elaboration.

Rethinking the Question of Rural Architecture

Rural vernacular buildings were represented in the grand narrative of Turkish architecture first in conjunction with the nationalistic imagination of the 1930s and early 1940s and again in the "pluralistic" mood of the 1980s and 1990s.[36] The first move was serious and pedagogical, intended to totalize and homogenize. It looked for architectural models at a time when the Turkish nation was in the making. The second is playful and celebrant and is located in the contemporary cityscape, where every building vies with the others for attention and "anything goes so long as it sells." Despite these differences, in both cases the complexity of rural Turkey is reduced to a few stereotypical architectural moves.

Since the early years of the republic, rural architecture has been muted through recurrent acts of reproduction by a large number of modernist strategies that avoid addressing issues of representation. I have attempted to highlight some aspects of the complexity of certain architectural and spatial conditions (which are further complicated by issues of ethnicity and gender) that architectural discourse in Turkey has hitherto refused to address. From this perspective, *gecekondu* environments provide insights into other ways of acting, speaking, and perceiving spatial conditions. Located at the intersection between city and village, between the visible and the sensible, they represent silent interruptions in architectural discourse and ideal urban visions.

My interest in the early phases of *gecekondu* settlements is not motivated by a desire to romanticize or aestheticize, which would reproduce earlier positions on rural architecture. As I have tried to make clear, I am interested in a long-overdue investigation of other ways of understanding architectural and urban space and in adopting a tone that neither celebrates nor condemns the phenomenon of urban migration, which is wrongly described as "the ruralization of cities." I am interested in the tactical spaces of the city because they are fluid and multiple and they resist totalization. They speak of architecture in different ways because they are nonpedagogical and nonappropriative. Most importantly, they call for reflections on space and architecture and different ways of writing, designing, and building that are neither pedagogical acts of totalization nor celebrated gestures of pluralism. The *gecekondu* environments do not offer instant formal clues for the architectural profession to adopt or to appropriate. Their contribution is much subtler and less direct. *Gecekondu* environments offer alternative ways of thinking about architecture and the city by calling out for the recognition of incommensurable differences.

Notes

1. I have explored certain ramifications of this phenomenon in "Between Civilization and Culture: Appropriation of Traditional Dwelling Forms in Early Republican Turkey," *Journal of Architectural Education*, November 1993, 66–74.

2. The term "Kemalist," derived from the name of Kemal Atatürk, the founder of the Turkish republic, refers to the cultural politics of the early years of the republic. Under the banner of "Westernization," political leaders of the period

launched a series of reforms ranging from the adoption of the Swiss Civil Code to the transformation of the alphabet from Arabic script to Latin, in order to break all past associations with the Ottoman heritage, the Middle East, and Islam.

3. Quoted in Homi K. Bhabha, "Dissemination: Time, Narrative and the Margins of the Modern Nation," in Homi K. Bhabha, ed., *Nation and Narration*, New York: Routledge, 1990, 320. Bhabha emphasizes Benjamin's insistence on the necessity of retaining fragments as fragments that will never constitute a totality.

4. For an extensive analysis, see Erdal Yavuz, ed., *Tarih İçinde Ankara* (Ankara in History), Ankara: Middle East Technical University, 1980.

5. I borrow the term "pedagogical" from Homi Bhabha, who makes the insightful argument that "in the production of the nation as narration there is a split between the continuist, accumulative temporality of the pedagogical, and the repetitious, recursive strategy of the performative." The people, according to him, occupy a double time as both the historical objects of a nationalist pedagogy and the subjects of a process of signification that must erase any prior or originary presence of the nation-people. See Homi Bhabha, "Dissemination," 297.

6. Herman Jansen, "Ankara Planı İzah Raporu" (Report on the Master Plan of Ankara), *Mimarlık*, vol. 5, 1948, 22.

7. Jansen, "Ankara Planı İzah Raporu," 11.

8. Yakup Kadri Karaosmanoğlu, *Ankara*, Istanbul: İletişim Yayınları, 1987 [1934], 107.

9. Recounted in Marshall Berman, *All That Is Solid Melts into Air,* New York: Simon and Schuster, 1983, 148–55.

10. Berman, *All That Is Solid,* 154.

11. Quoted from Gentizon, *Mustapha Kemal ou l'Orient en marche,* Paris, 1929, in Nilüfer Göle, *Modern Mahrem,* Istanbul: Metis Yayınları, 1991, 53.

12. Renata Holod and Ahmet Evin, eds., *Modern Turkish Architecture,* Philadelphia: University of Pennsylvania Press, 1956.

13. For an extensive analysis of this issue, see Sibel Bozdoğan and Gülsüm Baydar Nalbantoğlu, "Images and Ideas of 'The Modern House' in Early Republican Turkey," unpublished paper presented at the annual meeting of the Society of Architectural Historians, 1992, Albuquerque, New Mexico.

14. The term *Siedlung* refers to public housing projects built by modernist German architects in the 1920s. They were conceived as a response to industrial workers' lifestyles and were based on principles of efficiency and productivity.

15. Afet İnan, *Devletçilik İlkesi ve Türkiye Cumhuriyetinin Birinci Sanayi Planı* (The Principle of Statism and the First Industrial Plan of the Turkish Republic), Ankara: Türk Tarih Kurumu, 1933.

16. By "humanistic project" I refer to the project's relying on the individual's access to reason as the basis of communal existence and sociopolitical action without questioning the ideological process generating individuality and reason.

17. Nusret Köymen, "Köy Çalişmalarında Tek Müsbet Yol, Köylü Hanı" (The Only Positive Development in Rural Works, Peasants' Inns), *Ülkü*, vol. 7, no. 40, 1936, 299–302; and Nusret Köymen, "Köycülüğün Daha Verimli Olması Hakkında Düşünceler" (Thoughts on Increasing Productivity in Rural Reforms), *Ülkü*, vol. 13, no. 73, 1939, 27–29. *Halkevleri* (People's Houses) were urban institutions

founded in 1932 to educate the population along the lines of Kemalist reforms in civic life. Besides their monthly publications, they offered library facilities, organized art courses, supported sports facilities, and conducted research on various aspects of folk culture.

18. Köymen, "Köycülüğün," 27.

19. Zeki Sayar, "İç Kolonizasyon" (Internal Colonization), *Arkitekt*, vol. 6, no. 2, 1936, 47.

20. This distinction is based on Roland Barthes' notion of myth as a second-order semiological system that gets hold of language in order to build its own system. See "Myth Today" in his *Mythologies*, New York: Hill and Wang, 1984, 109–59.

21. Tansı Şenyapılı, *Gecekondu: Çevre İşçilerin Mekanı*, (Gecekondu: The Space of Peripheral Labor), Ankara: ODTÜ, 1981, 170; and Tansı Şenyapılı, *Ankara Kentinde Gecekondu Gelişimi: 1923–1960* (The Development of Gecekondus in Ankara: 1923–1960), Ankara: Kent Koop Yayınları, 1985, 58.

22. Şenyapılı, *Ankara Kentinde Gecekondu Gelişimi*, 57–58. Şenyapılı emphasizes that the minister, Şükrü Saraçoğlu, was one of the most sympathetic administrators regarding the illegal settlements, having realized that they did solve the problem of housing for the migrants, although not in an entirely acceptable manner.

23. John Berger (text) and Jean Mohr (photographs), *A Seventh Man*, New York: Viking, 1975, 43.

24. Michel de Certeau, *The Practice of Everyday Life*, Berkeley: University of California Press, 1984, xix, 34–39.

25. Adviye Fenik, "Altındağ Röportajları" (Altındağ Reports), *Zafer Gazetesi*, 19 May 1949.

26. Nursun Ertuğrul, "Gecekondu Yapım Süreci: Akdere'den bir Örnek" (Gecekondu Building Process: A Case Study in Akdere), *Mimarlık*, no. 3, 1977, 105.

27. İbrahim Öğretmen, *Ankara'da 58 Gecekondu Hakkında Monografi* (A Monograph on 58 Gecekondus in Ankara), Ankara: AÜSBF Yayınları, 1957, 25.

28. Latife Tekin, *Berci Kristin Çöp Masalları* (Berci Kristin: Tales From the Garbage Hills), Istanbul: Metis Yayınları, 1990, 13.

29. Adviye Fenik, "Altındağ Röportajları," 15 May 1949.

30. Abdullah Ziya, "Köy Mimarisi" (Village Architecture), *Ülkü*, vol. 1, no. 5, 1933, 370–74.

31. Adviye Fenik, "Altindag Röportajlari," 22 May 1949.

32. For a remarkable study of the emergence of a unique type of music from the *gecekondu* culture, see Meral Özbek, *Popüler Kültür ve Orhan Gencebay Arabeski* (Popular Culture and Orhan Gencebay's Arabesque), Istanbul: İletişim Yayınları, 1991.

33. Şenyapılı, *Ankara Kentinde Gecekondu Gelişimi*, 135.

34. İbrahim Yasa, *Ankara'da Gecekondu Aileleri* (Gecekondu Families in Ankara), Ankara: Ministry of Health and Social Welfare Publications, 1966, 46.

35. Mete Tapan, "International Style: Liberalism in Architecture," in Holod and Evin, eds., *Modern Turkish Architecture*, 106.

36. I have deliberately left out the 1960s and 1970s, when the interest in "vernacular architecture" was institutionalized, by and large, as an academic discipline dominated by structuralist and hermeneutical approaches. A critique of this phenomenon deserves a detailed analysis slightly outside the scope of this essay.

12/ Arabesk Culture

A Case of Modernization and Popular Identity

MERAL ÖZBEK

A type of popular music emerged in Turkey at the end of 1960s that captured the passions of rural migrants living in *gecekondus*, or urban squatter settlements. It is known as arabesk music, and it is a new hybrid genre mixing Turkish classical and folk elements with those of the West and Egypt. The term "arabesk" was originally coined to designate—and denigrate—these popular songs, but it later came to describe the entire migrant culture formed at the peripheries of Turkish cities.[1]

Since the late 1970s, various attempts have been made to explain the rise of arabesk culture and its social significance. In the majority of these explanations, arabesk is seen as a threat in its so-called impurity, fatalistic outlook, and degeneration. It is said to ruralize and contaminate the urban environment. Underlying these dominant appraisals is "classical modernization theory," which assumes a duality between the traditional and the modern and postulates a cycle that admits a basic backwardness of the traditional followed by a transition period in which tradition gives way to modernity. Arabesk culture has been portrayed as the product of this transitional period—an alien and malformed element marginal to society that is supposed to fade away as industrialization and urbanization proceed.

The basic premise of this essay is that arabesk is not an anomaly but is instead a historical formation of popular culture, constructed and lived through the process of spatial and symbolic migration in the Turkish path through modernity.[2] This culture of hybridity was first made popular by the masses of rural migrants, giving voice to experiences shaped by the rapid modernization of Turkish society since the 1950s. It is the much-disputed urban culture of the peasant generations whom the founders of the Turkish republic once revered as the authentic foundation of the new society but whose "uncultured" presence, after they had migrated to live subordinately at the fringes of the urban centers as a spare army of labor,

211

has been much resented by the various established urban others. The story of arabesk, therefore, tells also a specific story about the "Westernization" of the so-called Third World, and understanding arabesk is crucial to comprehending the contradictions and ambivalences of the project and process of Turkish modernity.

One way of thinking about arabesk is to see it as a metaphor for popular identity—for the responses of the urbanizing popular classes to the capitalist modernization process in Turkey. Official cultural politics, growing market forces, the development of a culture industry, and popular traditions and changing lifestyles at the margins of society have all prepared the ground and provided the materials for the gradual articulation of arabesk music and culture. But it was specifically the spontaneous popular response that simultaneously opposed and affirmed the modernizing practices that gave arabesk its hybrid form and its original, potent energy.

The first public representation of this popular response appeared in the arabesk music of Orhan Gencebay, the founding musician of the style. Crystallized in Gencebay's music is the ambivalent structure of feeling of the popular masses that found its well-spring in the experience of displacement, with its double-edged emotions of liberation and desolation under the process of modernization.

Although arabesk remained a hybrid musical genre, its form, content, production, reception patterns, and social significance have changed markedly since the mid-1960s. The ideological journey of arabesk in these years can be broadly periodized according to its relationship with the changing politics of capitalism in Turkey, from the politics of nationalist developmentalism to those of transnational market orientation after the 1980s.

The 1970s represent the zenith in arabesk's journey as a popular response. After that decade, arabesk culture began to lose its subversive originality and came under the hegemony of neoconservative ideologies and a neoliberal economic restructuring. As the popular urban masses who nurtured arabesk became cultural and political forces to be reckoned with, and as the culture industry developed, their cultural expressions were increasingly drawn into the ideological and political mainstream. The music itself became diffused, fragmented, and commercialized; while some of it was marginalized, some climbed the cultural ladder, reaching far beyond the original enclave in its appeal. The expansion of arabesk beyond *gecekondu* borders after the 1980s revealed also that arabesk, as an emotional vocabulary, addressed people from many different walks of life and cut across experiences of displacement far beyond the encounter between the rural and the urban—including other cultural exclusions and the unrequited Turkish love for the "West."

The responses of intellectuals to arabesk have themselves been a force in the journey of the genre. Their debates are important not because they explain the social underpinnings of the arabesk formation but because they reveal the dominant aspirations of Turkish modernity. The labeling of the identities of the migrant and subordinated others as "arabesk" and the discourses and conflicts built around it helped to expand the story of arabesk from the cultural to the ideological arena. Thus, arabesk became a contentious topic after the 1980s in debates over national and urban identities and lifestyles. Ironically, the intellectuals' questions of "who we are" and "how we should live" were precisely the same ones the arabesk-loving masses themselves were posing when their voices found an outlet in the music of Orhan Gencebay at the end of the 1960s.

The Hybrid Roots of Arabesk Music

Arabesk music was first produced in Istanbul during the mid-1960s, when the Turkish music industry was in its infancy and was providing an avenue of creative expression for those excluded from state-controlled media and culture. Orhan Gencebay was its most famous early exponent. The term "arabesk" was already known to the music community of the early 1960s when it was used to describe the work of the popular composer Suat Sayın. Sayın was writing light versions of Turkish "art" music—the name given to the derivative of classical Ottoman court music—and plagiarizing some melodies from Egypt. His major contribution was the way in which he orchestrated this music. Instead of using one each of the traditional instruments, as was the convention, Sayın multiplied their number and augmented them with a Western string section following the Egyptian style. Thus, in an interesting twist, Western influences seeped into Turkish art music via Egypt.[3]

Orhan Gencebay appeared on the scene in the mid-1960s. A self-taught musician, he was influenced by many other musicians, some excluded from official media and others more classical or mainstream practitioners of Turkish folk music and art music. In 1966, when Gencebay wrote his first popular song, "No Raft in the Ocean to Hold Onto" (Deryada Bir Salım Yok), he combined various folk and classical instruments with Western strings. Although the tune was not originally Arabic, its orchestration led orthodox classical and radio musicians to consider Gencebay an arabesk musician too, after Sayın. At that point, "arabesk" was a term confined to a small music community; it had not yet entered the public debates over Turkish cultural identity. But the connotations intended in its initial labeling—impurity, nonbelonging, and backwardness owing to Arabic influence—were to remain thereafter.

A migrant himself, Orhan Gencebay had left his Black Sea hometown of Samsun for Istanbul to achieve recognition as a musician at a time when the myth of the "golden rocks and lands of Istanbul" referred plausibly to actual conditions. Studies of arabesk have ignored the fact that its emergence coincided with a relative cultural renaissance in Turkish society that lasted until the late 1970s. This renaissance was a product of diverse struggles and cultural projects of earlier decades, and it culminated in the strengthening of democratic principles and fundamental human rights in the 1961 Constitution, and in a more equitable distribution of income.[4] The 1960s were a time of experimentation and innovation in popular culture and provided fertile ground for the creative exchange of influences among various musical traditions. After 1962, the fruits of these endeavors began to appear on the market, gradually feeding an expanding record industry. This wave of innovation owed itself also to the widening accessibility of state-owned radio, which, after the late 1930s, began introducing Turkish folk music and classical and art music across the country, along with Western classical and pop music. These musical genres had earlier been confined to regional production and consumption.[5]

One conspicuous result of this musical renaissance in the 1960s was the reinvention of, and renewed appreciation for, folk music and instruments. The primary folk music instrument, the *bağlama,* or long-necked lute, in particular became a musical icon for popular and radical musicians and for the leftist militants of the 1960s and 1970s. Folk elements began to be blended into rock music, culminating in a new musical genre called Anatolian rock music. The newfound popularity of Anatolian folk music played a crucial role in determining the future of arabesk music.

It was the incorporation of folk music elements into the lush Sayın-style orchestration of Turkish art music that characterized Orhan Gencebay's work and gave it the locus of its identity. Gencebay is a true virtuoso of the *bağlama* and has a unique playing style into which he has worked various influences. Indeed, he has said that what hurt him most in the 1950s, when American rock music and Turkish art music were reigning on the music scene, was the disdain shown toward the *bağlama.* He then began playing famous Turkish art and Western rock songs with it, especially the songs of Elvis Presley, trying to show that "this innocent instrument [was] capable of playing every kind of music."

In 1968, Gencebay wrote and performed "Give Me Consolation" (Bir Teselli Ver), and then "Nobody Is without Fault" (Hatasız Kul Olmaz), which made a breakthrough as something more than just music. Something in the lyrics and melodies of these works resonated with the oral vocabularies, musical traditions, and new lifestyles of the *gecekondu* populations. The music tapped into the new private language growing at the outer margins of the big cities, a language that expressed the rising expectations, desires, and frustrations of the urbanizing popular masses under the experience of the urban encounter. The culture of migration and subordination had found a voice in Gencebay's work and image, and that voice was carried via his music into public representation. Within a decade, the same music was to become an object of scorn in the judging eyes of the established urban others.

The hybrid quality of Gencebay's music was its foremost characteristic, both in its musical elements and in the ideas expressed in its lyrics. The "sliding" singing style performed in a dramatic voice, the use of counterpoint and lush orchestration, and the emphasis on rhythm created an alluring sound and feel quite new for the period.[6] Gencebay's music is very emotional and melodic, as is Turkish music in general. The dominant theme in the lyrics is love, and all other themes dissolve into lyrics about love or are spoken through the authority of love.

The pervasive theme of love forces the lyrics to center on the first person (I), the beloved (you), and the unique importance of their union (we) in the world. The "world" refers to different habitats: the inner world of the lover, the union of lover and beloved, and human life at large. The beloved "you" is often left abstract. She is the intimate fellow sufferer, as the beloved has always been in Turkish mystic poetry. Sometimes the "you" is displaced from the beloved and used to address God or fate. At other times it seems to be representing an abstract subject translatable as society or even state or any perceived oppressor. The "we" is also a vague collective category of "lovers" who are described as poor, lonely, homeless sufferers (*garip*) searching for "truth" in the form of love. The "I" is the conjurer, yearning for love and solace from the "you." And the "you" is capable of giving happiness as well as oppression, love as well as humiliation, solace as well as suffering. At times, the lover turns to God asking plaintively, is it "me who is baffled or you, my God?" When the beloved is just and compassionate, she is depicted as the sun, life, and happiness itself. The "I," who yearns to belong, feels completed by submission to and becoming one with the "you."

All through this tangle of meaning, the identity of the speaker "I" is problematized and becomes infused with questions of life and death, love and hate, and happiness and suffering. Despite this questioning, however, the "I" is always the innocent one, the one who has cause to blame and accuse the other of not allowing him to live in love. The "I" cannot bear the possibility of isolation from the beloved, which would break the bonds of love and suffering between the two. Though protesting against suffering in this "dreamlike world," the lover also endures and resigns himself to that state by considering it an "experience." Even the pain of unrequited love offers some solace, because love itself is the ultimate balance, the solution to the misery in the world—the world that obstructs one's right to live in love.[7]

The early lyrics of Orhan Gencebay's songs are usually composed of popular traditional concepts given a mystically religious voice that is secular in intent. But the articulation of the lyrics with the sounds of the melodies amounts to an invention of popular tradition containing connotations that were readily understood and in tune with the popular discontent and protest specific to the 1970s. Poverty, displacement, deprivation, and the harsh daily round of urban life are not explicitly described in arabesk lyrics, but they are expressed abstractly and through a feeling of disquiet and yearning that permeates the music. Although the lyrics do not speak directly of social inequities, they have struck a sympathetic chord in the people who receive their immediate contextual meaning.[8]

It is worth noting the difference between the types of themes that Orhan Gencebay used in songs shaped more by folk music and those in songs shaped by Turkish art music. His folk-style–dominated music was the vehicle for stirring social themes put to voice by the lover, whose laments to the beloved are against the suffering in the world. In his art music, private, personal love reigns supreme. Because love, in this symbolic discourse, is conceived of as analogous to the right to live in dignity, the harsh social conditions that prevent love constitute an obstacle to a fulfilling life.[9] Thus, in this symbolic network, both the personal and the communal levels are addressed through the vocabulary of love, which is itself offered ultimately as the imaginary solution for handling the "problem of meaning" caused by displacement under modernization. It was this new articulation of the long Anatolian tradition of popular justice that gave Orhan Gencebay's arabesk its democratic resonance. Gencebay's arabesk music created a specific "affective/moral vocabulary" for the urban popular masses who engaged daily in a struggle to survive, resist, and be recognized.[10]

The Popularity of Arabesk during Periods of Change

Orhan Gencebay found himself a popular hero at the end of the 1960s. He had become almost an urban minstrel (*aşık*). His image grew into that of a benevolent older brother who was manly, trustworthy, and tolerant and who spoke against injustice, humiliation, and poverty. His lyrics were concerned with the problems of life and love, usually put forth in plain, wise sayings clothed in Anatolian *aşık* tradition and folk mysticism.

The protest tradition in Turkish folk poetry and music had seen a revival beginning with the end of the 1950s. *Aşıks* were migrating to the major cities, bringing their *bağlamas* and new poems that no longer focused on the simple conflict between rich and poor but contained more sophisticated themes protesting what they called the "corrupt social order." Although the revived protest tradition coursed through Gencebay's arabesk music, he diluted and blended it, inventing a new tradition of humanism for mass consumption. The title of one of Gencebay's most famous songs, "Down with This World" (Batsın Bu Dünya), might seem to indicate an utter rejection of it, but in fact Gencebay liked to live in this changing world—he simply wanted it to be a better place. For him, change should come through fusion and compassion rather than through exclusion and force. The title is meant to strengthen people's emotional response against the human hosts and dehumanizing assaults of capitalist modernization.

The metaphorical response of Gencebay's work to modernization is, on the whole, an ambivalent one. There is an uneasiness in which modernization is both affirmed and denied, submitted to and resisted. His work has both welcomed the possibilities the process of modernization offers and denied the reality of the exclusion and injustice it has caused. Gencebay has mixed different musics, made use of modern technology, and incorporated popular traditions to voice this melange of experience. Ambivalence surfaces also in his music, especially in the soaring melodic lines that evoke a yearning simultaneously defiant, sad, and hopeful.[11]

The growth of the Turkish audiocassette industry and the importation and production of new music technology prepared the ground for the diffusion and proliferation of arabesk music beginning in the 1970s and especially during the 1980s. Although arabesk music was excluded from state-run radio and television because it did not fit into any of the officially sanctioned musical modes, by the mid-1970s it was everywhere. It could be heard in music halls and blaring from cassette players in minibuses and taxis, and it could be enjoyed in workplaces in the informal sector, in squatter homes, and in drinking establishments (*meyhanes*). Arabesk invaded virtually every private and public sphere, from theaters that showed movies of arabesk singers to thoroughfares where street peddlers sold cassettes. It traveled from squatter homes back to the city center in taxis and minibuses run by the migrants themselves. Truck drivers carried it from city to city. So closely associated with migration and with its literal means of transport was arabesk music that during the 1970s it was often called "minibus music" or "*gecekondu* music." Gaudily decorated minibuses took migrants through urban streets to jobs in the formal and informal sectors, where their music, language, values, and manners interacted and clashed with those of the urban middle and upper classes.[12]

The first generations of migrants were also travelers between urban squatter settlements and rural native villages, where they visited relatives and brought provisions for the winter. They seem not, however, to have maintained illusions about permanent return to the village, no matter how impoverished their lives were. Yet to satisfy their urgent daily needs, which ranged from building or renting *gecekondu*s to finding jobs, they created informal clusters and networks of kinship, townsmanship, and neighborhood relations within the larger urban setting. Migrants preserved their sense of individual and communal identity through these networks. The one main axis for a migrant's identity stemmed from these clusters and depended on the answer to the question, "Where are you from?"

The most famous arabesk singers came from outside Istanbul. Their fame and popularity corresponded more or less to their regional place of origin and the size of the migrant population coming from that area to Istanbul. Orhan Gencebay became famous during the late 1960s, when migrants were moving to Istanbul in large numbers from the middle and northern parts of Anatolia. Ferdi Tayfur and Müslüm Gürses reached their peak of popularity in the late 1970s, when the south and east fed Istanbul with migrants. Emrah and İbrahim Tatlıses were stars of the 1980s, when massive numbers arrived in Istanbul from the southeast. Although good arabesk singers inflected their music with the distinct accents, sounds, images, and moods of their respective regions, they all retained their general appeal to the poor and powerless. Gradually, these regionalisms were reworked in Istanbul and distributed throughout Anatolia, so that arabesk music became the most widespread popular genre in Turkey in the 1980s.

The end of the 1970s was a time of growing economic depression and deep political crisis. It was also a time when cultural tensions and social contradictions resulting from the process of migration came to the fore, and it was publicly realized that rural migrants were not mere visitors to the cities. Increasing the urban population density by about 50 percent, harboring radical leftist militancy, and focusing their infrastructural and social demands at the level of municipalities, the *gecekondu* populations proved that they had come to stay. The term "arabesk" then superseded the phrases "minibus music" and "*gecekondu* music" irreversibly. "Arabesk" began to encompass not just a musical genre but the entire lifestyle and mentality of the *gecekondu*s, including both migrant and nonmigrant urban popular classes. It provided an "arbitrary closure" for multiple popular identities, separating and positioning them as the urban "other."[13]

During the 1980s, the new political rulers played a conscious game of hegemony that revolved around manipulating and winning the support of the *gecekondu* masses, who were now seen as worth wooing for their votes. New right-wing populist policies began to be realized with the victories of the Motherland Party (Anavatan Partisi), implementing material rewards at the level of municipalities and securing the necessary ideological interpolations at the national level.[14]

Indeed, the political significance of arabesk was acknowledged by Turgut Özal well before he formed the Motherland Party and became prime minister in 1983. In 1979 he had written a major report to Prime Minister Süleyman Demirel of the Justice Party (Adalet Partisi) in which he pointed out that the very fluid votes of the *gecekondu*s held the key to the national elections (a point that proved true).[15] The Motherland Party formed a research unit called the Arabesk Group to study the cultural habits, likes, and dislikes of the *gecekondu* people. Later, the party hired a major public opinion research organization to develop a voter profile of the party, the outcome of which contended that those who had voted for the Motherland Party were, in general, conservative. But even the most conservative of these voters were sympathetic to liberal pluralism. The game of hegemony had its results, and the research found what it had looked for from the start—that the voters were neoconservatives or neoliberals.[16]

The 1983 elections in Turkey saw, for the first time, mass political advertising. Among other things, the Özalist political campaigns made widespread use of arabesk music. Özal, in fact, was genuinely fond of the music and employed it to support his themes that all Turks were "lovers" and that he respected and welcomed all of the four main political ideologies (extreme right, Islamist, center right, and social democrat) into Motherland's fold.[17] Just as Gencebay's music articulated the popular classes' demand for change through a fusion of the popular tradition and the new values, so did this neoconservative project do so by conjoining conservative values with the new market values.[18] But in this new political arena, the fusion of the old and the new shifted away from being a means of providing for the welfare of the popular classes toward becoming an avenue to victory for the powerful new entrepreneurs of the emerging financial, commercial, and trade arenas and their politicians. Against this background, arabesk lost its utopian connotations and became increasingly associated with pragmatic concerns such as registering squatter houses or "turning the corner without due labor."

Throughout the 1980s, therefore, the story of arabesk became increasingly complex as the popular classes partially tuned into the neoconservative politics of the new right. Clientelism and promises of legalizing *gecekondu* ownership rights manipulated *gecekondu* votes before each election. As land speculation became rampant, some former *gecekondu* dwellers took advantage of rising property values and built apartments, while a *gecekondu* mafia flourished in the real estate market. With the influence of mass media, arabesk also came to characterize the lifestyle, tastes, and sentiments of a newly rich group with provincial origins: new economic elites of finance, commerce, and trade. The sensationalistic media began broadcasting images of the new rich displaying incompatible arabesk tastes, epitomized in the stereotype of their drinking *alafranka* (Western) whiskey while eating *alaturka* (Turkish) *lahmacun*. The audience for arabesk music had expanded to include not only the masses of *gecekondu* dwellers and much of the rural population but also sections of the middle and ruling classes of the 1980s. Thus, during the second half of the 1980s, as arabesk became the most widespread music across the country, the earlier public awareness of poverty and subordination at the urban peripheries waned. Arabesk began to be used as a metaphor for Özal's regime.

Since the end of the 1970s, arabesk as a musical genre had evolved, mutated, and proliferated as it became more popular and gained, through improved technology, a wider and more diversified reception. Many of these changes can be seen in the musical output of Orhan Gencebay, who is still considered the "king" of arabesk. During the 1980s, although the theme of love remained a dominant feature of arabesk music, the political protest of earlier songs evaporated, as did the tension in the music between grief and hope. As it became a more commercial genre, spawning profitable subindustries in production, writing, performance, videos, and advertising, arabesk's themes became more worldly and concrete, and fame began to go to new, newsworthy singers. (Orhan Gencebay, however, remained writer, performer, and producer of his own music.) Recent technology and recording techniques have also changed the sound of arabesk and created variations on it; one of the most widespread forms in the 1980s was called "taverna" music.[19]

Arabesk music greatly influenced the genres of Turkish art music, folk music, and pop music—the established categories of Turkish music disseminated by the state-run mass media. Arabesk melodic patterns, rhythmic emphases, and performance styles seeped into these other genres, although arabesk itself remained prohibited. Until the emergence of private television and radio channels in the 1990s, only the leading singers were allowed to perform on national holidays.

After the mid-1980s, arabesk not only began to be used widely in political campaign songs and as theme music at football games but also was admitted to the world of "legitimate" entertainment and was assimilated by the culture industry. Orhan Gencebay was elevated to the status of "classic" arabesk. Ferdi Tayfur also gained wide and lasting acceptance as the second major star of arabesk, while Müslüm Gürses's transgressive music and image developed into a cult. Arabesk continued to produce protest singers, most notably Ahmet Kaya, who defined his music as "the opposition of emotions." Kaya, like Gürses, appealed most strongly to marginalized youths, the "lads" excluded from the dominant culture. The media began to talk of his music as "revolutionary arabesk," just as it called other new versions "Islamist" and "nationalist" arabesks. Common to all of them was performance style.

The imaginary collective identity of the migrant culture given voice by the arabesk music of the 1970s seems to have lost its "closure" in the mid-1990s. The hybrid quality of arabesk has penetrated other genres as arabesk has spread and lost its previous class anchoring in popular discontent and protest. Arabesk has been superseded now by a vibrant new pop music and culture that owes much to arabesk, as well as to MTV and a reinvention of the Turkish pop music of the 1960s and 1970s. Although the three now-classic arabesk musicians are still well received, audiences in general are no longer partisans of a single arabesk singer. Instead, there seems to be a desire to embrace more singers and styles, from arabesk to pop, and not to align oneself so passionately with a single performer.

The changing journey of arabesk is apparent not only in its widening appeal but also in the changing attitudes of its singers and followers toward the dominant appraisal that arabesk is uncultured. Even more than differences in class, region, and income, it is differences in educational assets that continue to overdetermine the discourses on arabesk culture and the identity clashes lived around it. A decade earlier, arabesk singers expressed their sentiments defensively; now, they seem more self-confident, and their followers are also more open in their rage against their non-arabesk counterparts. This defiance was clearly articulated by the end of the 1980s, when the terms *maganda* and *zonta,* originally created by cartoonists, entered the popular vocabulary to describe and denigrate arabesk aficionados as vulgar, sexist, and uneducated. Youths at the fringes of the dominant urban culture responded by coining their own term, *entel,* as a sarcastic nickname for preening, "sterile" intellectuals.[20] *Entel*s were defined as the natives of Istanbul, who were the antitheses of the Anatolian migrants.[21]

In interviews, Ferdi Tayfur often mentions the difficult circumstances of his life—the death of his father and the necessity of his foregoing an education in order to support his family by manual labor—and contrasts it with the lives of the educated rich, who humiliate the poor but are in fact no better than they. Such bitterness is also reflected in arabesk singers' refusal to describe their work as arabesk, because of the term's "dirty" connotations. Orhan Gencebay, for example, insisting that his music has nothing to do with the Arabs, refers to his own work as "free Turkish music," in opposition to the stilted, one-dimensional, officially sanctioned performances of Turkish music. He maintains that his music is more than an outgrowth of the migrant experience—he has created a new mixed genre that could address all Turks, rural and urban alike.

So, although arabesk singers have found honor in their work and their popular recognition, they have not embraced the label "arabesk" with enthusiasm. This is less true for later generations of musicians and migrants, who do not hesitate to assert their Anatolian origins. Their bolder attitude was expressed by the folk-arabesk singer İbrahim Tatlıses during the 1980s. Tatlıses became famous for his beautiful Kurdish voice and folk songs and was known to have underground supporters as well as sympathy for Turgut Özal, which was reciprocated by the late president. He emphasized bravado and masculinity, which resulted in much criticism and in his ultimately being branded a vulgar *maganda*. But Tatlıses was unfazed and began to parody himself, playing up the *maganda* stereotype and making fun of himself and his critics.

The role gender plays in the formation and popularity of arabesk music is a complex question. Orhan Gencebay, who implied in his arabesk that suffering would one day end, retained his image of sedate manliness. Ferdi Tayfur, who became famous after him during the depression years at the end of the 1970s, showed, in his gloomier arabesk, that men did cry in a society in which manliness was predominantly defined as being tough. Although a number of female arabesk singers have become popular and the music has been well received by women in general, the genre has re- mained closely bound to masculine culture. It is strongly associated with mustaches, masculine friendship, and *rakı*-drinking, cigarette-smoking rituals.

But this masculine ethos seems to have its ambiguities. Its bravado hides a sense of self-doubt, of a self devalued under the gaze of a dominant "other" that pushes these men into a vulnerable status in society.[22] Thus, the emotional disposition of a subordinated self positions these men along- side other excluded people and seems to admit, in effect, a crossing of the boundaries of gender and an acceptance of the permeability of iden- tities. The considerable number and popularity of transsexual arabesk singers, including the famous Bülent Ersoy, adds to this blurring of the conventional boundaries between genders. The dominant discourse on arabesk, on the other hand, is filled with gender-inscribed adjectives such as "passive," "depressed," and "yelling," indicting this ambivalent emo- tional disposition in arabesk culture.

Arabesk and the Debate over National Cultural Identity

Since the late 1970s, many writers have debated the origins and the mean- ing of arabesk culture in Turkey. The dominant appraisal has been that because Turkey was an "underdeveloped country," its path toward mod- ernization was "crooked," and arabesk, as a "degraded" genre, was sim- ply a reflection of this deviation. And because arabesk music was formed concomitantly with the growth of market forces in the musical arena, it was considered a mere entertainment administered to the semi-peasant masses.[23] In the *Encyclopedia of Music*, arabesk is defined as "a music of alienation"—the rural migrants could not leave their traditional values behind, could not adapt to the urban environment, and so nourished hatred toward it. Arabesk, the article continues, which has no musical value, provides the means for these people to "yell out" their distress and depression.[24] These attitudes toward arabesk led studies of it to be restricted by the "integration perspective." The musical characteristics of arabesk and the new lifestyles and subjectivities being constructed on the peripheries of urban culture have been left out of the research agenda.[25]

Bureaucrats, intellectuals, and artists of disparate cultural and political persuasions have shared the opinion that arabesk is a vulgar, degenerate genre, though their reasons differed. For bureaucrats in general, and producers of state-run television and radio in particular, any Turkish music that did not fit into the officially sanctioned categories of Turkish art music, Turkish folk music, Turkish light (pop) music, or polyphonic (Western) music was assumed to be arabesk music and therefore subject to censorship—alongside music with radical or leftist lyrics. Most leftist thinkers also distanced themselves from arabesk, which they viewed as a traditional (read, backward) genre that promoted a fatalistic viewpoint, provided a false, easily manipulated consciousness, and was devoid of the element of social protest. It was, in this sense, no more than "opium for the masses." Turkish classical and folk musicians, on the other hand, condemned arabesk for polluting the "pure" traditions with Arab and Western influences.

Indeed, the negative connotations of arabesk actually increased with time. Initially, the label "arabesk" had meant that the music was only an imitation; it did not belong to "our" culture, since it was of Arabic origin, and all things Arabic were thought to have been left behind as the country Westernized. After 1980, arabesk gained a negative political connotation as well, owing to its affiliation with the neoliberal practices of the Motherland Party. By the mid-1980s, influential writers had begun using the term "arabesk" to describe virtually anything in Turkish social life that they considered degenerate: arabesk democracy, economy, people, tastes, sentiments, and ways of thinking and living. It was as if the term had finally provided a name for the problem of Turkish identity in a society long struggling with its self-image as an underdeveloped state. It had almost become a metaphor for Turkey's unrequited love for the "West." The broad use of the term "arabesk" described a social reality that fit neither the ideal traditional (Eastern) nor the modern (Western) forms, relationships, practices, and values but instead was completely unforeseen, odd, and embarrassing. Because arabesk was considered backward in every way and fatalistic in its vision, it became a symbol of everything that must be jettisoned from society.

The debate over arabesk music and culture has raged so fiercely because this was the first massive popular cultural formation that grew in the hothouse of modernizing Turkey. It spontaneously transgressed and questioned accepted notions about Turkish cultural identity. That the debate centered on music was no coincidence. The origins of the debates on music go back to the closing of the military music center—the Mehterhane—during the abolition of the Janissary army in 1826, when the Ottoman government came out in favor of Western music. Republican reforms of the 1920s also influenced the traditional music scene. When the Ottoman dervish lodges were closed by the state in 1925 during secularization, the second most vital arena for the production of traditional music, after the Ottoman court itself, was eliminated. A year later, education in Turkish music was proscribed. For fifteen months in 1934–35, in the state's fervor to structure a national identity fixed on a Western cultural model, all Turkish music was banned on private radio.

The official cultural politics of the Turkish republic, especially in its early years, gave priority to Western classical music and—in its visions of populism—Turkish folk music, and it promoted a "Westernized" and "modernized" version of Turkish folk music as well. Behind such moves was the influence of the nationalist thought of Ziya Gökalp (1876–1924), who drew a sharp distinction between civilization and culture. According to Gökalp, the new civilization was universal and was represented by Western science, technology, and intellectual developments. Culture, however, was particular to a society and was represented by a people's spirit, values, and aspirations. For Gökalp, Ottoman classical music belonged to the realm of old civilization and was, moreover, of Byzantine origin with Arab inflections, so it could hardly represent the new Turkish national identity. Anatolian folklore and folk music, however, were outgrowths of Turkish culture before Islamization and therefore were the cultural resources around which a Turkish national identity could be formed. So it was a synthesis of Western civilization and Turkish folklore that formed the foundation on which the new identity was to arise.

During the early 1930s, a republican campaign was launched for a radio of "education, culture, and propaganda" to oppose the broadcasting policy of the then-private radio industry. Critics fervently accused private radio producers of acting merely as entertainers and commercial disseminators of "tasteless and fatalist" Turkish art songs, the so-called *alaturka* music of the period.[26] In 1936, when the state took control of private radio stations, it began broadcasting the products of cultural projects developed by bureaucrats and scholars in their efforts to build and impose a preferred national culture. Thus, the tension between *alaturka* and *alafranka* music has had a long history and lies at the heart of an on-going debate over the crafting of the Turkish national identity—an identity into which the tension between the traditional and the modern was easily integrated.

By promoting Western music and Turkish folk music while neglecting, censuring, and prohibiting Turkish classical and art music or any reinvention different from the state-sanctioned modes, the cultural politics of the Turkish state contributed to the development of arabesk music and to its social significance. The state's actions have put music and culture at the center of the national ideological and political struggle since the foundation of the republic. In doing so, they set the stage for the struggle among the intelligentsia, between the state and the people, and between the educated and the uneducated.

At the end of the 1980s, for the first time, under Turgut Özal's influence, there was a discussion about permitting the performance of arabesk music on Turkish radio and television. This softening of the state line on arabesk seemed to culminate in 1988 with the Second National Congress for Music, in which the subject of arabesk was at last included. In 1989, the Ministry of Cultural Affairs attempted to commission from an arabesk composer an arabesk song devoid of grief. It was hoped, rather naively, that this song could be used as a model for future production and would elevate arabesk from its general "vulgarity" and "tastelessness." The effort came to nothing.

With the 1990s, a major source of dissemination for arabesk has been the new private television stations, whose motto is "whatever sells well gets air time." The expanding neoliberal atmosphere and the emergence of a new, private mass media have provided fertile ground for a new appreciation of arabesk that competes with the earlier appraisal. This new appraisal accords with the mythical discourse of the Özalist regime, which maintains that Turkey has not just come a long way toward modernization but has in fact achieved it. Turkey has recently "jumped directly into modernity" in its own peculiar fashion. Following this line, if people want to buy arabesk music, there is "no problem," since this is a time of free choice, and it is thanks to the migrants that urban culture has become more pluralistic and colorful.

During decades past, under Kemalist authoritarianism (now referred to by some as First Republicanism), arabesk was suppressed and conceived of as a disquieting throwback to Eastern traditions, hardly comparable to anything from the West. Under the so-called Second Republicanism there is a more confident attitude that no longer fears everything from the East and is not obsessed with cultural purity. This new pragmatism, however, is indexed to market forces, which dispense with the norms of public responsibility and social justice. Moreover, by hiding the asymmetrical power relations that make and cut through different tastes and identities, it leaves them untouched and institutionalizes an easy, surface pluralism.

In the Turkey of the mid-1990s, the debates over arabesk have lost their cultural vibration. The rising Islamist Welfare Party (Refah Partisi) and the threat of Islamist fundamentalism are now at the center of the cultural and political agenda, while the Kurdish issue, as it pertains to ethnic identity or political solutions, is not yet a publicly debatable subject under a rising, popularized racist nationalism. By the late 1980s, arabesk had already lost its allure as a radical popular formation that used the materials of modernity to resist modernizing control from above. After the left-wing political milieu of the 1970s, in which arabesk had derived its subversive significance, was undermined by the military coup, the nodal point that articulated arabesk as a democratic discourse about the right to live in dignity was loosened. Arabesk sentiments in general became more easily incorporated into and revealed through different subjectivities and political orientations after the 1980s. Losing its original anchoring in "low modernism," arabesk has become so diffused that it is now considered a "transclass taste" and structure of feeling.[27]

Although arabesk culture was neutralized and its subversive elements marginalized, the state of poverty and subordination from which it sprouted has not been eliminated. Resistance and protest persist, in various forms, on the fringes of the urban landscapes and in the corners of the dominant culture—the more public manifestations of which have yet to show. Meanwhile, in the place of old shanty *gecekondu*s there have arisen shanty multistoried apartment complexes as subcities with virtually no urban amenities on their outskirts.[28] In recent years, the cleavage has markedly increased between the peripheral neighborhoods and the suburban villa-towns of the upper-middle class and, in the urban core, the commercial and financial centers, shopping malls, and five-star hotels. The new urban spaces constructed for presumably educated and high-income customers are promoted for their convenient and sterile lifestyles protected from the physical and "cultural" contamination of the city. The differentiation of living, working, and consumption spaces for different classes and groups in greater Istanbul signifies a social fracture that is splitting Turkey into at least two unequal societies, if not into more.

It is no coincidence that current political debate over the Islamist Welfare Party revolves around the term "lifestyle." The dominant camps in this conflict draw their bases of support from groups with quite different lifestyles. The Islamist Welfare Party, while developing its own bourgeoisie and its new intellectuals, grew by winning broad support from the old and new *gecekondu* populations with its populist motto of "pure and just order." Opposed to it is a loose group consisting of the radical bourgeoisie, state bureaucrats, the army, the urban middle classes, Kemalist intellectuals, the "Second Republicans," and some radical intellectuals. Secularism and the Western-modern way of life are about the only common ground this otherwise incompatible alliance has.

It is clear that class does not correspond "properly" to political culture because class boundaries in Turkey have been increasingly crosscut by contradictory and hybrid cultural constructs of religion, ethnicity, nationalism, lifestyle, and gender. The culture of the popular classes can be opposed as "alienated" or "backward" by their supposedly counterpart intellectuals, as has been the case with arabesk culture. At the same time, regressiveness and racism can become popular among the subordinated, as is epitomized in the Sivas massacre and the rise of a popularized nationalist fervor suppressing the Kurdish issue. It is not just because the official, public political sphere in Turkey is so very restricted that social conflicts have been increasingly expressed in the language of culture since the 1980s; the politicization of culture itself has been a major factor in and consequence of the project and process of Turkish modernity from its inception. In that sense, the contradiction that inheres in the formation and appraisals of arabesk culture continue with Turkish society: the contradiction between a dominant nationalist and paternalist incapacity to live with difference and a deep, unrealized popular capacity to change and accept difference through hybridization.

In conclusion, a few questions may be asked, based on the foregoing discussion, that allow a rethinking of the Turkish path toward modernity. How far can the mode of articulation of arabesk, during both its subversive and its hegemonic periods, be considered a metaphor for that path? Does the culture of migration of Turkish laborers living in Germany include a structure of feeling that resembles arabesk, although it may be lived in inflected forms owing to different social contexts? The two questions can be combined into the same question that Stuart Hall asks: "What stays the same when you travel?"[29] What has stayed the same in people's physical and symbolic travel along the capitalist modernization path, from the Ottoman Empire to the republic, from the village to the city, or from Turkey to Germany?

And what has happened to the popular democratic demand to live in dignity that was articulated in the visions and blueprints of the left-wing cultural and political movements of the 1960s and 1970s? If there was anything substantial in this modern demand, when and how will it return? What new subjectivities, languages, sounds, and counterpolitical public spheres will give it voice? And with what new attitudes and discourses will intellectuals and scholars receive this new subversive popular voice?

Notes

1. "Arabesk" (French, *arabesque;* Italian, *arbesco*), meaning "made or done in the Arabic fashion," refers to a complex, ornate design of intertwined foliate or geometrical figures used for ornamentation (*American Heritage Dictionary*, s.v. "arabesk").

2. Throughout this article the terms "popular," "popular culture," and "popular tradition" are used as they are defined by Stuart Hall in his "Notes on Deconstructing the Popular," in G. S. Jones et al., eds., *People's History and Socialist Theory*, London: Routledge and Kegan Paul, 1981, 227–40.

3. Because the main centers for producing classical music were closed down, there was no officially sanctioned arena for education in this genre until the State School of Turkish Music was established in 1976. When Turkish musicians working in the music market attempted to revitalize Turkish music, some of them looked to the Egyptian model, which was grounded in synthesizing Western and Ottoman classical musics. During the Second World War and into the 1950s, Egyptian and Indian films became immensely popular in Turkey. These films offered well-known singers as leading characters in stories about good, poor people who were oppressed by the evil rich. Lyrics from these movie soundtracks were translated into Turkish, and similar songs began to be composed by some Turkish musicians. Some of them, such as Sadettin Kaynak and Selahattin Pınar, were very famous and are now considered classical Turkish composers. At the time, however, they were not held in high regard by orthodox classical musicians.

4. See Korkut Boratav, "Türkiye'de Populism: 1962–1976 Dönemi Üzerine Bazı Notlar," *Yapıt*, no. 1, 1983, 7–18.

5. Although there was conflict between state-controlled radio and private music

institutions, the interaction between them cannot be ignored. From the end of the 1930s, both the music halls and recording studios, on one hand, and state radio, on the other, became de facto music schools in the absence of other public institutions. If musicians worked in both arenas, they adapted to two different modes of performance, one popular, the other official. Moreover, the singers performed both Turkish art songs and folk songs—the vast collection of which was made by experts working at the radio and in the People's Houses—until the 1950s, when musicians began to differentiate between these music traditions. These crossovers and the mixed music programs performed at the music halls had an effect in the blending of the folk and art music elements later in arabesk.

6. The vocal technique of sliding over notes is a characteristic feature of Turkish art music. This is most apparent in the classic *gazel* form, which was banned from state radio but was popular in *gazino*s (music halls) and films. A single rhythm eventually pervaded the arabesk scene and became known as "arabesk rhythm," which is typically a *düyek* played double time, although other variations of *düyek*, alongside different rhythms, were used by Gencebay himself.

7. A few examples of lines from Gencebay's most popular songs of the 1970s illustrate the yearning for a good life: "We are only guests in this world/So we can only behave like guests." "You may not like the *garip*s/But don't ever look down on them/It is such a shame that man serve man." "Love is happiness/Love is life itself/So you let us live." "Down with this world/Let the dream end/Shame to the days without love/Every drop of tear is a protest of my years/Every drop of happiness is a protest from my heart/Justice is what we are after/Oh God, let this cruelty stop/I don't ever want anything from the oppressor/But God, you are the Almighty/So you give me consolation."

8. The traditional view, for example, that it was shameful for man to serve man, which is articulated in Gencebay's lyrics, was even made into the political slogan "Enough with man serving man" by the Turkish Workers' Party in the mid-1960s.

9. Nature and social issues have long constituted a "decor" in the feelings of the folk poets, as Pertev Naili Boratav points out in his *Folklor ve Edebiyat*, Istanbul: Adam Yayıncılık, 1982, 356–59. In the *mani* form, social norms are upheld if they reinforce love, and one would be justified in resisting them if these norms appear to hinder love. See İlhan Başgöz, *Folklor Yazıları*, Istanbul: Adam Yayınları, 1986, 232–39.

10. Clifford Geertz, *The Interpretation of Cultures*, London: Hutchinson, 1973, 104–8, 218.

11. Beginning in 1971, musical films starring arabesk singers began to be called arabesk films. For the most part, these films did not differ from other musicals. In arabesk films, however—especially in Gencebay's—there was a real tension between traditional values and the need to resist injustice, generally caused by a traditional figure who was powerful and wealthy. The usual solution for Gencebay was to take justice into his own hands, as he did in his 1975 movie *Down with This World* (Batsın Bu Dünya).

12. Titles of songs and lyrics from Orhan Gencebay's repertoire entered popular culture as slogans and were also put on stickers. These stickers, as well as postcard snapshots of famous arabesk singers, were important decorations inside and outside the minibuses, trucks, and taxis run by the migrants.

13. "Arbitrary closure" is discussed in Stuart Hall, "Cultural Studies and Its Theoretical Legacies," in L. Grossberg et al., eds., *Cultural Studies*, New York: Routledge, 1992, 278.

14. See Korkut Boratav, *Türkiye'de Sosyal Sınıflar ve Bölüşüm*, Istanbul: Gerçek Yayınevi, 1991, 117–21.

15. Taha Akyol, "ANAP ve İdeoloji," *Tercüman*, 20–27 October 1988.

16. The two surveys were conducted by SİAR for the Motherland Party in 1987 and 1988.

17. Because all former political parties were banned by the National Security Council after the 1980 coup, this catch-all kind of politics worked well as political alliances were reconstituted under the few officially permitted new parties. The strength of neoconservative-neoliberal politics thus arose out of the 1980 coup, which also undermined the 1961 Constitution and the other major democratic laws. Leaders of the coup chose a "Turkish-Islamist synthesis" as the new binding ideology. Although this ideology was not all-pervasive, it had a strong impact on the shaping of political and cultural movements and institutions after the 1980s. The Motherland Party took 45 percent and 36 percent, respectively, in the 1983 and 1987 national elections. This included the majority of the *gecekondu* votes, which, in the 1970s, were going to the social democratic Republican People's Party. But in later elections Motherland Party's share fell to 20 percent of the votes cast.

18. There are some important similarities between Thatcherism and Özalism. When Stuart Hall describes how Thatcherism "stitched together a contradictory juncture between the logics of the market and possessive individualism, on the one hand, and the logics of an organic conservatism, on the other," he could just as well have been writing about Özalism. See Stuart Hall, "The Toad in the Garden," in Cary Nelson and Lawrence Grossberg, eds., *Marxism and the Interpretation of Culture*, London: Macmillan, 1988, 35–57; the quotation is from 53.

19. Taverna music, which takes its name from the music hall, grew with arabesk. It proved immensely popular after new technology import laws were enacted in 1983. The music is inexpensive to stage, relying on a single singer with a synthesizer and a drum machine. The musician sings different popular songs of the day, one after another, chatting with the guests in the intervals while they eat, dance, and entertain themselves.

20. Gencebay has said that the *entel*s are different from intellectuals in that they talk and write about social phenomena (arabesk, in this case) in ignorance and with lack of respect.

21. In the early 1990s, in the seaside public space of Ortaköy, a neighborhood of Istanbul, fights broke out between the marginalized youths of the area and the university students who had created a bohemian community there.

22. The issue of male identity in this vortex of change is a complex one. For rural migrant men, the former hierarchy of family roles began to disintegrate in the city. Men now had to deal with unemployment, working wives, and daughters who wanted to go more public. Women of all ages seemed to balance the contradictory demands better and gain a sense of empowerment, although this was not accomplished without pain. They became major forces in the demands for an

improved urban infrastructure and social services in their neighborhoods, as well as for strengthened human rights for their imprisoned or missing children.

23. At the very end of the 1970s, when the dominant discourse on the "taste-lessness and backwardness" of arabesk was being formulated, Engin Ergönültaş insisted that arabesk was an expression of the protest of the lumpen proletariat; see his "Orhan Gencebay'dan Ferdi Tayfur'a Minibüs Müziği," *Sanat Emeği*, no. 15, May 1979, 5–22. Murat Belge was the first to point out that arabesk is a composite genre and that its formation is more complex than the prevailing appraisals asserted; see his "Arabesk'in Öyküsü," in *Tarihten Güncelliğe*, Istanbul: Alan Yayıncılık, 1982, 399–415.

24. The issues of migration and of lifestyles in the *gecekondu* neighborhoods have been portrayed in both auteurist and popular commercial films. The tradition of alternative caricature has been the main area of insight in this matter, but *gecekondu* life was also uniquely narrated in Latife Tekin's novels.

25. The term "alienation" in the dominant discourse was used without scrutiny as a synonym for "anomie" or "degeneration." Studies based on marginality theory that affirmed the existence of "alienation" in the migrant attitudes were not supported by the empirical findings on migrant attitudes in the work of the prominent sociologists Mübeccel Kıray, Tansı Şenyapılı, and Kemal Kartal, who showed that "fatalist and traditional attitudes were not continuous." Kıray argued that more analytical research was needed. See her *Toplumbilim Yazıları*, Ankara: GÜİİBF Yayınları, 1982, 172–74. The sociologist Orhan Türkdoğan, however, who studied Erzurum *gecekondus*, took a "culture of poverty" approach and argued for a perceived "philosophy of resignation" that complemented the struggle to earn a living in the *gecekondu* "sub-cultures." See his *Yoksulluk Kültürü*, Erzurum: Atatürk Üniversitesi Basımevi, 1974, 174.

26. See Uygur Kocabaşoğlu, *Şirket Telsizinden Devlet Radyosuna*, Ankara: SBF Yayınları, 1980, 77–81.

27. For a fuller discussion of "low modernism," see "Introduction" by Scott Lash and Jonathan Friedman, eds., *Modernity and Identity*, Oxford: Blackwell, 1992, 1–30. A "transclass taste" was the way 1990s' arabesk was described by Can Kozanoğlu in his *Cilalı İmaj Devri*, Istanbul: İletişim Yayınları, 1992.

28. The 1994 "Fadime's Song" (Fadime'nin Türküsü), by Ferdi Tayfur, seems to reflect publicly, for the first time, a nostalgia for village life. When interviewed about this song, Tayfur complained of the crowded, dirty, ugly city and its water shortage and contrasted it with an image of the village as clean, friendly, and now packed with the latest in technology and facilities. See Cem Sancar, "Hadi Gel Köyümüze Geri Dönelim"," *Aktüel*, no. 159, 1994, 68–71.

29. See the discussion between Stuart Hall and James Clifford about "travel and dwelling," which follows Clifford's "Travelling Cultures" in Lawrence Grossberg et al., eds., *Cultural Studies*, 1992, 112–16.

13/ The Turkish Option
in Comparative Perspective

ERNEST GELLNER

My direct knowledge of Turkey is extremely limited, but I have
for many years been concerned with its long-distance neighbors: the neighbors in one direction, across the Mediterranean
on the northern shore of Africa, as examples of Muslim society, and equally
Turkey's neighbors to the north, as examples of Marxist ones. This is the
excuse for my undertaking what I am about to do, namely, discuss the
Turkish option, the Turkish path, to whatever that thing called modernity may be. My main point will be something like this: to stress the fascinating uniqueness of Turkey, or the multiple uniquenesses of Turkey,
and the interconnectedness of the various unique aspects of the Turkish
political and social experience. The uniqueness is found in at least four
fields: in religion, in state formation, in the pattern of nationalism, and
in the diverse styles of modernity. These four things overlap, of course,
and are interconnected.

Let me begin with religion. Here already there is a kind of double uniqueness: Islam is unique among world religions, and Turkey is unique within
the Muslim world. The uniqueness of Islam, so far as I can see, is very
simple. One of the most famous theses of sociology is the secularization
thesis, the idea that under conditions of modernity and industrialization
and associated political changes, which one can lump together as modernity, the hold of religion over society and over the hearts and minds of
men diminishes. This generalization is far from completely true: there
are all kinds of countercurrents, and the patterns of secularization vary;
nevertheless, by and large, if one has to say yes or no, the answer is yes,
secularization on the whole does occur. But not in Islam.

In Islam, in the last hundred years, the hold of religion over society
has not diminished, and by some criteria it has probably increased. Other
societies may have their Bible belts, but Islam *is* a Koran belt; it has no
particular Koran belt. And the hold of the religion over society seems in-

233

terestingly independent of other aspects of society; it applies equally to societies still under traditional regimes and to those under regimes that embrace or embraced radical socialist policies. In either case, secularization has not occurred, with one interesting exception—Turkey.

Why has secularization not occurred in Islam in general? Nobody really knows the answer, but I am prepared to offer a theory. I am not sure it is true, but I think it deserves to be considered. It is a relatively simple theory, and it runs as follows. The connection, the Weberian connection, between modernity and "Protestantism," using this as a generic concept, does indeed obtain. Modern societies, through economic growth, occupational mobility, rationale of production, and so on, have a tendency to move toward the "Protestant" features of religion, by which I mean symmetry, absence of religious hierarchy, simplicity, unitarianism, puritanism, scripturalism—the kind of syndrome that, in the European tradition, is associated with Protestantism. This is the first point.

Point two: Of the Western monotheisms, Islam is the most Protestant. That is, at least high and "proper" Islam, Islam as codified by the people who, within the religion, are treated as authoritative, has certain appropriate "Protestant" features: rule orientation, strict unitarianism, a kind of completeness, the stress on doctrine, and the finality of doctrine. It is significant that there is an actual name for the sin of pretending to mediate between a human and God; mediation, or the cult of personality and religious hierarchy, is formally proscribed, even though it is practiced. Equally significant, there is a name for the sin of innovation. And there is the completeness and equal accessibility of the message in writing, which makes for a kind of religious egalitarianism weighted slightly in favor of literate men—all this is highly significant. Now, if this is a correct sketch of Islam, and if the Weberian thesis is correct, then they already go some way toward explaining why Islam has suffered less from modernization and the impact of the modern world than have all the other major religions, not to mention the minor ones.

But there is more to it than that. The main characteristic of Muslim religious life has been the polarization between a high tradition of scholars—unitarian, puritanical, scripturalist, antimediationist—and a folk tradition oriented basically toward saint cults and therefore mediationist, ecstatic, unpuritanical, and with an ethic of loyalty rather than an ethic of rules. These two elements within the faith frequently cohabit peacefully and harmoniously, interpenetrating each other without conflict. At other times the latent stress between them comes out into the open, and hence there is a kind of oscillation in the history of Muslim societies. When we come to the modern world, however, for the first time we get, instead of an oscillation, a definite and final swing of the pendulum in the direction of the "higher" form.

In my view, this occurs basically because the social underpinning of the "lower," or folk, variant diminishes or disappears. (When I say "high" and "low," I am not making a value judgment but am using the terms in a kind of technical, sociological sense.) The low, or popular, form of Islam has as its underpinnings those mutual aid, mutual insurance, semiautonomous units generally appearing in the literature as "tribes," whose internal organization is naturally inclined toward what one might call a Durkheimian style of religion—a religion that is, so to speak, the choreography of social organization, that provides the punctuation in space and time of social life. When these units are eroded by political and economic centralization, by incorporation of the local units into a well-centralized state, by the destruction of local units—their atomization—and by their inclusion in large, bureaucratic, administrative units and in a large market, then the folk variant of faith loses its underpinning and tends to wither away or become much weakened. It does not disappear completely, and it continues to have all kinds of therapeutic functions, but it is weakened. This social transformation appears at the level of consciousness as a kind of sudden rediscovery of the principles that had always been recognized in theory but had not been followed—the proscription of mediation, the technical absence of clergy, and so on.

If you accept all this, it has a further important implication that I think helps to explain the vigor of Islam throughout the twentieth century and its escape from the secularization fatality. Muslim societies, when in the position of underdevelopment—when finding themselves in a temporary economic and military inferiority vis-à-vis other societies possessed of more powerful technology—escape what might be called the classical East European dilemma, which has its supreme expression in Russian literature of the nineteenth century: the opposition between Westernizing and populism. Most undeveloped societies, confronted suddenly with an irritating and humiliating technical economic superiority on the part of some outsiders, face two options that might be expressed this way: we can imitate them so that we will be as strong as they are and can send them back where they belong, or we can reaffirm our own values. If we imitate them, we shall acquire their strength, but psychologically it is a bit unpleasant because it means expressing contempt for our own tradition. Alternatively, we can say that our own values, though they may not be materially as effective, have some deeper merits and deeper significance. You might call this the Tolstoyan answer. It is difficult to idealize the local ancien régime at the top, because it is in decline. But we can idealize or value the local *folk* tradition, and that is what many people in this situation have done; it is a characteristic East European reaction. This is the dilemma, and it is the basic story of East European underdevelopment.

Islam was different, and for a simple reason. In order to affirm itself against outsiders, a genuinely local tradition *was* available, and it had most of those modern features, at least by Weberian criteria: it was unitarian, it had a low loading of magic, and it was scripturalist and individualist and thus well adjusted to a mobile and therefore egalitarian modern society. It required discipline, and so one could blame backwardness on the folk tradition, which in any case could always be described, with some plausibility, as an aberration, as crypto-paganism. Thus one could find a genuinely local tradition, perhaps not quite so old as fundamentalist Muslims like to believe—insofar as the high tradition may not, in fact, be identical with the actual practice of the Prophet and his companions—but still, one that *is* genuinely old and genuinely local. There is no need either to go to the *muzhik* or to imitate the Westerner; one could combine both aims (self-respect and the imposition of the new self-discipline) by using a genuinely local tradition that had always been respected, though not widely followed, and that had previously been a minority accomplishment of the privileged urban stratum of society.

This is the theory I offer to explain the extraordinary vigor of Islam in the last hundred years. Turkey is an exception, because Turkey is the one important case within Islam of an elite's turning convincingly, and with some permanence, to a semisecular tradition. Why is Turkey the exception within the exception?

In the sphere of state formation, Turkey is exceptional probably by any standard but particularly within the Muslim world. By and large, I am an enthusiastic follower of Ibn Khaldun, and I think basically he was right: his sketch of Muslim society up to the coming of the impact of the industrial world, his sketch of the mechanics of its political life, of the rise and decline of political authority, was correct. His argument is well known. It constitutes a most interesting contrast to the main theme of European or what might be called Western or Atlantic sociology.

That theme is the transition from Gemeinschaft to Gesellschaft, from community to society, from the closed community—the integrated world in which vision of the world and social hierarchy and social life all interlock—to the mobile, open, progressive, growth-oriented, centralized society. One either likes this transition, if one is a "progressive," or dislikes it, if one is a romantic traditionalist. But for Europeans, this is the basic direction of history, and it is the concern with this long-term secular trend that is at the heart of sociology.

Ibn Khaldun differs from this view in that, although he too is preoccupied with this very contrast, he does not for a moment think of it as a long-term *trend*. Each of the two elements is permanently present in his mind and in the world he knows. To him, rural communities—self-administering and unpoliced, and therefore cohesive and martial, but economically unspecialized—coexist with urban societies, which are specialized, productive, and economically essential, but for that very reason politically emasculated. This is the human condition.

Ibn Khaldun is the most *wertfrei,* the most neutral, of sociologists; he just "tells it like it is" and offers little in the way of a recipe for correcting. He just analyzes. And both elements are, in his view, essential for society. Interestingly, urban society is *economically* essential, which is not a European view. Country folk, paradoxically, *need* the specialists of those clustered habitations of traders and artisans protected by the citadel. They need them economically, but politically it is the other way around. Politically, the towns need the cohesion and discipline of the countryside. The townsmen are nearly powerless politically and militarily, and the only way order can be maintained is by the provision of rulers from the rural reservoir of political and military talent. So far as Ibn Khaldun is concerned, this is how it is and how it will always be.

I think he was right. Hence, one of the criticisms to which my theory, based on Ibn Khaldun's, has often been subjected is simple: it does not apply to Turkey. The corollary of Ibn Khaldun's position is that political power is unstable; rulers are supplied from the reservoir of virtue and political talent in the countryside, but this virtue is destroyed by its very political success, so that every few generations it has to be replaced. Thus there is a kind of permanent rotation of elites, and political instability. But if that is so, then how does one explain an empire that dominated the eastern Mediterranean, or most of it, for four or five centuries and was markedly stable? On the surface, Turkey indeed constitutes an exception.

I think my answer to this would be that under the surface, in large parts of the Ottoman Empire, the world of Ibn Khaldun was alive and well.

This was so in most of Algeria and the Ottoman-dominated part of North Africa, in the Arabian peninsula, and in most of eastern Anatolia. The only areas that were more effectively centralized were parts of the Balkans and the Nile Valley, and maybe some of the sedentarized parts of the Middle East and regions lying along the routes that had to be kept open. The rest of the nominally Ottoman area was governed in the Ibn Khaldunian manner, in a tacit and varying degree of incorporation with the center. But that is not a debate I want to enter now. The fact is that at the center, there was indeed a different kind of regime, and the Ottomans perfected a different political principle in marked contrast to the Ibn Khaldunian doctrine that the only way to govern society is to accept the state as a gift from the tribe, that the only way to acquire political virtue is in the rude life of self-help in the savanna or the mountains.

As an alternative to that, there is the Platonic recipe for how to govern society—that is, how to create cohesion—not by the "natural" process of self-help in the desert but by sustained education. The first famous blueprint for this is Plato's *Republic*. According to it, we can stabilize society and maintain order provided we have really virtuous rulers, and the only way of making them really virtuous is by having thorough and sustained education from the beginning, producing a kind of meritocratic elite that at the same time is safe from temptation by being communistic, free from the temptations of kin and property. Such a communistic, spartan elite owes its virtue both to its training and to its social position, which frees it from temptation.

The nearest example of, or the nearest approximation to, Plato's recommended way of running society was Sparta, which, in Xenophon's and Adam Ferguson's words, made virtue the business of the state. It did have an elite trained in these ways, virtuous to an exceptional extent, and it came closer to practicing these ways than did the more relaxed neighboring societies. But on the whole, in that kind of Durkheimian society based on local kin groups and local ritual, it is difficult to impose virtue with great conviction. The Platonic recipe for running society really had a good chance of widespread application only with the coming of what Karl Jaspers called axial religions, a notion recently revived by S. N. Eisenstadt.

Axial religions are scriptural and puritanical. Their focus on written texts and their provision of institutions for preserving texts allows for sustained training. The sacred texts also externalize authority—that is, give it a kind of extra-ethnic, extra-political standing—so that sustained training of a nonreligious sort can be carried out. All this seems to have come together in the Ottoman Empire, which combined sustained training with the Mamluk principle of selecting rulers individually rather than tribally. For once, there was a strong and stable state, which lasted much longer than the Ibn Khaldunian model would allow.

There were other Mamluk societies as well, but the Ottoman Empire was the one where this kind of detached elite, systematically trained and disconnected from the productive part of society, was brought to the height of perfection, and it led to remarkable political results in terms of stability. This Platonic-axial way of running society perhaps helps to explain the first puzzle, why Turkey was an exception within an exception. It was precisely because the state was relatively strong when the predicament of underdevelopment came—when Western domination became manifest in the nineteenth century—that the local high religious tradition was less tempting as an escape than it was elsewhere. In a strong state, that religious tradition was itself compromised: it was part of the same ancien régime that was blamed for the new relative weakness and for its aggravation. There was no escape in that direction.

Roughly the following generalization holds: the better located and better placed the religious scholars were, the less they provided an option for escape from what I call the East European dilemma—for the use of the high tradition as an escape, a new identity, a means of self-discipline, a means of achieving against the outside. So the very success of this unique political experiment also stopped Turkey from moving in the direction in which most of the rest of the Muslim world has gone.

Furthermore, and connected with this, there is nationalism. In my view, nationalism is not something universal, something inherent in the human condition, as nationalists like to present it. Neither is it some kind of aberration, or a by-product of an ideological disease, as my friend the late Elie Kedourie presented it. Nor is it a revival of atavistic forces going back to the very roots of human being. It is, I think, a consequence of modernity. It is a consequence of the fact that in the kind of economy in which we live, a *high* culture, a literate and educationally transmitted culture, is by far the most important characteristic and possession of a person.

In agrarian society, work is physical. With us, work is *semantic*. In order to be employable, but also in order to be an effective citizen, two conditions are required. First, you have to be competent in the idiom employed by the surrounding educational, economic, and administrative bureaucracies. Second, your personal characteristics must be compatible with the self-image of the culture in question. If you master the idiom—and it is an abstract idiom that can be mastered only through formal education—and are also acceptable to it through your personal characteristics, then full citizenship is open to you. If not, your life is a series of humiliations.

And this dilemma, this basic situation of modern humans, forces people to be nationalists, because either they are in the satisfactory condition, having mastered the high culture of the institutions surrounding them, or they are not. If not, then they have a number of options: to assimilate, to migrate, or to become irridentist nationalists and try to change the situation. The society has similar options toward those who do not fit its local dominant characteristics: to assimilate them, to expel them, or to "ethnically cleanse" them, whether by murder, by forcible expulsion, or by intimidation. These are the processes we have been witnessing in the twentieth century.

This is the basic underlying pattern of nationalism, which requires, for a viable polity, congruence between state and culture. It is a completely new situation. It was absent in the past in the agrarian world, where, on the contrary, culture was required to be highly differentiated because its main function was to underwrite nuances of status in societies that had complex hierarchies. Vertical differences in culture were encouraged in order to mark the different statuses, and lateral differences were encouraged by the sheer fact that the majority of the people were agricultural producers living in closed communities that tended to differentiate themselves from each other by a kind of automatic cultural dialectal drift. By contrast, in the modern world, culture does not mark status; it marks the boundaries of political units and the kinds of pools within which individuals can move freely in what is inherently an unstable occupational structure.

Paths to this blessed marriage of state and culture vary a great deal, according to the availability and condition of the partners. Within Europe, there are three or four "time zones," and the relationship of the partners to each other differs from zone to zone. In the westernmost time zone, along the Atlantic coast, the two partners have, by historical accident, been cohabiting for a long time, long before the marriage was prescribed by the new logic of the situation. The fairly strong dynastic states based in Lisbon, Madrid, Paris, and London correlated roughly with cultural zones anyway, so that come the age of nationalism, nothing much needed to be done. The only major change in West European boundaries under the impact of the nationalist principle has been the creation of the Republic of Ireland. Otherwise, the frontiers have not changed much and are really more closely related to dynastic wars of the prenationalist age than to details of the ethnographic map.

In the next time zone to the east, the bride was beautifully tarted up and ready at the altar, but the bridegroom was missing. In other words, a high culture, codified and *staatsfähig,* ready for the modern world, was available to both the Italians and the Germans. Italians had had it since roughly the time of Dante, and the Germans since Luther or perhaps even earlier. There was a fairly compact catchment area of peasants speaking dialects not too distant from the language of the high culture in question. The cultural bride was ready; the political groom was missing. But in the nineteenth century, he was found in Piedmont and Prussia, and the marriage was in due course arranged without excessive violence. The amount of violence and manipulation practiced by Cavour and Bismarck was not all that much greater than that which was customary in dynastic wars, not to mention religious wars, which had been much worse.

It was in the eastern part of Europe, where *neither* bride nor groom was present, that nationalism was bound to create the greatest havoc because it required both political and cultural engineering. Here there were no national states but only dynastic political units and religious ones. And where you have a mass of variegated dialects, most of them not *staatsfähig,* uncodified, and not immediately eligible for a modern, centralized, bureaucratic, single-market state, you are in trouble. Moreover, East Europe could be subdivided into two further time zones according to whether there was, for forty or seventy years after the collapse of the old dynastic religious system, a new secular ideocracy.

Again, none of this applies to the Muslim world. If my diagnoses of Muslim fundamentalism and nationalism are correct, then the two have the same root: the switch from a society based on food production and storage, with a stable technology, a majority of peasants, and no expectation of growth, to a modern society in which work is no longer physical, agriculture is just one profession among others, growth is expected, occupational instability is inherent, and semantic standardization is required. This is the underlying force, which for some reason manifests itself primarily as nationalism in Europe and primarily as fundamentalism in the world of Islam. I say *primarily* because, of course, fundamentalism and nationalism are intertwined in Europe: nationalism uses religion in cases where the nation happens to be religiously defined and contrasted with its neighbors. Still, the stress in Europe clearly is on nationalism rather than fundamentalism, and in Islam it is the other way around.

The difference between the two is that nationalism consists of the worship of a differentiated high culture *without* the religious doctrine once linked to it. The doctrine has been shed. In early modern times, the two were linked. Bernard Shaw comments on this eloquently in *Saint Joan,* where he requires Joan to be burned as a Protestant heretic by the church and as a nationalist by the English. There are other examples of the linkage of the two themes, but all in all, the two elements usually became separated, and modern European nationalists are committed to an apotheosis of a national culture without linking it to a doctrine. In the Muslim world, the linkage of faith and high culture has remained firm. It is not clear why this should have happened.

Once again, the Turkish case is profoundly eccentric. If you take my parable of the bride and bridegroom, the Turkish case seems to be the opposite of that of the two great nations of the erstwhile Holy Roman Empire, where the bride was there but the groom was missing, where political organization was fragmented but cultural homogeneity was considerable, and where the cultural machinery was present. The Turkish Ottoman case seems to be one in which, on the contrary, the *groom* was present. There was a state elite, but so far as I know, it was not deeply identified with Turkish ethnicity. The elite spoke Turkish, but it did not single out the Anatolian peasantry as its favored object. It was a state elite, linked to the *state,* and it just happened to speak Turkish. It was in the past identified with Islam, but it controlled an ethnically and religiously variegated population.

Whereas in Italy and Germany, a self-conscious culture had to look for its political patron (Prussia and Piedmont were available), in Turkey it was the other way around: a political elite was looking for a way out of relative decline and needed to find an ethnic group. The way to religion was blocked because the religion was too closely linked with the declining ancien régime, so the elite had to look for an ethnic bride. The Anatolian peasantry was available. The bride hardly knew what was happening to her and continued to think for some time in religious rather than political terms. But again, the pattern contrasts interestingly both with the rest of Islam and with the three or four different patterns of relationship in Europe.

What were the consequences? So far as I can see, what crystallized was a distinctive new political system. The Kemalist revolution adopted the Western path and was lucky in that, unlike Turkey's northern neighbors, the Russians, it did so without adopting an overspecific sociopolitical doctrine, something that in the Russian case turned out to be economically and politically catastrophic. What the Kemalists chose was a relatively nebulous emulation of Western political principles: nationalism, constitutionalism, and whichever other features Western societies possessed that were, by association, rightly or wrongly credited with being the sources of their strength. These principles were taken up by the old political elite, by the groom in my parable, and applied in the spirit to which the elite was accustomed. So Westernization was carried out in the spirit of high Islam.

My first experience of Turkey was a fascinating occasion that I owe to the patronage of Şerif Mardin. It took place sometime in the 1960s, when members of the first generation of the Kemalist elite were still alive. I was able to observe their state of mind when I was invited to a conference on society and religion. The invitation said something quite innocuous like "religion is a terribly important phenomenon and ought to be studied"— nothing one could possibly contest. When I came, I found that the real content of the conference was far more specific: how do we stop the peasants and the small towns from voting for parties which then flirt with religion?

The basic dilemma was, so far as I could see, that the Kemalist heritage was committed to the Western sociopolitical system, but if that system was implemented, then sooner or later people who flirted with religion and betrayed the Kemalist tradition would win the elections. Either you give up democracy and in doing so contradict the principles you are supposed to be applying, or else you implement it, in which case you allow people to win who will, in turn, betray it. Under the impact of this dilemma, a new cyclical political system emerged, which for a time seemed to be institutionalized. It was quite different from the Ibn Khaldunian cycle. First, the army, the guardian of this new democratic tradition, allows free elections to take place. A party wins that would betray the Kemalist tradition, so the army steps in and hangs its leader. Then, after a time, it hands the government back again, and so on. I think it was Mark Twain who said, "Giving up smoking is easy, I've done it so many times." The Turkish army could say, "Reestablishing democracy is easy, we have done it so many times." And so this cycle appeared as if it were institutionalized.

At that conference it was very interesting to watch these Kemalist ulamas. They discussed, for instance, an advertisement that had appeared in a newspaper, endorsing one of the coups. The advertisement said the coup was legitimate for certain reasons. And somebody at the conference said, this clearly was the Kemalist *fatwa* (in its usual sense, a Koranic legal ruling). Then someone else stood up and said, this wasn't a *fatwa* for reasons A, B, C, D, and E. This man was clearly an excellent *alim* (Koranic scholar); he knew exactly the theological principles concerning what was and was not a *fatwa*. And he was not only an *alim* of Kemalism, he was also an alim *sans phrase*. He knew his stuff. And it was clear that he was practicing Kemalism in this kind of ulama spirit.

It is interesting to contrast this spirit with that of the next generation, including people such as Şerif Mardin and Nur Yalman, who are no longer so committed to a Kemalist secularism but, on the contrary, are trying to find a way out of the dilemma that led to this circle in politics. The argument is, we were wrong to identify Islam with the rigid, administrative ulamas, linked to the central power. Out there in Anatolia, one can find a more liberal, more humane, more elastic, more pliable, and perhaps more modernizable Islam to which we can turn and which will enable us to escape from that dilemma.

It is not for me to say how plausible and effective these alternatives are. All I can say is that I am pleased that the new circle, the new rotation that I thought I was observing—this periodic return to purification by the army and then a return to democratization—now seems to have ended. At least, the last cycle seems to be going on for quite a long time, and one may hope that the spell is broken. This, then, is the manner in which I see the uniqueness of the Turkish experience, vis-à-vis Europe, vis-à-vis its northern and now tragic neighbor, Russia, and also vis-à-vis the Muslim worlds to the south, in which, for better or worse, the fundamentalists seem to be winning.

14/ Modernizing Projects
in Middle Eastern Perspective

ROGER OWEN

When I first read the conference papers that became the chapters of this book, I was very much struck by their overall coherence—by the way in which they seemed to speak directly to one another. And this, it seemed to me, could only be a result of the fact that there was general agreement among the participants about the nature of Turkey's modernity project, as well as a belief that it would be difficult to discuss twentieth-century Turkish history from any other point of view.

I was also struck by the opportunities the papers offered for comparison with other projects elsewhere in the Middle East, where new states were provided with basic blueprints for their future moral and material progress by elites who were often led by some important historical figure, such as Atatürk, Reza Shah, David Ben-Gurion, or Habib Bourguiba. What they all seemed to share was a common response to twentieth-century colonialism and dependence, leading to a common desire to find a place for themselves and their peoples within the larger community of independent nation-states.

So much can be easily said. But if the comparison is to be pushed any further, it is necessary to elaborate the modernity project itself a little more fully and then try to situate it more securely in its Middle Eastern, as well as its Third World, context. I will start by seeking to establish some of the features that seem common to all such modernizing schemes.

First, the type of modernity project we have been discussing can be imagined only in terms of a state and a people. In other words, before there could be such a project, it was first necessary either to create its particular site de novo, as in the case of Turkey or Israel or Syria, or to re-shape an existing site, as in the case of Iran or Egypt or Morocco. It was also necessary to transform the existing inhabitants into a homogeneous people, sometimes by forcibly excluding some and forcibly including oth-

245

ers, and always by appealing to a common history and a common culture reinforced by a common educational system.

Second, the definition of the project often went through several stages. As a rule, the first nationalists were concerned simply to get rid of foreign domination, without thinking much about what would happen next, beyond the passage of a new constitution and the creation of a few truly national institutions such as banks and universities. Later, as the twentieth century progressed, there came more elaborate notions concerning the peoples to be modernized and their future progress. Hence, after a while, it came to be quite common to associate colonialism with political division and the deliberate encouragement of narrow sectoral interests, and thus to associate nationalism and progress with the healing of social wounds, with unity, and with spiritual regeneration. In many cases, such views were the result of positive interaction with Marxism and communism, which encouraged nationalist intellectuals to analyze their societies in terms of their component classes, without, as a rule, positing any necessary contradiction between them.

Third, there was a similar development in the central notions of moral and material progress, in terms of both definition and how they were to be brought about. For material progress, the elite took its cue from what it perceived to be the central features of the larger economic world in which the country found itself, aiming at some times to interact with that world as openly as possible, and at other times to protect the national economy from what were identified as harmful international influences. The usual passage was from a mainly "open" foreign trade and investment regime to a mainly closed one, and then back again. In any case, it was the elite, using the machinery of the state, that tried to set the terms of this pattern of exchange as well as to define the way its progress was to be measured, in terms of improvements in income, in welfare, in productive capacity, or, sometimes, in national self-reliance. The elite seems to have been motivated by an urgent sense of haste—the need to catch up with the industrialized economies, often by means of an organized economic and social revolution.

Fourth, and finally, the notion of moral progress was much more difficult to pin down. It could be found in any number of different formulations and reformulations until, by and large, it dropped from the state elite's own vocabulary, only to be rescued, on occasion, by various types of liberal or religious opposition. In the anticolonial period there was usually no major problem in defining the notion. As Michael Aflak and Salah a-Din Bitar, the founders of the Ba'ath Party, sought to define it in French-mandated Syria, the promotion of such progress was part and parcel of the nationalist struggle itself, which, to be effective, "had to involve a change of mind and of thought, a deepening of national consciousness and of moral standards."[1] Later, as the actual practice of power dimmed the luster attached to most of the first generations of nationalist politicians, similar notions found their way into the vocabularies of other groups—sometimes the army ("the moral guardian of the nation"), sometimes the monarch (for example, in Morocco and Jordan), sometimes the more radical elements who seized power in the name of revolution, positive neutralism, and social justice—before they, too, proceeded to discredit themselves by their dictatorial, self-serving, and often corrupt ways.

These are what I take to be the main components of the modernity project as it received political and practical expression among the various countries of the Middle East. Let me now turn to a few of its more controversial, but still general, features. The first set of these features concerns the project's historical and international context, and the second involves some central characteristics of modernity itself.

Given the need to create a state as a site for the project, much depended on how this task was carried out, particularly for its significant longer-term consequences. The Middle East provides a number of examples. In some cases, notably Turkey and Israel and to a lesser extent Iraq, the very founding of the new state was accompanied by the expulsion of large numbers of persons previously resident within its borders, whether Greeks and Armenians, Palestinians, or Assyrians, and the forcible incorporation of others into a project to which they owed only unwilling allegiance. In other cases, notably many of the Arab countries at the eastern end of the Mediterranean, the new boundaries established during the colonial period were not only disputed by many but also contained a mix of groups which, though mainly Arabic speaking, proved resistant to attempts to turn them into a homogeneous Syrian, Iraqi, or Lebanese people. In other cases again—for example in the Persian Gulf—the coupling of a people with a land was presented in the somewhat unusual formula of the historical right of a family (or tribe), rather than of a people, to dominate a particular space, in such a way that Kuwait became synonymous not with the Kuwaitis but with the Al Sabahs, and Saudi Arabia with the house of Saud. The result was to build into the project of modernity from its very inception certain fundamental rigidities and ambiguities regarding its scope and uniformity.

The international context also had an important impact in that the interpretation of modernity itself, and even the territorial space in which it was carried out, was shaped by world economic and political forces. One obvious example is the way in which colonialism and dependence could be used to generate their own counterprogram in the postindependence period. That is, if colonization was defined in terms of division, industrial backwardness, and minimal spending on education and welfare, then the new state had to concentrate on uniformity, rapid industrialization, and much larger social expenditure. The same processes can be seen in the rival influences of the capitalist and communist models, in the intrusion of Cold War pacts and alliances into the Middle East from 1947 onward, and in the spreading effect of oil wealth throughout the region in the 1970s and 1980s. Not only did such forces have a profound impact on the internal balance of power within the separate states, but they also changed some of the basic definitions of the project itself—for example, by allowing it to be identified on some occasions with capitalism, on others with socialism, and on still others with some third way such as etatism, neutralism, or the Arab Socialism of Gamal Abdel Nasser or the Syrian Ba'ath Party.

Turning more explicitly to the character of the modernity project itself, I would like to make three points. First, as I have mentioned, it seems to contain, in its twentieth-century, Third World context, an implicit sense of needing to "catch up" by means of some transformative economic and social revolution. The presence of such an imperative could explain some of the sudden enthusiasms generated by certain aspects of the project—for example, those often associated with the early stages of state-engineered import substitution, when progress up the technical ladder seems as easy as it is inevitable. Such excitement was well captured by a slogan of Egypt's first five-year plan in 1960–65: "From the needle to the rocket."[2] The need for speed could also account for some of the lack of enthusiasm for party democracy, a practice that was seen both as divisive and as standing in the way of the strong, effective government that the project itself was thought to require.

Second, the introduction of the modernity project alone was enough to transform domestic politics, licensing new vocabularies and opening up new possibilities for recruitment, organization, and contestation. One thing the project could not avoid was a high degree of definition, a feature that worked to its advantage so long as it monopolized the ideological terrain but which could provide a tempting target for oppositional forces as the project's achievements began to seem less compelling. As a rule, the project was initially identified with Westernization and secularism, something that not only proved offensive to many but also threatened the authority of preexisting sources of religious authority, with whom compromises often had to be made. These compromises might take the form of, for example, the Israeli agreement over continuing religious control in matters of family law, or the more radical Saudi attempt to dissociate scientific progress from the maintenance of what were taken to be the existing moral and cultural norms. On at least one occasion, in Iran in the late 1970s, dissatisfaction with the project of modernity itself, both in theory and in practice, was sufficient to encourage nationwide protest by almost all sections of the population, who were united only in their opposition to the Shah and his much-advertised policies and achievements.

Third, there are several senses in which the modernity project can be regarded as necessarily incomplete. One, which finds support in the essays in this book, is the argument that in the Turkish context, the project lacked an explicit program for creating a democracy based on well-defined rights of citizenship, a state of affairs that still awaits proper implementation. In this sense, the notion of incompletion could also be used to provide a political agenda for the future, not only in Turkey but also in many other parts of the Middle East, on the grounds that it can be said to have achieved its aims only when it has gone on to create the legal and ideological base for full popular participation in the political process.

But there are other ways in which the notion of incompleteness could be employed as well. For example, the relatively common idea that modernity required its opposite is central to several of the architectural chapters in this volume, demonstrating how the traditional, the old, could be presented as "bad" in such a way as to encourage an exaltation of the modern, not simply as something new but also as something essentially "good." Another example is the way in which the realities associated with the exercise of political power rarely permit the imposition of the types of universalities and uniformities upon which modernity, in most of its definitions, must necessarily insist. Typically, twentieth-century regimes came to rely on the support of a heterogeneous mix of social and political forces, all standing in quite different relationships to the economy and the outside world and requiring different strategies for control and incorporation.

If space allowed, it should now be possible to use the larger notions just outlined to illustrate key aspects of the recent political history of a number of Middle Eastern countries. What I would like to do instead is to focus attention on just a few of the ways in which the comparative approach can be made to yield interesting results. Starting with the historical part of the analysis, it seems to me that it is only when a state elite is pursuing a project of this type that the state itself, as an instrument of management and control, appears as a coherent actor and can be talked about and analyzed as such. In contrast, where there is no such self-declared project, the concept of state lacks consistency, and the machinery of government can more easily be analyzed in terms of the relationships among its component parts. The Middle East, like other regions of the non-European world, offers a variety of historical examples in which the coherence, or lack of it, of various types of statist structures can be compared and contrasted over time and in different country settings.

Something of the same type of argument can also be applied to the study of the present and the future. As the preceding essays show, Turkey's modernity project is under attack from many directions, and the same is true elsewhere in the Middle East. For one thing, the world economy contains a huge variety of forces, all of which impinge on the domestic economy and on domestic policy-makers in an often bewildering variety of ways. For another, rapid economic and social change has made the imposition of a single, coherent vision increasingly difficult to sustain. In such circumstances, those who seek a new consensus seem to have to look for it in some notion of revived community, sometimes based on religion, sometimes to be founded on a society of legally constituted citizens acting within a framework of properly democratic institutions. But in either case, two things are sure. First, the process of modernity itself is unstoppable and will continue, however it is interpreted and performed in a national context. Second, almost all Middle Eastern religious movements are perfectly congruent with the material aspects of modernization and will preserve most of its central features if they ever come to power.

As the essays—and discussions at the conference where they were first presented—make clear, these are exciting and yet increasingly uncomfortable times in which the historians of a new state's twentieth-century history cannot avoid becoming engaged in some of the most highly charged political issues of the day. On the one hand, historians have recognized the strength of the hopes raised by independence and by the promise of rapid economic and social development; on the other, they have to chart the actual experiences of the millions of people whose lives were changed in ways over which they had little control and that in many cases created great disruption and disturbance. Analysis presents formidable problems and may lead to unexpected and perhaps unwelcome conclusions. Judgment is unavoidable.

Notes

1. Quoted in Patrick Seale, *The Struggle for Syria: A Study of Post-War Arab Politics 1945–1958,* London: Oxford University Press, 1965, 149.

2. Quoted in John Waterbury, *The Egypt of Nasser and Sadat: The Political Economy of Two Regimes,* Princeton, New Jersey: Princeton University Press, 1983, 81.

15/ Finding the Meeting Ground
of Fact and Fiction

Some Reflections on Turkish Modernization

JOEL S. MIGDAL

The modernity project is one of both fact and fiction. Its facts lie in the tremendous cultural and political power concentrated by leaders with like-minded notions of how society could (and should) be organized.[1] From the halls of science to the streets of the city, that power has involved knowing the physical and social world in which humans live and then dominating and controlling it. Michael Keren, in a book about Israel that I shall return to later, captured the duality of modern power—its knowledge and domination—in his title, *The Pen and the Sword*.[2] In Turkey, as elsewhere, leaders have used modernity's steamroller to create nations out of the remnants of ancient empires.

Modernity's fiction resides in the myths that it has generated about the limitlessness of that power. The project proclaims, for example, its own inevitability and universality; through words ending in "ization"—modernization, centralization, secularization, and a host of others—it has appeared as an inexorable force, transforming all in its purview in all facets of their lives. Another myth involves homogenizing all those who somehow were missed in the first pass of the modernizing steamroller to some uniform residual category, such as "traditional peoples."

Marshall Berman contrasted the two faces of nineteenth-century Paris, which captured the fact and the fiction of the modernity project in that city. The planned, modern city was expressed in the new, wide boulevards, where "great sweeping vistas were designed, with monuments at the boulevards' ends, so that each walk led toward a dramatic climax. . . . Paris [became] a uniquely enticing spectacle, a visual and sensual feast." But "alongside the glitter, the rubble: the ruins of a dozen inner-city neighborhoods—the city's oldest, darkest, densest, most wretched and most frightening neighborhoods, home to tens of thousands of Parisians—razed to the ground. . . . The setting that makes all urban humanity a great extended 'family of eyes' also brings forth the discarded stepchildren of that family. The physical and social transformations that drove the poor out of sight now bring them back directly into everyone's line of vision."[3]

In recent years, modernity itself has been a subject of dispute, losing its aura as the fated future. It is not surprising that proponents of the project have tended to emphasize the facts of modernity—increased food production, the elimination of smallpox, greater productivity of labor, the wide boulevards of the new city. They have regarded society itself as a human artifact that could be known and reshaped for the betterment of humankind. And equally unsurprisingly, its critics have focused on the fiction, including its totalizing discourses, its creation of the exotic "other," its disempowerment of the discarded stepchildren of the family. They have despaired at the hubris of those who would seek to remake society according to human plans and blueprints.

In many ways, unfortunately, the debate between proponents and critics has been an argument between advocates of oranges and apples. They have more often spoken past one another than with one another. At one dissertation defense in which I sat, the postmodern candidate lambasted the totalizing discourse on the Green Revolution in India and called for a sympathetic reading of villagers' magical agricultural rites. He argued that poor farmers used such rites, much more than the experimental results presented by government agents, to make important decisions about planting and harvesting. The Ph.D. examiners, on the other side of the table, wanted to talk not about discourses but about which methods—those of the Green Revolution or the magical ones—were more likely to increase food for the villagers' bellies. Those on both sides of the table, I think, left the exam oozing frustration. Both the examiners and the candidate would have agreed that modernity had cast a long shadow, reaching to the distant villages of India. Their frustration with each other stemmed from their different perches as they tried to assess the project's impact.

It is impossible to understand social and cultural change in the Turkish republic, or any other twentieth-century state for that matter, without confronting the effects of the modernity project. But where do the dynamics supporting social stability or prompting social transformations lie? Is it in the facts or in the fiction, in the structural bases of power or in the dominant discourses? Are we relegated to choosing one or the other and thus to talking past each other? Do we look to state leaders and the grand boulevards they create or to the discarded stepchildren in their wretched and frightening neighborhoods? Answers to these questions, I think, can be found not in an examination of elites and their institutions exclusively, nor in a focus solely on the poor or marginal groups of society, but on those physical and social spaces where the two intersect.

The project of modernity has not always gobbled up those in its path or discarded those who resisted absorption; it has often engendered protest and resistance, reorganization and adaptation, in a rich variety of ways. And while the forces of modernity have been powerful agents of change, they themselves have not been impervious to obstructions and reconstructions on the part of those touched, but not necessarily absorbed, by the project. At the critical interstices of society, we can find the unexpected effects of people's resistance and reorganization on modernity's instruments of power, even on its core beliefs.

Modernity encapsulates physical and social space. Indeed, the project of modernity is aimed at creating and constantly enlarging a space in which people can establish new contractual relationships free from the binding social ties of the past—of family, tribe, and religion. On the paved walkways that meander under the modern bridges spanning the Nile in Cairo, married and unmarried young couples walk hand in hand, forging relationships that would have been impossible several centuries, even several decades, ago. Urban planning and architecture can delineate and define public and private space in ways that promote the new social relationships.

But for all the technological and aesthetic power that is part and parcel of modernity, the project's goals have not been totally achieved; gaps have remained. As it has encapsulated, it has also created frontiers leaving some people on the other side. Those caught in the gaps and on the far side of the boundaries have not been unaffected by the project, as Berman's reference to Paris's destroyed neighborhoods attests. Nor has the project of modernity itself been unaffected by encounters with those outside its frontiers. In its creation of gaps and spaces, the project has cut these people off from their pasts, from their connections. They have had to forge new social relationships, indeed a whole new social world, for themselves. And they, in turn, have changed the nature of modernity. The seemingly totalizing project has been buffeted, eaten away, changed from inside and out.

In her article "Irreconcilable Landscapes," Zeynep Kezer captures the sparks in Ankara's gaps and spaces. Standing on one side were those who found, in the words of a modernizer, "a dilapidated town ailing in neglect . . . one that we are determined to heal and build anew in the image of a modern city." The new capital city would, as another put it, "symbolize the breakaway from the old which would demonstrate . . . what can be done in a hitherto backward Turkey."[4] Still, those standing beyond the new boulevard also had a say in what the new Ankara would be, even if they did not sit on the new municipality's commissions and boards. Or, to paraphrase Kezer, those who came to build the new Ankara were vulnerable to the reality that they set out to frame.

Ankara never quite became all that its modern planners hoped it would be. Its bright new buildings and planned streets resembled a Hollywood set, at first glance representing depth and a total community but on closer inspection becoming just a facade with little behind its placard fronts. Those inhabiting the crawling lanes beyond Ankara's new boulevards were not simply excluded from the modern project; they, too, had a say in what Ankara was to become and thereby shaped the project of modernity as it shaped them.

Too often, observers have failed to note those spaces where fact and fiction have met, where the project of modernity and those outside its walls have intersected and transformed one another. Nowhere has this been more true than in the Middle East, where powerful, often charismatic political leaders have merged the project of modernity and a fiery nationalism into their personal programs of rule. The Shah of Iran, Gamal Abdel Nasser of Egypt, David Ben-Gurion of Israel, and others all sought to present the project of modernity not only as an inevitable end in its own right but also as the means to revive the nation. Indeed, nationalism and modernity have been the odd couple of the last two centuries—one parochial and exclusive, the other cosmopolitan and universal.[5] Key leaders and social classes have used them to sustain each other. The powerful tools of modernity—technology and rational organization— have been harnessed to empower nations. At the same time, the idea of the nation has mobilized poor and other vulnerable peoples into the service of modernizing sectors.

Using their personal charisma to lend a sanctity to the idea of the nation, the Shah, Nasser, and Ben-Gurion were able to muffle dissenting voices or to label them as subversive. Protesting, resisting, or obstructing modernity came to be seen as a traitorous act to the nation. In Mexico or Ecuador or any other number of other countries, Berman's stepchildren, those on the far side of the project's frontiers, were idealized as the future soldiers of modernity's army. But as Berman noted, alongside the glitter, the rubble; these marginal groups' troubling encounters with modernity were often hidden from view. Intellectuals, themselves mesmerized by the powerful leader, the passion of nationalism, and the al-

lure of modernity, did little to cast light on those spaces beyond the boulevards and the glittering lights of the city where the actual encounters
with marginal groups took place. The great leaders' forcefulness, their
stature, and the breadth of the stage upon which they strutted frequently
obscured critical social dynamics in their societies.

Keren's account of Israel points to Ben-Gurion's overwhelming role in
obfuscating those spaces where fact and fiction met. Once Israel achieved
independence in 1948, the new prime minister insisted that the new era
would demand more than modern scientists creating the resources for
the nation and its new state. "The whole intellectual community must
participate in heart, soul, and deed."[6] Ben-Gurion saw writers, teachers,
academics, and scientists alike as parts of a single pursuit to transform
the Jews into a modern, normal people. The idealized figure was the *oleh,*
the broken Jew who had somehow made his or her way from oppressive
lands up to the promised land. Once these people reached Israel, the focus
was less on their actual encounters with the harsh realities of settlement
in remote towns and their relations with an unresponsive bureaucracy
than on an idealized picture transforming them into *halutzim,* or pioneers.

Ben-Gurion's personal role went far beyond the political arena into a
running commentary on what was acceptable or unacceptable in the country's cultural, aesthetic, and scientific life.[7] He wanted writers to develop
the notion of the *halutz* and thereby fortify the image of a modern Jewish nation. He intervened in the debates of historians and endlessly suggested what the proper subjects for essayists and fiction writers might be.
No corner of cultural life, let alone politics, was beyond the range of his
sweeping interests.

Even after the inevitable revolt against Ben-Gurion's domineering
methods—indeed, into his retirement and after his death—the wily
leader seemed to dominate the agenda on countless scientific and cultural issues. Intellectuals lined up for or against his positions, and they
continue to do so until this day. Little thought went into the possibility
that Ben-Gurion's agenda obscured key dimensions of social change in
Israel and that unexpected, marginal forces, such as Arabs and immigrant
Jews from Arab countries, were changing his cherished project as much
as they were being changed by it.

In Turkey, Mustafa Kemal has played at least as dominant a role as Ben-
Gurion did in Israel or as the Shah and Nasser did in Iran and Egypt. For
Turkey's intellectuals, Atatürk has been like an elephant sitting in the liv-
ing room. Whether one likes the elephant or not, it is very difficult for

others in the room to see around it or, for that matter, to speak about anything else. More than half a century after his death, Atatürk has continued to set the agenda, provoking ongoing veneration, along with a sometimes vituperative opposition. Indeed, as Reşat Kasaba points out in chapter 2, criticism of the Kemalist program of modernization became a vocal and persistent theme in political discourses in Turkey. For the most part, critics have stayed within the parameters that the Kemalist plan established, more than they have peered beyond it.

Yeşim Arat's analysis of the feminist movement in Turkey, in chapter 7, reflects Atatürk's continuing domination of the cultural agenda. On one side have stood the early feminists, devoted to the Kemalist project. Nermin Abadan-Unat, the first female political scientist in Turkey, remarked that "if Mustafa Kemal did not exist, perhaps I would not exist." And on the other side have been the anti-Kemalists, such as Şirin Tekeli, who saw Atatürk's support of women's rights as little more than a ploy to further his own larger goals. Yet Arat's analysis leads one to ask just how far apart the two feminist groups are. For all the criticism that the new feminists have heaped on Atatürk, they still are firmly planted within the boundaries of the program he established.

When Atatürk was alive, his emphasis on *devlet*, or stateness, combined with Jacobinism to delegitimize the sound of dissenting voices outside the republic "une et indivisible." Those voices were simply from "feudal remnants" and could be discounted or muffled as atavistic cries. Şerif Mardin's argument in chapter 5 for the study of the "everyday," I believe, is a call to recent critics of Atatürk as much as to his admirers. A focus on the "everyday" will pull intellectuals away from the Kemalist agenda, pro or con, to the spaces that the agenda veiled. It is here that the power of modernity's facts and the overstatement of its myths will be most obvious.

The vast distance between what the peoples of Israel, Egypt, and Turkey were and what their great leaders envisioned for them, between the fact and the fiction, lent a utopian quality to the modernity project in these cases. For Ben-Gurion, this was expressed in a kind of secular messianism. He transformed the traditional Jewish belief in a great figure who would usher in the end of days into one emphasizing a national redemption through collective initiative and the tools of science. Although Ben-Gurion never claimed to be the Messiah in a religious sense, he was not above projecting himself as a "Messiah-like" figure, chosen to effect the redemption of the Jewish people into a modern nation, indeed, into a light unto other nations.

Nasser's vision also had a utopian dimension, although it was less clearly set out than Ben-Gurion's. Here, too, redemption and revival played critical roles, as the Arab nation would return to its previous glory. Through a distinct brand of Arab socialism, again with the use of scientific techniques, the degrading dimensions of recent history would be shed. Nasser saw himself as the towering philosopher-king who could break through the barriers of resistance to the nation's unity and to the promises that modernity held.

Atatürk faced a challenge as monumental as Ben-Gurion's or Nasser's. Fashioning a nation out of the core remnant of the Ottoman Empire demanded a utopian image of the future. Atatürk did not stand as the messianic messenger of redemption in the mold of Ben-Gurion or as Nasser's philosopher-king. Rather, he became the embodiment of the nation. His personal being represented the possibilities of the future. As the title of one publication indicated, the new nation was to be *La Turquie Kemaliste.*

Several years before his death, he insisted that all citizens take on a family name. His own choice was instructive—Atatürk, the father Turk. To the shaky concept of a Turkish nation he lent his personal being as a representation; his aim was to achieve a sense of sanctity and inviolability for that developing idea of the nation. "Atatürk had above all created a legend," wrote his biographer, Lord Kinross. "In a land needing heroes his mystique was such that a child, blessed by his handshake, would for weeks leave his hand unwashed, lest the virtue depart from it; that an old peasant woman, once asked what her age was, replied, 'Seventeen,' for her life had begun only when she first saw him with her eyes during the War of Independence."[8]

Like Ben-Gurion, Atatürk insinuated himself into issues far beyond normal politics. Creating a nation, in his mind, demanded an embrace of the West and its project of modernity. That project was a package including not only the hard core of science and technology, the facts, but also the trappings of style, the fiction. His reach extended into unlikely crevices of the country's cultural life. He took an interest in linguistics, pressing for the cleansing from the language of the "linguistic capitulations" of Arabic and Persian. Sitting with dictionaries piled high around him, he sought to create an elevated, modern Turkish language. He also harangued the historians, at one point summoning them to a Turkish Historical Congress in Ankara. "Its task," noted Lord Kinross, "was to carry out research with a view to 'proving' the theory that the Turks were a white Aryan race, originating in Central Asia, the cradle of human civilization. As their lands progressively dried up they moved westwards, migrating in waves to various parts of Asia and Africa and carrying their civilization with them. Anatolia had thus been a Turkish land since remote antiquity."[9]

It was inevitable that intellectuals and others would eventually rebel against this sort of cultural tyranny. The critiques of Atatürk's project in recent years were aimed first at the fiction—Atatürk's insistence on the entire package of modernity—and later at the facts, the positivistic science of the Enlightenment. But too often these criticisms have been narrowly conceived, reacting to Atatürk's cultural and political agenda rather than seeing beyond it. Kasaba complains that the official versions of history often portray a narrow, sterile path—one that excludes those on the far side of modernity's frontier and even the majority of those who were ostensibly included in the project. But it is not enough to cast light on those formerly excluded groups. The challenge is to illuminate their encounter with the modernity project—the changes in them that this encounter produced and their surprising ability to transform the project itself. Toward that end, this volume takes a giant first step.

Notes

I would like to thank Tom Lewis for his helpful comments on an earlier version of this chapter.

1. Perhaps no one has written more incisively about the integration of elites, institutions, and values than Edward Shils, *Center and Periphery,* Chicago: University of Chicago Press, 1975.

2. Michael Keren, *The Pen and the Sword: Israeli Intellectuals and the Making of the Nation-State,* Boulder, Colorado: Westview Press, 1989.

3. Marshall Berman, *All That Is Solid Melts into Air: The Experience of Modernity,* London: Penguin Books, 1982, 151–53.

4. Zeynep Kezer, "Irreconcilable Landscapes: Vision and Division in Early Republican Ankara," unpublished paper presented at the MIT conference leading to the present volume, 1994.

5. For one view of the linkage between the two, see Liah Greenfeld, *Nationalism: Five Roads to Modernity,* Cambridge, Massachusetts: Harvard University Press, 1992.

6. Keren, *The Pen and the Sword,* 35.

7. Michael Keren, *Ben-Gurion and the Intellectuals: Power, Knowledge, and Charisma,* Dekalb: Northern Illinois University Press, 1983.

8. Lord Kinross, *Atatürk: The Rebirth of a Nation,* London: Weidenfeld and Nicolson, 1964, 474.

9. Lord Kinross, *Atatürk,* 468.

Contributors

YEŞİM ARAT is a professor in the Department of Political Science and International Relations at Boğaziçi University, Istanbul. She is the author of *The Patriarchal Paradox: Women Politicians in Turkey* (1989). Her current work is on contemporary feminist activity in Turkey.

SİBEL BOZDOĞAN is an associate professor of architecture in the History Theory Criticism section of the Department of Architecture at the Massachusetts Institute of Technology. She teaches courses on the architecture of the nineteenth and twentieth centuries. She is the coauthor of *Sedad Eldem: Architect in Turkey* (1987) and is currently working on architecture and nationalism in the making of modern Turkey.

ERNEST GELLNER was a professor of philosophy with special reference to sociology at the London School of Economics from 1962 to 1984, professor of anthropology at the University of Cambridge from 1984 to 1992, and head of the Centre for the Study of Nationalism at the Central European University, Prague, at the time of his death in 1995. He wrote more than twenty books, among them *Nations and Nationalism* (1983) and *Anthropology and Politics* (1995).

NİLÜFER GÖLE is an associate professor of sociology at Boğaziçi University, Istanbul. Her current research interests and publications concentrate on the place of religion in modern Turkish society. She is the author of *Forbidden Modern* (1997; in Turkish, 1991).

HALDUN GÜLALP is an assistant professor of sociology at Boğaziçi University, Istanbul. Among his recent publications are articles on the crisis of Westernization in Turkey and on Islamism and postmodernism. His research interests center on Third World studies and political sociology, with a current project on social and political change in contemporary Turkey.

DENİZ KANDİYOTİ is a senior lecturer in the Department of Anthropology and Sociology, School of Oriental and African Studies, University of London. She is the editor of *Women, Islam and the State* (1991) and *Gendering the Middle East* (1995) and the author of numerous articles on gender and ideology in Turkey and the Middle East.

REŞAT KASABA is an associate professor of international studies at the University of Washington. He has published *Ottoman Empire and the World Economy: The Nineteenth Century* (1988), *Cities in a World System* (1991), and articles on the social and economic history of the late Ottoman Empire and the early Turkish republic. Currently he is researching state policies toward labor migration in the Ottoman Empire and its successor states.

ÇAĞLAR KEYDER is a professor of sociology at Binghamton University. Among his publications are *Turkey: The Definition of a Peripheral Economy* (1981), *State and Class in Turkey* (1987), and numerous articles on the history and politics of modern Turkey.

ŞERİF MARDİN is a professor of sociology at the School of International Service at American University. He has written extensively on Ottoman and Turkish cultural history, including *Religion and Social Change in Modern Turkey* (1988).

MICHAEL E. MEEKER is a professor of anthropology at the University of California, San Diego. He has conducted several research projects in Turkey, in Trabzon and Antalya from 1966 to 1968 and in Istanbul from 1986 to 1988. He has also published books and articles on the oral traditions and social institutions of pastoral peoples. He is now completing a book on local elites in the eastern districts of Trabzon.

JOEL S. MIGDAL is the Robert F. Philip Professor of International Studies at the University of Washington. He writes on the interaction of Israelis and Palestinians and, more generally, on state-society relations. His books include *Strong Societies and Weak States* (Princeton University Press) and, with Baruch Kimmerling, *Palestinians: The Making of a People* (Harvard University Press).

GÜLSÜM BAYDAR NALBANTOĞLU teaches architectural history, theory, and design at the School of Architecture, National University of Singapore. She is co-editor of the forthcoming book *Postcolonial Space(s)* (Princeton Architectural Press) and has published articles on various aspects of modern architecture in Turkey and postcolonial architectural conditions outside the West.

ROGER OWEN is the A. J. Meyer Professor of Middle East History at Harvard University and director of the Harvard Center for Middle Eastern Studies. He works primarily in the economic history of the Middle East and has published *The Middle East in the World Economy 1800–1914*.

MERAL ÖZBEK is an assistant professor of sociology at the Mimar Sinan University in Istanbul. Her research interests are in cultural studies. She is the author of *Popular Culture and Orhan Gencebay's Arabesk* (in Turkish, 1991).

Index

Boldface numbers refer to illustrations.